UNDERSTANDING THE BR

Peter Donaldson read politics, philosophy and economics at Oxford and graduated in 1956. He taught for two years in a college of technology before taking up a university appointment at Leeds. He was a lecturer in the Department of Economics at Leicester University from 1959 until 1962 and also worked for the Leicester and Nottingham University adult education departments and for the Workers' Educational Association. In 1962 he was appointed, for two years, Visiting Reader in Economics at the Osmania University, Hyderabad, and subsequently stayed there until 1967. He returned to England to teach at Ruskin College, Oxford, where he is now Senior Tutor in Economics. In recent years he has done a considerable amount of broadcasting for radio and television. His many books include *Guide to the British Economy*, *Worlds Apart*, *10 × Economics*, *Economics of the Real World* and *A Question of Economics*, all of which are published in Penguins.

John Farquhar's first degree from Aberdeen University was in forestry, a profession that he followed in the Middle East and East Africa until 1962. He then worked as a forest economist for the United Nations and also gained a doctorate in economics from Southern Illinois University in the United States. In 1968 he began a second career as a teacher of economics at Enfield College, now part of Middlesex Polytechnic in London. After retirement in 1985 he acted as temporary tutor in economics at Ruskin College, Oxford, while Peter Donaldson took leave of absence to prepare *A Question of Economics*.

UNDERSTANDING
THE
BRITISH ECONOMY

Peter Donaldson and John Farquhar

PENGUIN BOOKS

PENGUIN BOOKS

Published by the Penguin Group
27 Wrights Lane, London W8 5TZ, England
Viking Penguin Inc., 40 West 23rd Street, New York, New York 10010, USA
Penguin Books Australia Ltd, Ringwood, Victoria, Australia
Penguin Books Canada Ltd, 2801 John Street, Markham, Ontario, Canada L3R 1B4
Penguin Books (NZ) Ltd, 182–190 Wairau Road, Auckland 10, New Zealand

Penguin Books Ltd, Registered Offices: Harmondsworth, Middlesex, England

First published 1988

Made and printed in Great Britain by
Richard Clay Ltd, Bungay, Suffolk
Filmset in Monophoto Ehrhardt

Contents

List of Tables and Figures

FIGURES

Preface

This book has been written 'for the general reader who would like to have some grasp of what economics is about and what makes the economy tick', to quote from the introduction to its predecessor, Peter Donaldson's *Guide to the British Economy* (first Penguin edition 1965). Such a reader, it was felt, might find the standard textbook approach too abstract and too arid, so that it was important to provide a factual description of the British economy as a context into which concepts and theories could be placed.

All this is still true, and that general reader is still our intended audience. But now there are large numbers of young people (and some not so young) studying economics at GCSE and A-level, or in further and higher education. It is very important that their theoretical studies are complemented and enhanced by a feel for the size and shape and structure of the real British economy.

For both these groups of intended readers we have made a generous provision of statistical information in the form of tables and figures, supported by a good deal of purely descriptive text. This would make very little sense, however, if there were no explanations of the underlying concepts of economics and no consideration of the economic theories in which they appear. Theory is necessary to make sense of the figures; the figures illuminate and illustrate the theoretical concepts; and most of the theory covered by an introductory text will be found in the chapters which follow.

Books can be used in various ways. The most obvious is to start at the beginning and read through to the end, and the reader who does this should end up with the background information she or he needs to understand, and even to take part in, the contemporary debates about the state of the British economy and the economic policies which governments should pursue.

As a guide to more selective use we may say that the size and shape of the British economy are sketched (using a fairly broad brush) in Chapters 2 to 5. Chapter 5 explains the common 'measures' – national income and national product, for example. By contrast Chapters 6, 7 and 8 provide a simple theoretical explanation of the way in which the economy works, focusing on two topics which are central to recent and current debate, namely unemployment and price inflation. Chapter 9 sums up by reviewing the recent performance of the economy.

In an economics textbook most of the preceding material would be found under the heading of 'macro-economics' – the study of the economy as a whole, looked at from the outside. A great deal of economics, perhaps more than half of the typical textbook, would however be concerned with markets and prices and with the economic behaviour of individuals, households and business firms under the heading of 'micro-economics'. Part II of this book therefore begins with a brief theoretical discussion of markets in Chapter 10 and then goes on to describe the more significant organizations and institutions which operate within our market economy. Chapters 11 and 12 are about firms, whether privately or publicly owned. Chapter 13 is about the market for labour; Chapter 15 about the market for money. Money, a complicated subject in itself, forms the subject of Chapter 14.

The major, if not dominant, role of the government in our economy is described in Chapter 16, and the international context within which the British economy must operate forms the subject of Chapter 17.

So the reader who wishes to use the book to supplement a textbook, or even as a substitute for a textbook, can concentrate on the appropriate chapters of Parts I and II, and clothe the bare bones of theory with some up-to-date empirical flesh.

Part III deals with economic policies, and is therefore more controversial. People differ and disagree, often quite violently, about economic goals or objectives and about the means by which they might be achieved. The reader whose main reason for reading the book was to improve his or her understanding of debates and disputes in the press or on television could start with Part III, referring back whenever necessary to the explanations and descriptions in Parts I and II.

Such a reader should be warned in advance that there is no such thing as a neutral or unbiased book about economics. Even the most arid-looking work, full of diagrams and mathematical equations, reflects its author's prejudices, and this must be even more true of a popular introduction. It will quickly become clear that neither author is a committed monetarist, and that both would criticize a good deal of recent policy, though we hope we have given a fair description of its aims and methods. And there are dangers even in using economic statistics which no one, however careful, can avoid.

Almost all the statistical material used in the book comes from the official statistics published by the Central Statistical Office (CSO) of the government. The major source is *The United Kingdom National Accounts*, 1985 and 1986 editions. This is invariably known as 'The Blue Book' from its original (and present) colour. One of its companions, 'The Pink Book', is officially entitled *UK Balance of Payments* and is the source of our data on trade and payments. Two other annual summaries are extremely useful: *Social Trends* provides a wealth of information about income, wealth, housing, health, leisure and education; and *Regional Trends* presents a wide range of information region by region. There is also a new summary called *Key Facts*.

Financial Statistics is published monthly by the CSO, but the figures on employment, unemployment, wage rates and so on appear in the monthly *Employment Gazette*, issued by the Department of Employment. Similarly health and education data come from the respective ministries, and banking information from the Bank of England's *Quarterly Review*.

The CSO has published a very useful guide to the national accounts and an explanation of how they are produced: *A Short Guide* (1981) and *Sources and Methods* (3rd edition 1985).

Unless some other source is indicated, the reader can assume that the tables and figures are derived from these official sources. Even so, they need great care and understanding in use. First of all, they are subject to considerable revision after their first publication. Some of the data for 1983 or 1984 which we have given have been taken from the statistics published in the year immediately following, and all our 1985 figures are from the 1986 publications. These will be (or have been) amended in the light of more recent information, and some examples of the magnitude of such revisions are given in the table opposite.

Changes of this size can make a difference of up to 1% more or less in rates of growth, and initial impressions about the state of the economy and its direction of movement might be very much in error.

A second reason for caution in interpreting the figures is that they are

Revisions in the 1986 edition of the national accounts
to figures for previous years (£ million)

	1982	1983	1984
Consumption expenditure	+ 750	+ 670	+ 1,038
Exports		+ 362	
Imports	+ 608	+ 411	+ 538
Gross domestic product	− 750	+ 385	+ 822
Net property income from abroad			+ 853
Gross national product	− 905	+ 366	+ 1,675

all estimates, with a larger or smaller degree of uncertainty attached to them. The best estimates, the statisticians admit, could be as much as plus or minus 3% in error; many will have a possible error of between 3% and 10%, and some are worse even than that. Most of the estimates of expenditure on gross domestic product should be less than 3% out, except for the data on capital formation and in particular the estimates of changes in stocks; the latter are in the 'more than 10% uncertainty' category. Estimates on the income side are generally less reliable; only income from employment would be within the '3% over or under' category, and data on profits and property income are admitted to be very unreliable.

Hence, of course, the need for considerable revisions as more and better data come in, and this results in another problem: that of the 'residual errors' or 'balancing items' in the accounts. In theory flows of expenditure or income between all the sectors of the economy should balance, but in practice they do not. There is an overall discrepancy, which is itself the net result of discrepancies in the flows into and out of particular sectors. The 'balancing items' really reveal the extent of our ignorance, consisting as they do of all those errors and omissions which cannot be accounted for. Some figures for the past three years will show how large some of these uncertainties are for some of the important totals in the economy (see the table overleaf).

With all this uncertainty in mind we have done a good deal of rounding of figures, and for all these reasons the very careful reader may detect some inconsistencies in the figures within, and between, the various tables. But it should now be clear, we hope, why absolute precision is unattainable.

Composition of the balancing item	1983	(£ million) 1984	1985
Personal sector	− 2,410	− 3,864	− 5,071
Company sector including public corporations	+ 1,753	+ 3,322	− 21
Government	+ 72	+ 152	+ 674
Overseas sector	+ 1,539	+ 5,124	+ 3,694
Total	957	4,734	3,276

Introduction

A couple of decades ago, in the mid-1960s, British economic performance could be regarded with considerable satisfaction on many counts. There were three main grounds for a certain amount of self-congratulation.

In the first place, we had by then enjoyed the longest uninterrupted period of full employment in modern British economic history. For a quarter of a century, the vast majority of people who wanted a job and were capable of work were able to find it without great difficulty. Despite a very large increase in the numbers joining the work-force, unemployment had never during these years been greater than some 2% – and the parts of the country where this national average was exceeded were seen as a major problem deserving the special assistance afforded by positive 'regional policies'.

The contrast with what had been experienced in earlier times was quite dramatic. In the inter-war years, the number out of work had averaged some 14%. But now it seemed that the conquest of mass unemployment had finally been achieved and that no longer would millions of people have to bear the indignity of being unable through their own efforts to support themselves and their families – or to suffer the poverty and deprivation associated with being unable to find work. A whole generation had joined the labour force confident that they would be able to obtain jobs of one kind or another for the rest of their working lives. They paid little attention to their elders' tales of the bad old days of the Jarrow March, the scavenging of slag-heaps for pieces of coal, the fear and demoralization wrought on society by the unemployment that was described in a 1943 *Times* leader as, next to war, 'the most widespread, most insidious and most corroding malady of our generation: it is the specific social disease of western civilisation in our time'.

Secondly, the post-war years were a period of steadily increasing material prosperity, a rising affluence enjoyed not just by a lucky few but by the great majority of the population. Mass consumption was the outcome of an economy that had seldom in the past worked so consistently well; it was also the basis of the mass *production* on which its effectiveness depended, with output rising steadily during the two previous decades. Partly of course this simply reflected rising prices. The *cost* of living had gone up. But after allowing for inflation, the *standard* of living – the amount of goods and services which the average family could buy with its income – had substantially increased. Ownership of a motor car, television, washing-machine, refrigerator and telephone was now for the first time becoming commonplace. And the higher standard of living comprised not only private consumption. Also to be taken into account was what later became known as the 'social wage' – the element in well-being due to the availability of health, education and other social services on a scale never before achieved.

What made all this possible was sustained economic growth: the ability of the economy, year after year, to increase its capacity to produce. This was a process which had been taking place since the Industrial Revolution. The post-war years were exceptions in that their growth rate of some $2\frac{1}{2}\%$ was higher than had ever been managed in the past, enough more or less to double the amount of output every twenty years.

The third source of satisfaction in Britain's earlier post-war economic performance was, for many, that we seemed to be moving towards a fairer, more egalitarian society. Although great inequalities remained, it would be claimed that redistribution was taking place, albeit very slowly, through the mechanisms of the tax system and the Welfare State. And there was widespread acceptance that it was *right* for the extremes of inequality to be removed, that it was no longer acceptable for millions to be condemned to poverty while a handful commanded a huge slice of available income and wealth.

There was, none the less, no shortage of contemporary critics of how the economy was faring. Combined with the British capacity for 'economasochism', this meant that shortcomings rather than successes most often dominated discussion. Thus there was the recurring problem of the balance of payments, Britain's difficulty in paying its way internationally, which led to periodic calls from the politicians for a tightening of belts and the need for greater efficiency. There was the fact that, although Britain's growth performance was historically unparalleled, our major competitors appeared to be doing even better. And there was the niggle of constantly rising prices, with inflation frequently running at 2% or 3% a year.

But despite these doubts, there was an underlying optimism that continued improvement was possible. Moreover, there remained a strong belief that our economic destiny was *manageable*, that economic forces were amenable to rational control and that government policies therefore had a major role to play in ensuring future economic progress. Symbolic of this confidence was the initiation in 1965 of Britain's first 'national plan'.

A decade later and that confidence had been shattered. The Yom Kippur War between Israel and the Arab States had led to a cementing of Arab unity which enabled the fourfold hiking of oil prices by the major Middle Eastern producers. Industrial economies based on cheap energy, such as that of Britain, were suddenly faced with huge cost increases and enormous difficulties in paying for necessary fuel imports. With the oil-producing countries accumulating surplus earnings faster than they could spend them, there was a decline in world demand, which in Britain and many other countries led in 1974–5 to the first post-war decline in national output.

At the same time, there was an explosion of the price level, with the rate of inflation sharply increasing to the point where in 1975 it exceeded 25%, with a general expectation that the same or worse was to come. With Britain suffering to a greater extent than its major competitors it was not long before a crisis of confidence arose about future prospects. This was reflected in a steep decline in the exchange rate, the amount of foreign currency that could be bought with pounds sterling. By 1976 Britain had to approach the International Monetary Fund for loans to cover its mounting deficits, and had to accept the terms on which such loans were made available.

These terms involved placing reins on government spending and the introduction of tight financial discipline. But it would be wrong to claim that the restrictive economic policies pursued during the subsequent decade resulted solely, or even mainly, from externally imposed constraints. The Labour government of the time went further than was required by the IMF in curtailing the level of spending in the economy; its Conservative successors, from 1979 onwards, went very much further along the same road.

Thinking and policy changed, gradually to begin with and then dramatically. In the first place, this change was one of priorities. With prices rising so sharply by the mid-1970s government policy increasingly focused on the need to reduce inflation. With the advent of the Thatcher administration in 1979 'squeezing inflation out of the system at all costs' had become the absolute policy priority, if necessary overriding any commitment to full employment.

But with regard to employment it anyway came to be held that governments were able only to provide a framework within which job creation was likely. The idea that by manipulating the level of demand they could positively influence the level of employment was now dismissed derisively as 'throwing money after jobs' and likely to lead to inflation rather than work.

What happened, in other words, was that the 'Keynesian revolution' on which the post-war consensus had been based was overthrown in a counter-revolution of economic thinking reasserting the old orthodoxy that unemployment was simply a matter of workers 'pricing themselves out of jobs'. Coupled with this was a resurrection of the belief that inflation was caused by too much money in the economy – an old view known in its modern guise as 'monetarism' – and that it was government's prime responsibility to regulate that quantity. Beyond that, it was felt that government intervention in the economy should be minimized and that efficiency would best be enhanced by leaving 'market forces' to do the job to the greatest possible degree.

Alongside these changes in ideas and techniques during the decade from the mid-1970s to the mid-1980s was a further profound change from what had gone before. Britain struck oil. The first discoveries in the North Sea were hailed as potentially freeing Britain both from its long-standing balance of payments weakness and from its disability inflicted by the great oil price increase which had taken place. Such a bonus would surely enable us to look forward to a period of unparalleled prosperity and give a breathing space in which it was possible to regenerate the economy at a time when international competition was becoming increasingly fierce.

What has been the outcome? How does the economic scene today compare with that of ten or twenty years ago? Which are the significant differences that someone revisiting the economy after that space of time would be most struck by?

The first must surely be the reappearance and persistence of mass unemployment, that ghost of the 1930s which Keynes seemed successfully and finally to have exorcised. The number out of work rose steadily in the 1970s from 600,000 to 1,200,000, and then accelerated sharply in the early 1980s to reach a level unprecedented in modern times, which would have been unimaginable a decade earlier.

A second great difference which could hardly be overlooked lies in the structure of the British economy and its relationship with the rest of the world. The great manufacturing base of earlier years has been significantly eroded. The economy is now heavily and increasingly dependent on imported manufactured goods to meet domestic demand. Moreover, Britain is more deeply locked than ever before into the structure of the world economy, epitomized by its integration into the European Community and by the uncontrolled ability of multinational corporations to shift the location of their operations between countries in accordance with their own global strategies. Such factors can severely circumscribe the ability of any one nation, like Britain, to determine its own economic destiny.

Probing a little deeper reveals the third way in which the British economy of today contrasts with that of ten or twenty years ago. Inequalities have greatly increased. Far from slowly reducing the gap between the richer and poorer members of the community, recent government policy has deliberately widened it. The burden of the 'recessionary' years was far from evenly shared. And when the economy enjoys rising prosperity, this is now denied to a large proportion of the population. The division between the 'haves' and the 'have-nots' is more sharply etched today than at any time during the post-war years.

A glance at any popular description of the British economy during the early 1970s* reveals the fundamental nature of the changes which have taken place. Understanding the British economy of the mid- and late 1980s requires different emphases: on inequality rather then levelling-up; on industrial decline, rather than economic growth; on the control of inflation rather than the maintenance of full employment.

* Such as *Guide to the British Economy*, by Peter Donaldson. The present book began as an updated version of that guide, the last edition of which is dated 1976. But it rapidly became apparent that a completely new book would have to be written.

PART I

ℒℒℒℒℒℒℒℒℒℒℒℒℒℒℒℒℒℒℒℒ

THE ECONOMIC MECHANISM

1

ᶜᶜᶜᶜᶜᶜᶜᶜᶜᶜᶜᶜᶜᶜᶜᶜᶜᶜᶜᶜ

Concepts and Definitions

Some technical terms have already made their appearance in the preceding Introduction, and a number of concepts and ideas need a first explanation. We shall try not to be too detailed at this stage but just give a preliminary taste of the language we need to describe and analyse the British economy.

BRITAIN AND BRITISH

'Britain' and 'British' are the first things to define. What exactly do they mean? Geographers identify two large islands off the mainland of Western Europe as the British Isles. One of these is Ireland, in its geographic sense; the other is Britain, or Great Britain. Each island is made up of a number of separate countries. Britain consists of three countries: England, Wales and Scotland, with the first two of these commonly linked as a statistical unit. Ireland is divided politically into Southern Ireland – the independent state of Eire – and Northern Ireland or Ulster, which is politically part of the United Kingdom of Great Britain and Northern Ireland: the UK for short.

This is the land area and the political unit with which we shall be concerned, and whenever we wish to be precise we shall use the term United Kingdom or UK. Northern Ireland, however, is often treated separately, as befits its special constitutional status, and a lot of statistical data deals with Britain; i.e. it excludes Northern Ireland. Scotland, too, is often separated from England and Wales.

The title of this book is therefore somewhat ambiguous. What exactly do we mean by 'British'? We shall in fact often use the word loosely, as we have done in our title, simply because 'Britain' and 'British' are easy words to use. The tables and diagrams always make it plain which unit is covered.

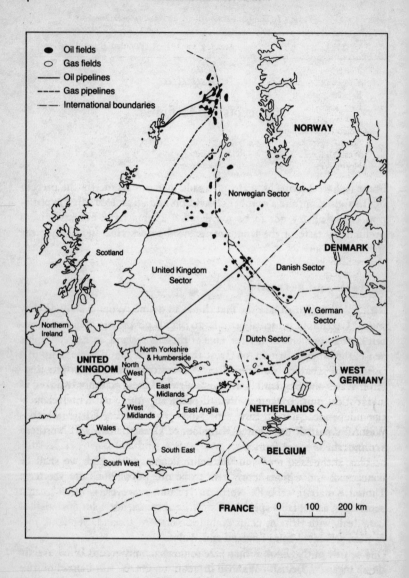

Table 1.1. The United Kingdom, area and population

Unit	Area (sq. km.)	Population 1983 (millions)
North	19,300	3.1
Yorks and Humberside	14,200	4.9
East Midlands	12,200	3.9
East Anglia	12,600	1.9
South-East	27,400	17.0
of which Greater London		(6.75)
South-West	23,700	4.4
West Midlands	13,000	5.2
North-West	8,000	6.4
England	130,400	46.8
Wales	20,800	2.8
England and Wales	151,200	49.6
Scotland	78,800	5.2
Great Britain	230,000	54.8
Northern Ireland	14,100	1.6
United Kingdom	244,100	56.4

(Note the dominance of the South-East region, which contains 36% of England's population in 21% of the area.)

Something which we have already glanced at is the distribution of income between *regions*. For statistical and other reasons England is divided into eight regions: South-West, South-East (within which London is sometimes treated separately), East Anglia, East Midlands, West Midlands, North-West, Yorkshire and Humberside, and the North. Within this regional framework Wales, Scotland and Northern Ireland become the ninth, tenth and eleventh regions. The map on page 4 sketches their locations, and their areas and populations are given in Table 1.1.

AN OVERVIEW OF THE ECONOMY

One way to gain a view of the whole of the economy would be to take an aerial trip, though it would be difficult to detect the details of the economic activity which was going on below. Indeed the first problem is how we pick out the specifically *economic* activity from the rest of the bustle that is going on below. The traditional response has been that economics is concerned with activity involving the use of money: with those parts of society's affairs which can be brought within the measuring rod of money, to paraphrase a famous definition. Myriads of transactions between individuals and organizations take place during the year which involve payments, and it will be these which are at least our prime consideration.

But not all these transactions are linked to the production of goods and services. Sometimes money changes hands without any corresponding exchange of goods or services. Some of us get money (like a pension cheque or a win on the football pools) without working for it, and without selling anything. And sometimes the exchange of money is a payment for some previously produced goods (second-hand cars, old-master paintings) or for a piece of paper which is a claim on money, often at some future date (a savings certificate, perhaps).

Here, then, is a basic preliminary distinction to be made – between transactions involving the production of new goods and services, and other transactions which are simple transfers of assets, and which are therefore known as 'transfer payments'.

We could visualize the economic activity as consisting of a flow of economic resources into the 'firms' or productive organizations, and a corresponding flow of payments from firms which constitute the bulk of people's incomes. Using these resources, the firms produce a flow of goods and services, which are bought by individuals and families, by government and firms to expand their productive capacity, and by foreigners. The last of these subdivisions we usually call 'exports', and there is a corresponding inflow of goods and services which are called 'imports'.

Resources, income, production and expenditure are four fundamental concepts around which we shall organize our description of the economy. We turn now to some problems of measurement.

THE SIZE OF THE ECONOMY

In assessing the size of the economy an important concept is 'gross domestic product'. There is in fact a family of similar measures – gross national product, net national product, national income and so on – which attempt to do this, and which we shall define in detail later (see Chapter 5, page 69). The gross domestic product (or GDP) quantifies the flow of products and the range of services that the economy produces each day, week and month throughout the year. In principle it would be possible to watch all this production taking place and to add up the number of motor cars of various types, the amount of coal mined or oil pumped, the number of times people used the services of doctors or hairdressers, the tonnage carried and the mileage covered by trucks and trains and aircraft. The total list would be a very long one indeed.

However, there is a difficulty. It is possible to 'add up' the land area in square kilometres, and count the number of people at a periodic census. But there is no common *physical* measure for totalling the great number and variety of products in a modern economy. The economist and the statistician are forced to use the prices of the goods and services produced – that is to say, *money* – as the unit in which to add up the flow of products.

Unfortunately, money is not as constant and unchanging a measure as are metres or kilogrammes. This means that corrections have to be made to allow for the changing 'size' of the unit of measurement itself. We have to distinguish carefully between the *concept* of national product and the figures in millions or billions of pounds sterling which are used as the *measure* of it. Initially, the statisticians must evaluate the flow in terms of the actual prices for which the goods and services are bought or sold, and so each year's estimate of national output will be labelled 'at current prices' in any tables or diagrams. Thus, for example, the gross domestic product of the UK economy amounted to £352 billion in 1985.

It would be useful then to compare figures like this with the last year's, to see whether the economy – the flow of goods and services – had increased or decreased, and by how much. In this particular case, the previous year's figure, for 1984, computed on the same basis, was £320 billion. The increase was £32 billion, or 10%.

But only part of that 10% was the result of a genuine increase in the quantity of goods and services, and the rest was simply a reflection of the fact that the prices of goods and services were rising. The way round this problem is to apply a *constant* set of prices, and statisticians have now agreed to use the years ending in 0 or 5 as the 'base years' whose prices will be used in these calculations. So if you want to know how much our economy *really* grew between 1984 and 1985 you must look for a table (Table 1.2, for example) headed 'gross domestic product at constant (1980) prices'. There you would find a figure of £253 billion for 1985, and £244 billion for 1984, giving an increase of just under 4%.

This distinction between current prices and constant prices, or between monetary and 'real' magnitudes, is crucially important throughout

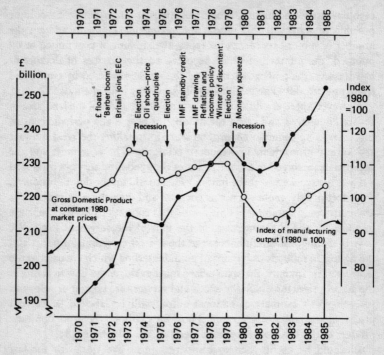

Figure 1 The progress of the British economy, 1970–85

this book, because we are covering a period of years during which prices rose very quickly indeed.

Before leaving this topic it is worth mentioning another simple but useful device which makes it easier to appreciate the changes taking place from year to year. The numbers we have just quoted are very large indeed, and if we expressed them in millions of pounds as £252,800 million and £243,684 million it is not always easy to see how much bigger the second number is, or to detect a change in the rate of increase.

To make it easier to grasp such matters, *index numbers* are used. This method takes the actual amount for one year (e.g. £230,329 million for 1980) and represents this by the figure 100. The next question to ask is what the actual amount for another year (e.g. £243,684 million for 1984) would be if expressed in the same terms? The answer in this case would be 105.8. We would then say that GDP in 1984 was 105.8 (1985 = 100).

Table 1.2. The progress of the British economy, 1970–85 (see also Figures 1, 2, 3, 4)

	1970	1971	1972	1973	1974	1975	1976	1977	1978	1979	1980	1981	1982	1983	1984	1985
Gross domestic product at current market prices (£ billions)	52	58	64	74	84	106	127	146	168	197	230	254	276	301	320	352
Gross domestic product at constant (1980) prices (£ billions)	190	195	200	215	213	212	220	223	230	236	230	228	230	239	244	253
Net national product or national income at constant (1980) factor cost[a]	150	153	155	170	167	163	170	169	174	178	171	169	171	179	183	190
Index of manufacturing output (1980 = 100)	103	102	105	114	113	105	107	109	110	110	100	94	94	97	101	104
GDP deflator (Index of Home Costs 1980 = 100)	27	30	32	34	39	50	58	66	73	84	100	112	120	126	131	139
Increase in Retail Price Index during previous year (%)[b]	5.0	8.6	8.0	8.0	12.9	20.3[c]	22.5	16.5	9.5	9.6	19.1[d]	12.6	11.1	4.7	5.2	5.5
Unemployment: % of labour force, 1st quarter	2.5	2.6	3.7	2.7	2.2[e]	2.9	4.8	5.1	5.3	5.0	5.0	8.5	10.6	11.8	12.4	13.0
Number unemployed (millions)	0.59	0.60	0.84	0.63	0.58	0.68	1.14	1.23	1.28	1.21	1.21	2.07	2.56	2.85	3.00	3.14
Employment in manufacturing industry (index 1980 = 100)	120	115	114	115	113	106	107	107	106	104	100	93	88	83	81	80

[a] For an explanation of these measures of the size of the economy, see Chapter 5, page 69, 'The national accounts'.
[b] Figures are based on the first quarter of each year.
[c] Peaked at 26.5% in the 3rd quarter.
[d] Peaked at 21.5% in the 2nd quarter.
[e] Change in definition. There are also a number of changes in the 1980s which on balance reduce the number recorded as unemployed.

The comparable figure for 1985 would be 109.75.*

Figure 1 and Table 1.2 illustrate the changes in the total output of the UK economy since 1970. We have gone back this far so that the sudden sharp contrast between the relatively rapid growth between 1970 and 1973 and a fall in GDP – a shrinking of the flow of goods and services – in 1974 and 1975 shows up clearly. Growth was then resumed, but at a slower rate, and the advent in 1979 of a government committed to squeezing inflation out of the economy triggered off another fall in output in 1980 and 1981.

UNEMPLOYMENT

A little earlier we proposed viewing the economy from an aerial trip. Suppose instead you are a visitor to Britain, and that after driving through Europe you have landed on the south coast, at, say, Southampton or Portsmouth. You have a choice of routes to the North: you could take the traditional road up to London, through Hampshire, Sussex and Surrey; you could drive through Berkshire and Oxfordshire towards Birmingham; or (being a real tourist) you could take in Salisbury, Stonehenge, Bath and Gloucester and turn north via Worcester. You would, whichever route you took, be driving through farmland, towns and cities very much like those you had left in France or Germany: modern, busy and prosperous.

Beyond your second or third day's drive, however, the picture would change. You might, if you drove up the M1 or A1, notice the cold silent steel works at Corby or Sheffield, and the motionless pithead gear of the coal-mines in Yorkshire around Doncaster or Barnsley. On the M6, driving through what used to be the throbbing industrial heartland of Britain in the West Midlands, you would be struck by the multitude of empty, shuttered factory buildings, the flattened areas of industrial dereliction, the numbers of men with nothing to do. Cross the Severn into South

---

* The arithmetic calculation is: $\dfrac{230{,}329 \times 100}{230{,}329} = 100.$

Now, if the same is done for 1984: $\dfrac{243{,}684 \times 100}{230{,}329} = 105.8.$

And for 1985: $\dfrac{252{,}800 \times 100}{230{,}329} = 109.75.$

These index numbers are usually rounded, so that one would say that GDP in 1985 was 110 and in 1984 was 106 (1980 = 100)

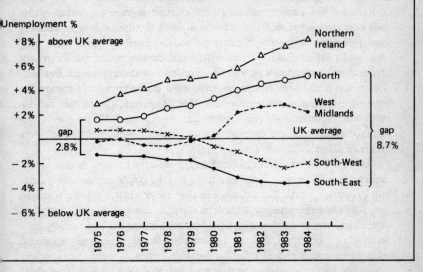

Figure 2 The widening gap between regions (measured by percentage unemployed)

Wales, or visit Liverpool or Glasgow, and the picture would be depressingly similar. The impression of 'two nations' would begin to come sharply into focus.

You might recall at your port of entry the bustling activity of 'roll-on, roll-off' ships taking trucks and containers to and from Europe. You could see the same again at Harwich or Felixstowe in East Anglia on a side trip from Norwich, Cambridge and Ely. Contrast this with the almost deserted ports of Liverpool or Glasgow, and you can appreciate the changes that have resulted from the redirection of much of Britain's trade towards Europe and away from the Atlantic. Liverpool has a declining industrial hinterland and is 'facing the wrong way'.

In Figure 2 the horizontal central line denotes the average level of unemployment in the United Kingdom. (NB Don't let the horizontality mislead you: as we shall see, the average national rate of unemployment rose during these years from 2.9% in the first quarter of 1975 to 13% in the first quarter of 1985. The diagram is designed to illustrate the growing regional *divergences* from this rising trend.) The Northern region has always had a somewhat higher level of unemployment than the national average: 1.6% higher in 1975, for example. By contrast, the South-Eastern region has consistently had a lower than average percentage of its work-force unemployed: 1.2% lower in 1975. By 1984 this 'gap' of 2.8% had grown to 8.7%; the South-East had an unemployment rate 3.5% below the national average; the North had a rate 5.2% above. Northern Ireland, as always, shows a much higher level of unemployment than any other part of the UK, but perhaps the most striking aspect of Figure 2 is the very sudden appearance of the West Midlands among the regions with an unemployment rate higher than the average. This is the consequence of the massive drop in manufacturing employment which took place in the early 1980s.

To gain a clearer understanding of the emotive concept of unemployment it is necessary to look behind the flow of goods and services which we have just discussed and to ask *how* they are produced. Agriculturalists, product engineers and cost accountants would provide us with a technical set of answers to such a question, but economists are not usually concerned with that level of detail. Instead they classify 'economic resources' into three broad groups – land, labour and capital – and examine how they are used to produce goods and services. We shall define these resources more strictly when we come to discuss how much of them the UK possesses (see Chapter 2); here all we need say is that we clearly do not have an unlimited supply of any of them. Land or space is limited by the size of the country, and the amount of labour by the size and composition of the population. Capital may be briefly defined as 'artificial aids to production' such as tools, equipment, machinery, buildings and roads; it too is limited in quantity at any one point in time, though unlike the other two it can be increased if we devote resources to producing these things.

There is therefore an upper limit to the quantity of goods and services which the economy is capable of producing – a limit set by the amount of economic resources available, by their quality and by our collective ability to combine them effectively in production. This upper limit represents the capacity of the economy when all its resources are being used, and it can be quantified, albeit not very precisely, as the 'full employment level of national income'.

Just how high the level is depends, however, on conventional views about many matters like the age of entry to and exit from the work-force, the school-leaving age and the age of retirement. It depends on how many hours a day, days a week and weeks a year we are prepared to

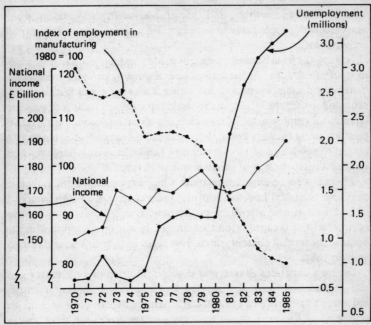

Figure 3 Unemployment

work, and on whether we keep machinery running longer through shift working. The production engineers could give us some ideas about plant capacity, using the commonly accepted norms of working, and this is probably as near as we could get to defining what we mean by 'full employment'.

During the Second World War the British nation worked its economy close to the absolute limits. Almost every able-bodied man and woman worked or fought, and hours were lengthened so as to work machinery to its maximum potential. The only limits were those imposed by the risks of breakdown, mechanical or human, and the shortage of materials. When peace came the pace slowed down again to conventional levels, but output was maintained at a level which required the participation of most men between the ages of 15 (then the school-leaving age) and 65, and a smaller though growing proportion of women. In many sectors of the economy there were complaints about labour shortages, and the proportion of the work-force registered as unemployed was very small (2% to 3%), remaining so right through the 1950s and 1960s. It was this level of economic activity, and this proportion of the work-force employed, which people came to have in mind when they talked about 'full employment'.

In 1976 the level of unemployment made a sudden jump to 5%, where it stuck until 1980. As we can see in Figure 3, national income was increasing during this period, but either it was not rising fast enough to provide jobs for the whole of the work-force (which itself was growing) or the 'full employment' of the other economic resources, or 'factors of production' as they are called, left some labour unused. A given level of output of goods and services could now be obtained with fewer workers, because the technology of production had changed.

There is a continuing debate about which explanation is the right one, or (more precisely) how much of the present level of unemployment is caused by too low a level of production, and how much by a lower requirement of labour per unit of output. It is a very important debate because the level of unemployment rose again in 1981 to 8%, and reached 13% in 1985.

Figure 3 illustrates all this, and shows in addition that the most recent rise is associated with a sharp fall in employment in manufacturing industry. The use of percentages can lessen the human seriousness of the problem, so Figure 3 shows that 13% means well over three million people without work.

These national averages conceal much higher levels of unemployment in some regions and cities. They also mask a very considerable change in the type of *employment* which our economy is now providing. Broadly speaking there has been a large drop in male, manual, unskilled or semi-skilled employment in manufacturing and construction, and a rise in the employment of females in the service industries, often on a part-time basis. Even within the overall shortage of jobs there is a mismatch; the work on offer is not in the right place, nor of the right kind, for those who are seeking employment.

INFLATION

Despite the scale of unemployment, which would have been unthinkable in 1975, the central topic of public debate for much of the period illustrated in Figure 4 was undoubtedly the rate of inflation. Since this switch of attention coincided with, or brought about, a corresponding shift in the concerns of economic theory and policy, we need briefly

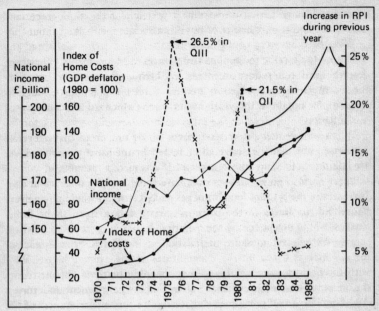

Figure 4 Inflation

at this stage to introduce price inflation, a topic to which we shall return in Chapter 7.

Inflation conjures up the picture of a child's balloon being blown up at Christmas, and at one time the word was applied to the general expansion of economic activity in a 'boom', as opposed to its decline in a slump. As often happens, words go out of favour or change their meaning, and the debate about inflation almost needs a glossary to itself. We shall use the word to denote a rise in the average level of prices. The rate at which such a rise takes place is the 'rate of inflation', and it can be increasing or accelerating, decreasing or decelerating or even constant. During the 1950s and 1960s, for example, prices rose fairly steadily at a constant rate of 3% to 4% a year.

'Slump' has an unpleasant sense of finality about it and came to be replaced by the word 'depression'. But in turn, because of its association with the severe and prolonged fall in economic activity and employment in the 1930s, the latter term too has largely fallen into disfavour, and a decline in the economy is now usually called a recession. 'Boom', on the other hand, is still used to describe a period of high employment and output and incomes, whether or not it is associated with price inflation.

What becomes very confusing is the use of the terms 'deflation' and 'reflation' to describe the actions and policies of governments. 'Deflation' describes action to reduce an excessively high level of activity; 'reflation' the attempts to encourage or increase output and employment. The opposite of 'inflation' therefore has to be the awkward and rarely used 'dis-inflation'.

When we say that prices have risen, we do not mean that *all* prices have risen nor that they have all increased by the same percentage. We are talking about some sort of average. If it is to be a meaningful average then the various goods and services have to be 'weighted' in some way. Increases in the price of food, or of gas and electricity, would affect every household; increases in the price of caviare and oysters, or of Rolls-Royces, would not be felt by the majority.

The commonest measure of inflation is the Retail Price Index, or RPI, which is based on the expenditures of the average household – with the necessary information about spending patterns obtained from the ongoing Family Expenditure Survey that the government undertakes. An 'index' in the sense we are using it here is a weighted average, and the 'weights' should reflect the importance of the included items to the average family: the percentages of total household expenditure on each of the various categories of goods and services which the average household buys.

Each year's retail price indices are calculated on the basis of the previous year's expenditure weights, which are therefore constantly kept up to date. A good indication of price inflation can thus be found by looking at the *difference* between the RPI for the latest month or quarter and the RPI for the corresponding month or quarter one year earlier. This also has the merit of showing up two marked peaks in the rate of inflation in 1975 and 1979.

These peaks are prominent features in Figure 4, but the steady rise in the level of prices can best be seen by looking at the difference between gross domestic product at current prices and GDP at constant prices. This difference – a measure of how much you have to reduce the 'current price' figure to obtain the 'constant price' figure which has the price inflation removed – is called the GDP deflator or the Index of Home Costs, and provides a measure of inflation which is not confined to the goods and services bought by households. It is also plotted, as an index, in Figure 4, and if you look carefully you can detect the increases in the slope of the line corresponding to the peaks in the R P I increase.

Figures 2, 3 and 4, together with the statistical data on which they are based, set out in Table 1.2, illustrate the significant economic events of the past decade and show in broad outline how the economy reached its present state: a story which the rest of this book will attempt to explain in more detail. The only major omission is foreign trade and payments, which are taken up in Chapter 8.

2

££££££££££££££££££££

Economic Resources

Although, as we have already seen, economics is generally concerned with that part of activity which falls within the *measuring* rod of money, it is usually the politician or accountant who is principally concerned with the financial cost of a particular programme or project – where the money comes from. The economist is more likely to think in terms of its 'resource cost', about the quantities of the three factors of production – land, labour and capital – which it will use. So the obvious first stage in a more detailed survey of the British economic landscape is to assess just how well endowed we are with these economic resources.

LAND AND SEA

Land has a wider meaning for an economist than the plain square kilometres of surface detailed in Table 2.1. The concept includes natural resources such as forests and fish; mineral deposits; sites for water power generation; even climate and scenery. This land resource supports one of the major sectors of the economy, agriculture, but only about half of it is suitable for intensive farming. Table 2.1 summarizes the pattern of land use.

A more detailed subdivision would show that the greater part of the farmland is in England, and that most of the rough grazing and forest is found in the North and West of Britain. This reflects a fundamental division into 'highland' and 'lowland' Britain: a line joining Plymouth and Newcastle is often used to divide them. There is, of course, a lot of good agricultural land in Wales and North-West England, and in Central and Eastern Scotland, but the line, which reflects the underlying geology and the amount of rainfall as well as the relief, makes a useful working boundary.

Table 2.1. Land use in the UK

Type of use	Area (000 ha)	United Kingdom %	England %	Wales %	Scotland %	Northern Ireland %
Crops	5,100	21	34	4	9	6
Temporary grass	1,860	8				
(Subtotal arable)	(6,950)	(28)				
			41	76	73	76
Permanent pasture	5,100	21				
Rough grazing	6,600	27				
(Subtotal agriculture)	(18,700)	(77)	(75)	(80)	(82)	(82)
Forests	2,250	9	7	12	13	5
Urban	2,890	12	18	8	5	13
Other uses	210	1	—	—	—	—
Total land area	24,100		100	100	100	100
Water	300	1	—	—	—	—
Total area	24,400	100				

Until quite recently the land area as we have just described it would have been more or less the same as the 'area of national jurisdiction' or the area over which the government of the United Kingdom held sway. There was a territorial sea lying within a three-mile limit of the shore, but beyond that the 'high seas' were open to all. Beginning with attempts by some states to take control over valuable fisheries, and then speeding up as valuable offshore mineral deposits, especially of oil, were discovered, more and more claims were made to the 'continental shelf' – the area of shallow seas contiguous with, and geologically a part of, the dry land. Two-hundred-mile limits began to replace the old three-mile limit, but in an area like the North Sea this meant overlapping claims, solved by the device of drawing a boundary half-way between the coastlines of neighbouring states. So in a legal sense the area of the UK includes this continental shelf, and whatever wealth is found there forms an element of our 'land' resources.

Part of this wealth consists of the fish that frequent our neighbouring waters, and in most economic classifications one finds fisheries next to agriculture, as another basic food provider. Considerable bickering has taken place between nations over the division of these marine spoils between the fishermen of Europe.

MINERAL RESOURCES

The British landscape bears the scars of 2,000 or more years of mining, often for metals such as lead and copper which are now no longer exploited. Cornwall was a source of tin thousands of years ago, and mining has continued to the present day on a diminishing scale. But mineral extraction in modern Britain means one of two things: either the extraction of sand, gravel and clay and the quarrying of slate and road-stone; or the extraction of coal, oil and natural gas.

The first of these activities serves the construction industry via the manufacture of cement, the production of aggregates for concrete and the manufacture of bricks, tiles and pipes. Clay is also the raw material for pottery, and the mining of china clay in Cornwall has left spectacular hills of white sand around St Austell.

The second activity – the extraction of mineral sources of energy – is by far the more important. Coal has been our largest source of energy for the past two hundred years, and will be so again perhaps when our oil resources run out. Britain's coal reserves, and its coal production, are the largest in the European Community and new coalfields are still being de-veloped to take the place of those which have reached the end of their economic life. Production has fallen in recent years, and at the present level of about 100 million tonnes (less than half the 1950 level of output) known reserves should last for a very long time.

The output of coal has fallen as the output of natural gas and oil has risen. These, of course, have represented a dramatic expansion of Bri-tain's known natural resources over the past decade. The gas fields of the southern North Sea were the first of the offshore discoveries, and gas is now also being extracted from under the Irish Sea. Very large quantities of gas are associated with the more northerly oilfields too, but not all of this is currently 'economically recoverable' because of the length and cost of the necessary pipelines.

All the estimates of the size of these underground resources must be fairly tentative, with a large margin of error. In particular, what is or is not 'recoverable' depends on the available technology and on the cost of extraction compared with the price of the product. Our gas reserves, however, are estimated at between 1,229 and 2,472 billion cubic metres, to which could be added a further 150 to 475 billion cubic metres 'undiscovered' but confidently believed to be there. Some of this has already been used, so we are left with between 875 and 2,443 billion cubic metres. This would last for over twenty years, based on the lower estimate of reserves and the current level of extraction. Using the higher figure the gas would last sixty years, and since we could certainly use it less wastefully than we do now we could extend this figure as well.

The line which divides the British half of the North Sea from the Norwegian half (see map, page 4) runs through the middle of several of the oilfields, leaving us with recoverable reserves estimated at:

1,500 to 2,650 million tonnes 'discovered';
330 to 2,825 million tonnes 'undiscovered';
1,830 to 5,475 tonnes total;
and allowing for oil already extracted, 1,130 to 4,780 million tonnes remaining.

The lower level of estimate, compared with the current, peak level of extraction of 120 million tonnes a year, gives a mere ten years' life to the resource. Realistically the level of extraction will slowly decline, so that the oil will not suddenly run out, and the commonly accepted estimates about the future of North Sea oil suggest that output will decline to coincide with UK domestic demand in the early 1990s. Using the much more likely higher estimates we may extend the period of self-sufficiency well into the next century, but of course the present export surplus would disappear, or at least be very much reduced, before then.

Despite their importance to the UK economy, and despite the large effect that their discovery has had, and their decline will have, on a world scale, the North Sea oilfields are relatively small. Our reserves are a mere 2% of the world total.

HUMAN RESOURCES

The second category of economic resources, labour, represents the contribution of the human population of the UK to economic output. 'People' are the resource, and the size of the population ultimately determines the amount of labour available.

Two things will influence this relationship: the age at which people enter and the age at which they leave the labour force, in other words the school-leaving age and the retirement age; and the proportion of the population of working age who actually work, which is known as the participation rate.

The dynamic elements derive from changes in the underlying popula-

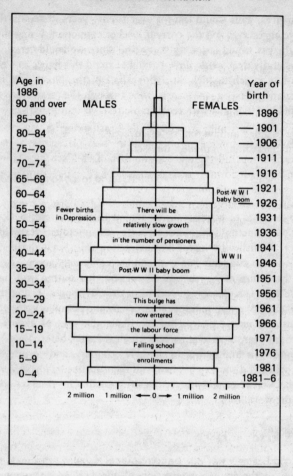

Figure 5 Structure of U K population (1986 estimates)

tion structure; changes in the participation rate, particularly of women; and shifts in employment between different sectors of the economy. The first of these factors is dominated by the surprisingly large changes in the annual number of births over the past eighty years. This is illustrated in Figure 5.

Immediately after the First World War, for example, comes a bulge: a post-war baby boom. This bulge of people are in their sixties, and most of them will by now have retired from the work-force. But this marked change from a period when few retired to a period when very many did so is one of the factors which affected the size of the labour force during the early years of this decade.

There is a very similar dip and bulge associated with the Second World War: few births in the early 1940s, but a marked increase in 1946–8. The present importance of this stems from the fact that when the female half of this bulge reached child-bearing age in the late 1960s, a secondary increase in the number of births took place. The birth rate did not increase, nor did the average number of children in a family; both these in fact went down. It was just that there were so many more potential mothers in the population in those years.

So a relatively large number of children were born in the mid-1960s. They caused a big increase in the school population in the 1970s, and then entered the work-force in the early 1980s. Sadly this did not mean 'entered employment', because the two population-related factors (relatively few retirements and a very large number of entrants) coincided with a very severe economic recession, and between them gave rise to levels of unemployment not experienced for fifty years.

Will this secondary bulge give rise to a tertiary bulge in its turn? The population forecasts predict another rise in births. In the immediate future, however, our problems arise from the very steep fall in the number of births in the mid- and late 1970s. At the moment this means empty classrooms, but in a few years' time it will mean a marked fall in the number of new entrants to the labour force.

Table 2.2 shows the impact of these demographic changes, and particularly the effect on the size of the labour force of the increasing number of young people entering it for the first time. The columns headed 'population' indicate the net effect of new entries and retirements during these years, but this is not always reflected in the overall growth of the labour force because of changes in the proportion of the population which makes itself available for work – the activity rate or participation rate.

The table shows how the advent of the recession in 1979–80 led large numbers of people, especially men, to withdraw from the labour force, while at the same time the shift in the pattern of employment drew in large numbers of women, often into part-time employment.

A more detailed breakdown by age and sex shows that the drop in the activity rate is most marked among older people. The only significant

Table 2.2. Changes in the size of the labour force (annual averages, 000s)

Period	Male			Female			Male and female		
	Overall change	Population	Activity (residual)	Overall change	Population	Activity (residual)	Overall change	Population	Activity (residual)
1971–7	+2	+41	−39	+166	+8	+158	+168	+49	+119
1977–81	+16	+81	−65	+66	+65	+1	+82	+146	−64
1981–3	−147	+104	−250	−18	+73	−91	−164	+177	−341
1983–4	+127	+145	−18	+385	+73	+312	+512	+218	+294
1984–5	+56	+92	−36	+135	+58	+77	+192	+151	+41

Table 2.3. Change between 1981 and 1985 in the percentage economically active (selected age groups)

Age group	Year	Men %	Married women %	Other women %	All persons (000s)	%
16–19	1981	68.6	47.8	63.6	2,309	65.5
	1985	72.3	38.4	69.4	2,431	70.1
50–59	1981	92.4	57.7	65.7	4,607	75.5
	1985	86.8	58.4	59.0	4,277	72.5
60–64	1981	69.6	23.2	23.6	1,272	45.0
	1985	54.4	19.4	16.9	1,083	35.6
All age	1981	77.8	49.4	43.7	25,737	61.9
groups	1985	75.4	52.2	44.3	26,468	61.8

Table 2.4. The economically active population, 1985

Economic status	All persons (000s)	%	Males (000s)	%	Females Married (000s)	%	Other (000s)	%	Total (000s)	%
Economically active:	26,500	49	15,500	59	7,200	52	3,800	27	11,000	40
in employment	23,700	44	13,800	53	6,600	48	3,400	23	9,900	36
unemployed	2,800	5	1,700	6	600	4	500	4	1,100	4
Inactive:	27,600	51	10,800	41	6,600	48	10,200	73	16,800	61
16 and over	16,400	30	5,100	19	6,600	48	4,700	34	11,300	41
under 16	11,200	21	5,800	22	—		5,500	39	5,500	20
Total	54,100	100	26,400	100	13,800	100	13,900	100	27,700	100

change apart from this was an increase in the participation of married women aged between 20 and 49, not shown in Table 2.3.

Table 2.4 shows how the population as a whole is divided between 'economically active' and 'inactive'. More detailed figures from the 1981 Census show that a large proportion of the females described as inactive are engaged in running a home and looking after a family. 'Economically inactive' is not the same as 'idle'; it can mean 'working but not earning a wage'. It is also worth noting that 40% of females in employment are part-time workers.

There are some persistent regional variations in participation rates, which for men vary from lows of 74.3% in Wales and 76.6% in the North and South-West regions up to highs of 79.8% in the South-East (excluding London) and 79.7% in East Anglia. For women the lows

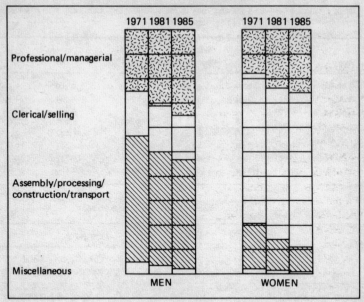

Figure 6 Employment by category

were also in Wales (42%) and the South-West (44.15%), and Northern Ireland has the low figure of 44%. Highs for women were 48.9% in Greater London and 48.55% in the North-West, a legacy of a long tradition of female employment in the textile industry.

Finally we must ask, what sort of work do all these people do, and which branch of the economy do they work in? There is a long-standing division into 'white-collar' occupations – professional, managerial, clerical – and 'blue-collar' occupations – assembly, processing, construction and transport.

The changing pattern shown in Figure 6 must in part be due to people 'upgrading' the jobs they do, but it also illustrates the decline in the traditionally male blue-collar occupations. Incidentally a very high proportion of the women in the professional/managerial category are professionals in health care and teaching.

Members of the labour force are considered to be 'qualified' if they hold some formal qualification beyond the Advanced level of the GCE. Overall some 10% of the population over 18 possess some such qualification, and they are heavily concentrated in the professional/managerial

Table 2.5. Qualified man- and woman-power in Great Britain
(1981 Census, 10% sample, 000s)

Qualifications level	Men	Women	Total
Higher degree	159	40	197
Degree or equivalent	1,225	650	1,870
Other post-A-level	810	1,000	1,810
Total qualified	2,190	1,680	3,870
Total number over 18	19,020	20,800	39,830
% qualified	11.5	8.1	9.7

Table 2.6. Employment and self-employment by industry

Industry group	Employed (000s)	%	Self-employed (000s)	%	Total (000s)	%	% of total work-force Male	Female
0 Agriculture	310	1.5	270	12.4	580	2.5	3.0	1.3
1 Energy and water supply	760	3.6	—	0.1	760	3.3	4.3	1.0
2 Minerals, metals, chemicals	930	4.4	10	0.6	940	4.0	4.4	1.8
3 Engineering, vehicles, metal goods	2,860	13.7	60	2.7	2,920	12.5	14.9	5.1
4 Other manufacturing	2,490	11.9	100	4.7	2,590	11.1	10.9	10.1
5 Construction	1,130	5.4	430	20.0	1,570	6.7	11.4	1.6
6 Distribution, hotel/catering repairs	3,600	17.2	690	32.0	4,290	18.4	16.1	25.4
7 Transport and communications	1,360	6.5	100	4.8	1,460	6.3	8.3	3.0
8 Banking, finance, business services	1,560	7.5	190	8.9	1,760	7.5	8.6	10.2
9 Other, mainly government services	5,650	27.1	270	12.5	5,920	25.4	17.9	40.3
Total[a]	20,900	100	2,160	100	23,050	100	100	100

Note: [a] Including some not classified by industry.

group of occupations, as one would expect. In education, welfare and
health over 70% are qualified. Outside that group, however, the level of
qualification is negligible except for male employees in clerical and sales
occupations, where it reaches 8% to 9%.

The data are shown in Table 2.5, but the gross figures hide some of the more interesting detail. For example, a great deal of importance is attached to that portion of the work-force which is qualified in science and technology, so we may note that of the 1,225,000 men with degree-level qualification 155,000 hold a degree in science and 310,000 in technology: 38%. Of the 810,000 with other post-A-level qualifications, by contrast, 680,000 or 84% hold science or technology qualifications. The one million women in this category work almost exclusively in health (580,000) and education (300,000) and hold nursing or teaching certificates.

As one would expect, the proportion of qualified people is rising as more and more of each group gain access to post-school education: 18.8% of men in the 30–34 year age group are qualified; 16.2% of women in the 25–29 age group are qualified. Taking the work-force as a whole, the 25–29 age group is the best qualified with 17%.

There is a standard method of grouping industries into categories, which will be discussed at greater length in Chapter 3. The broadest division is into ten major groups, 0–9, and the distribution of the work-force between these industrial categories is shown in Table 2.6. Unlike previous tables, this one distinguishes employed from self-employed, and shows how self-employment is concentrated in agriculture, construction, distribution, hotels and catering, and repair work.

The total number of people at work – employed and self-employed, full-time and part-time – has actually risen slightly in recent years while attention was still focused on the numbers *un*employed. But concealed within this is a marked fall in employment in industry groups 2, 3 and 4, and an offsetting rise in groups 6, 7, 8 and 9. Since nearly half the workers in this second group are women, this has meant a fall in male full-time employment and a rise in female employment, much of it part-time. The 'service' sector of the economy – groups 6–9 – now accounts for nearly two-thirds of all jobs.

CAPITAL

We come now to the third of the categories into which the economist classifies the resources which combine to make goods and services, and it is the one which is the most difficult to define and quantify. Its constituent parts are distinguished from 'land' because they are man-made, not of natural origin; but the line is hard to draw. Is the reclaimed land near the Wash in Lincolnshire and Norfolk natural? Or is it man-made capital? It is even possible to regard part of human labour as 'man-made' – as 'human capital', because of the educational investment that has taken place before the special capabilities become available.

Capital and labour are similar in another respect. Just as we considered the flow of new recruits into the labour force at 16 or 18 or 22 years old, and the drift into retirement of the 60-year-old, so we must think of the creation of new items of capital equipment, and of the wearing-out or obsolescence of other items. Capital, in other words, is a *stock* of man-made aids to production, constantly being depleted via depreciation, and constantly being renewed via new investment.

Both these terms justify a moment's attention, because like so many other terms in economics they are words in common use, but words used by economists in a strictly limited way. 'Depreciation' does not mean here the sums of money written down in the accounts of businesses; it describes the capital 'used up' during the year in the course of producing a flow of goods and services. The more descriptive term 'capital consumption' is often used.

Similarly 'investment' does not mean here buying securities or putting money into a building society account. As we are using it, it means the construction or manufacture of capital items like roads, buildings, machine tools, trucks, power-stations: real, tangible, physical things.

The problem we face is how to measure or how to 'add up' such a heterogeneous collection. Again, we are reduced, while recognizing the difficulties we create in doing so, to using money as our unit, and to measuring capital in monetary terms. But we are thinking all the time about the physical realities: the kilometres of motorway, the capacity of the nuclear power-station, the output of the machine tools or the square feet of office accommodation.

Infrastructure

There is in all developed, industrialized economies a very large amount of capital which serves the economy as a whole rather than being linked with one specific productive process. An idea of the huge extent of the infrastructure can be gleaned from looking at the 1984 figures for some of its main components: transport, energy, water and information distribution.

Transport is clearly a key part of the economic system. Raw materials

Table 2.7. Energy consumption

Energy source	billion therms				
	1970	1974	1978	1982	1985
Gas	6	12	15	17	19
Petroleum	27	27	27	23	22
Solid fuel	18	12	9	7	7
Electricity	7	7	8	7	8
All fuels	58	59	59	54	56

These figures conceal the fact that most electricity is derived from burning coal, as the figures below reveal.

	million tons coal equivalent	
	1983	1984
Coal	116	79[a]
Petroleum	106	135[a]
Natural gas	75	77
Nuclear power	18	20
Hydroelectricity	2	2
Total	313	312

Note: [a] Affected by miners' strike.

and finished products must be transported to and from the manufacturer and the consumer; there must be a system of ports, roads, railways and airports, and the trains and trucks and aircraft to use it.

The transport industry, which includes road, rail, sea and air transport, possessed capital resources in 1984 valued at £60.8 billion at 1980 prices. £36.1 billion (at current, 1984, replacement cost) was the value of vehicles, ships and aircraft then being used. Each employee in the industry thus had some £70,000 of capital equipment to work with.

Road transport is now far the most important way of moving goods around, and the number of vehicles may be surprising:

public transport vehicles: 115,000;
goods vehicles: 587,000;
agricultural tractors and similar equipment: 386,000.

Developed, industrialized economies are also distinguished by their lavish use of energy. Again, the whole economy is dependent on an electricity distributing grid, a system of gas pipelines and a petrol or diesel pump every few miles.

Figures for UK energy use in 1984 are considerably distorted by the coal-miners' strike, so 1983 figures are given in Table 2.7 as well. 'Energy' is one thing which can be added up in units other than money, and the units used here are 'million tons coal equivalent' (the energy used by our nuclear power-stations, for example, was the equivalent of 19.5 million tons of coal in 1984) and billion therms.

The supply of energy requires vast amounts of capital. The extraction of oil and gas needed a stock of capital worth £27.9 billion (1984 quantity at 1980 prices), which gave each worker in the industry the phenomenal amount of £825,400 worth of plant and equipment. The remainder of the energy sector had £114.6 billion worth of capital in 1984 (at 1980 prices), representing almost £200,000 worth per employee.

It is too often forgotten that another commodity which industry uses in very large quantities is water. Industry produces a comparable volume of dirty water too; its waste has to be disposed of, usually down the drain, so that a supply of clean water and a sewage system are essential. The water supply industry supplied 19.1 megalitres of water per day in the UK in 1984, a figure which is perhaps more meaningful when translated into 432 litres per head.

The final item in the stock of capital we call 'infrastructure' forms the information distribution system, and many people will argue convincingly that 'information' is the most important product of our modern society. It needs a telephone or data transmission system, and a postal system; otherwise the flow of information and the whole system will quickly seize up.

Posts and telecommunications in 1984 had £30.3 billion worth of capital equipment and buildings at their disposal (1980 prices), or £72,400 per employee. Ten billion letters were sent, and 22.6 billion telephone calls were made, in 1984.

Social overhead capital

The sort of capital we have described in the preceding paragraphs is not for the exclusive use of industry. Water and sewage are needed by people too, as are communication and transport facilities. Society as a whole needs capital, particularly to maintain the human input to the economy, the labour force.

Some writers therefore use the term 'social overhead capital' to describe the schools, universities, hospitals, libraries, museums and so on which make up the stock of capital equipment which our society requires to maintain and renew itself generation by generation. The accumulated stock of knowledge or 'know-how' which a society possesses is, in a very real sense, a stock of capital. In part it is embodied in individual members of the work-force, when we call it 'human capital'; in part it resides in books and blueprints and data banks, available for use in exactly the same way as a truck or machine tool is available for use.

As a rough measure of the amount of social overhead in existence we may look at that part of capital – vehicles, plant and machinery, and other buildings and works – attributed to the central government and to local authorities. In 1984 this capital was worth (at 1984 replacement cost):

Vehicles, etc.	£0.9 billion
Plant and machinery	£9.6 billion
Other buildings and works	£127.4 billion
Total	£137.9 billion

This excludes houses, as well as private cars and other items of personal equipment. It includes items such as police stations, law courts and defence establishments, as well as schools and hospitals. In size it is almost identical with the £142.6 billion attributed to the 'energy' sector as a whole.

Unfortunately it is virtually impossible to think of a way of quantifying this sort of capital more accurately, which is perhaps one of the reasons why its maintenance seems to be neglected, and expenditure on it begrudged.

Housing

Government statisticians separate out one other element from the total capital stock, namely domestic housing. Housing is bought or rented by individual households, and one might wonder why the purchase of a house should be treated differently from the purchase of a car or a television, both of which are, we hope, long-term pieces of equipment from which we will derive a flow of service for some years. Houses are very long-lived, however, often outlasting the generation which built them, and so are legitimately treated as capital: another element in social overhead capital, perhaps.

Table 2.8. Gross investment in capital goods, by type and sector, 1984
(£ billion, current prices)

Category of investment	Private sector	Public corporations	Government	Total
Vehicles, ships, aircraft	5	1	—	6
Plant and machinery	15	4	1	20
Other new buildings and works	7	3	5	15
Dwellings	9	—	2	12
Total	37	8	8	53

Table 2.9. Total capital stock of the economy (£ billion at current, 1984, replacement cost)

Category of investment	Personal sector	Industry, commerce[a]	Government	Total
Vehicles, ships, aircraft	5	30	1	36
Plant and machinery	13	204	10	226
Other new buildings and works	25	190	127	342
Dwellings	224	17	93	334
Total	267	441	231	939

Note: [a] Including public corporations.

Housing is a well-documented area of the economy, and domestic housing is one of the biggest single items in the inventory of Britain's capital stock. Privately owned housing was valued (at replacement cost) at £230 billion in 1984, and publicly owned housing at £104.3 billion, a total of £334.3 billion. (Cf. the total for energy and manufacturing industry: £349.5 billion in 1984, valued at 1980 prices.)

This sum represents 22 million dwellings, of which 13 million were owned in whole or part by their occupiers, 6½ million were rented from local authorities or new town corporations and 2½ million fell into other categories.

Because there are so many data available about it, we can use housing to illustrate an earlier discussion about 'capital' and 'investment'. Each year a number of new houses and flats are built, and this is the 'gross' investment in housing. Each year too a number of old houses and blocks of flats are demolished – which represents 'capital consumption' or depreciation. The difference between these two numbers is 'net' invest-

Table 2.10. Gross and net investment and capital stock, by industry (£ billion)

Industry group	Investment in 1984 at current prices		Capital stocks at 1980 cost		
	Gross	Net	1974	1984	Index 1984[a]
0 Agriculture	1.28	+0.03	22	25	113
1 Energy and water supply	6.96	+0.70	108	142	131
(of which 1,300 oil and gas)	(3.22)	(+0.90)	(4)	(28)	775
2, 3, 4 Manufacturing	7.08	−0.90	175	199	114
5 Construction	0.57	−0.09	11	13	118
6 Distribution, etc.	4.58	+2.12	48	69	146
7 Transport, except 78/79	2.62	−0.20	68	61	90
communication	1.86	+0.10	23	30	134
8 Banking, finance	8.60	+5.20	46	93	204
9 Other, mainly government	7.05	+3.90	145	190	131
Dwellings (not in above)	11.93	+6.00	288	365	127
Total	52.53	+16.86	931	1,188	127.5

Note: [a] 1974 = 100.

ment, which can be positive or negative. If it is positive, the stock of capital at the end of the year will be greater than it was at the beginning of the year. For housing, some illustrative figures are:

Period/year	(000 dwellings) New construction			
	Public sector	Private sector	Total	Net gain = net investment
	170	198	368	258
1961–70 (annual average)	142	178	320	226
1971–5 (annual average)	110	130	240	209
1980	55	143	198	181
1983				

In money terms, gross investment in housing in 1984 was £11.93 billion = £6.0 billion net. Figures for gross investment through the economy as a whole are included in Tables 2.8, 2.9 and 2.10, together with estimates of the total capital stock and its breakdown into various categories.

Tables 2.9 and 2.10 illustrate the difficulty of reconciling statistics

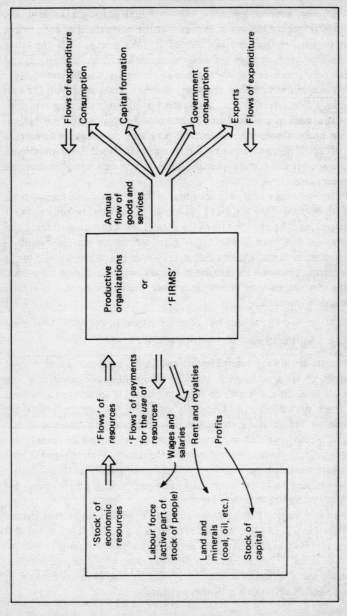

Figure 7 Stocks and flows of economic resources

from different sources, since we have two figures for the value of the total capital stock. One would expect that the one valued at 1980 prices would be smaller than the one valued at 1984 prices, since the latter includes four years of price and cost increases; but in fact it is larger, and one can only conclude that the method of compilation is different.

This is a minor technical problem, however, compared with the evidence in Table 2.10 that the capital stock is not always being replaced. There is a marked concentration of net new investment in distribution, banking and finance, government services and dwellings, whereas the stock of capital in manufacturing and transport declined. New investment in these sectors did not compensate for wear and tear, obsolescence and scrapping.

The ten-year data of growth of capital in Table 2.10 shows manufacturing at the bottom of the list, and a run-down in transport (mainly railways and shipping). The growth rate of the capital stock in manufacturing and construction has been barely 1% a year; and as we saw in Figure 3, employment in manufacturing fell steeply over the same period. One of our recurring themes – the decline in Britain's manufacturing industries, and the concentration of growth in finance and distribution – is vividly portrayed in this table.

STOCKS AND FLOWS OF RESOURCES

Economists are always careful to distinguish between *stocks* and *flows* of resources, goods or services. A 'stock' is the quantity accumulated at any given point of time; a 'flow', on the other hand, is an amount measured over some period of time. Generally this is a year, so that when for example we are thinking about the flow of labour (i.e. the use of our stock of labour), we talk in terms of man-years or woman-years, man-hours or woman-months, or some similar 'quantity × time interval' unit of measurement. It is perhaps because we do not usually do this explicitly that stocks and flows are commonly confused – with employment, for instance, referred to in simple numbers.

When in Chapter 1 (page 5) we took an imaginary flight over Britain and looked down on the economic activity going on below we noted that the production was carried out by organized groups of people, which we may call 'firms'. They produced a flow of *output* of goods and services, and made use of a flow of *inputs* of economic resources in order to do so. Figure 7 makes this idea a little more explicit.

The labour resource – that is, the active or potentially active portion of the total population – has been discussed at length in the section on human resources above, but in 'stock' terms. The 'flow' – the actual man- and woman-hours worked during the year – is best measured and understood by looking at the flow of payments which the firms or productive organizations make to their employees. This is not too difficult to estimate, since records of wages and salaries have to be kept for tax purposes. The 'guesswork' or imputing appears when we deal with self-employed people: how much of a farmer's income should be classed as rent, as wages or as profit? And there is an 'informal economy' in which work is done for payments which are not declared. Even so, there was a recorded flow of payments of wages and salaries totalling £195 billion in 1985, corresponding to the 21 million employed people or, more precisely, to the hours these people worked. The self-employed, just over 2 million strong, were estimated to have earned £30 billion, but this might not all be a 'return to labour' in the strict sense.

The 'land' resource, we saw, is partly the agricultural land on which our food, or a part of it, is grown and the land on which we build houses and factories and roads and railways. In both cases it is very difficult to separate land from capital, and perhaps not very useful to try. The second element of land, discussed in the section on mineral resources above, is now a very important one, because to the traditional coal we have to add the more recently discovered oil and gas reserves under the surrounding seas.

Payments for the *use* of land – i.e. the money payments corresponding to the *flow* of the resource into production – are called 'rent', and the owners of mineral resources are paid a rent (usually called a royalty) by those who exploit them. The owner of both coal and oil is now the state. We can therefore obtain an alternative measure of our 'land' resources by looking at the total annual payments of rents and royalties, which in 1985 totalled £26 billion. This figure necessarily contains a good deal of guesswork, because very often the users of the land are also its owners. Since they would not pay rent to themselves, someone has to 'impute' a rental payment.

It is also necessary to make a distinction between the use of a resource in the sense of 'using it up', and use in the sense of utilizing or 'making use of'. Some of our oil, gas and coal resources were 'used up' or depleted during 1985 and can never be replaced. Some of our capital equipment wore out, but that can be replaced, and even increased – though as we have just seen, some of it was not. Some of the stock of labour (and indeed some of the land and capital) was not used at all – it was unemployed. And as far as the labour force was concerned it probably deteriorated or 'depreciated' through *not* being used.

Capital poses the biggest conceptual problem. This is partly because it includes domestic housing, which is not used in the production of goods and services, but mainly because the 'return to capital' is the residual income after the identifiable rent and wage payments have been made. There is no reason why this residual should correspond to the 'use of capital', but we assume that the £60 billion of gross trading surplus or profit in 1985 approximated to a return to the economic resource 'capital'. Again this is a payment for the *use* of the stock for a period of one year.

When we add up all these payments made to the owners of the economic resources which were used in the production of goods and services during 1985 we have a total of all the incomes earned in the economy during that year. One would expect this total to be called the 'national income', but it is not. In the official statistics this total flow of payments to the factors of production is regarded as another way of estimating the volume of goods and services which these factors produced. It is an 'income-based' estimate of the gross domestic product. These technicalities are explored later. Our concern in this chapter has been with the *stock* of economic resources which the British economy has at its disposal, but from now on the focus will be very much on the use which is made of them, i.e. on the *flows*. This section will help the reader to keep this important distinction clearly in mind.

3

LLLLLLLLLLLLLLLLLLL

The Process of Production

We have just been looking at the extent to which the United Kingdom is endowed with economic resources: our 12 million hectares of farmland; our 23 million workers; and our £1,000 billion worth of equipment, buildings, power lines, railways and other items of capital. These constitute the *stock* of the factors of production needed to produce the goods and services that we require. Resources are the starting-point to those flows within the economy that we outlined in Chapter 1. We must now consider in more detail the way this stock is used each year to produce a massive *flow* of goods of all descriptions, and an equally wide range of services.

The producers who co-ordinate the use of the factors of production – who decide what should be produced, by which technique and with which combination of inputs – are to be found in Figure 7 in the box labelled 'firms', that being a convenient title for the various individuals and organizations involved; our concern in this chapter is basically with what goes on inside that box.

In the process of production, firms engage in a very large number of transactions between themselves, and indeed in many cases *within* themselves, because so many are large organizations with numerous branches and subdivisions.

Eventually a flow of goods and services emerges which is not used by other firms as an intermediate input, but which is 'consumed' or finally used. It is this flow of goods and services into final consumption which constitutes the 'domestic product' of our economy, and we describe it in more detail in Chapters 4 and 5. Here we are concerned with the production process itself, rather than with the end product.

THE STRUCTURE OF OUTPUT

At any one time there are many possible techniques available for producing goods and services. These will involve the use of machinery of a
particular kind and the employment of a number of people with differing
skills and knowledge, plus land, buildings, raw materials and so on. A
detailed description of each and every product, and each and every
technique of production, would fill an encyclopaedia, let alone a book.

Economists faced with this complexity must generalize, and you will
find that textbooks of economics deal with technology in a most general
way, talking only about 'capital-intensive' or 'labour-intensive' methods
of production. Oil and gas extraction is a good example of an industry
which uses an immense amount of capital in the shape of drilling rigs
and pipelines, but very little labour; each of the 33,000 employees had in
1984 £825,000 of capital to work with. In contrast the distribution of
finished goods to consumers through wholesalers and retailers uses a
great deal of labour (over 3 million in 1984) but relatively little capital:
only £16,000 per worker for this whole section of the economy.

The input of land – the third of the economist's factors of production –
is in practice not very significant except in agriculture, forestry and the
provision of housing. But this, of course, is to interpret 'land' in its
narrower sense. When widened to include mineral resources it plays a
much more far-reaching role.

All three factors of production are generally needed to create a flow of
output. A key decision is in what proportions they should be employed.
Economists use mathematical equations and diagrams to illustrate the
outcome of combining them in various quantities in order to decide
which is the 'best' mix. And in the real world firms have to take similar
decisions in which, as well as purely technical considerations, the prices
of the various factors will be a vital consideration.

The accounts of a firm record all the flows of goods and services in and out,
using money values as the common unit. One of the functions of money, as we
shall see, is to act as a 'unit of account'. At the level of one firm or enterprise we
find an annual profit and loss account; adding together the accounts of all the
similar firms which make up a sector of the economy produces 'sectoral'
accounts; and finally by adding up (with due allowance for double counting)
all the firms in the economy we obtain the 'national accounts'.

So it is useful to look at the production process by examining the
accounts of a typical productive enterprise. These will show:

(1) what it produced during the year, and how much this output was sold for, i.e. the total revenue;

(2) how much it paid out during the year for

    (a) raw materials, energy, etc. (goods and services bought in),

    (b) labour (wages and salaries),

    (c) land and buildings (rent),

    (d) capital.

(How is capital paid for? Conventionally the firm's capital belongs to its owners, the shareholders, and the net revenue or profit is considered to be a return to, or the cost of, the capital input.)

A much simplified revenue and expenditure account of, say, a flour miller might look like this (in arbitrary units):

Sales of flour	400,000	Purchase of wheat	80,000
		Purchase of sacks, bags, etc.	20,000
		Electricity, water, etc.	20,000
		Rent of buildings	5,000
		Wages and salaries	200,000
			325,000
		Net revenue = profit	75,000
			400,000

Slightly rearranged this becomes:

Purchase of raw materials, etc.	120,000
Value of final product	400,000
'Value added' in the course of production	280,000

Consisting of: Rent	5,000 to factor land
Wages and salaries	200,000 to factor labour
Profit	75,000 to factor capital

As can be seen, the 'value added' by the flour miller in the course of production is the difference between the cost of the materials bought in by the firm and the value of the final output which it produces. This addition comes about because of the further application of land, labour and capital that takes place within the flour mill. Naturally, therefore, 'value added' and 'payments to factors' amount to the same total: 280,000.

A flour miller comes somewhere in the middle of a chain of productive activities linking the farmers who grow the wheat to the consumers who eat the bread or biscuits. Farmers, at the beginning of such a chain, are

FARMERS

Wheat	80	[Other inputs]	
		Net revenue 80* divided into	
		Rent	30
		Wages	40
		Profit	10
	80		80

FLOUR MILLER

Flour	400	Wheat	80
		[Other inputs]	
		Wages	200
		Rent	25
			305
		Net revenue	95
	400		400

BAKER

Bread	1,000	Flour	400
(goods for final consumption)		[Other inputs]	
		Wages	400
		Rent	110
			910
		Net revenue	90
	1,000		1,000

* Farmers often own their own land and work it themselves; their income has to be arbitrarily split into rent, wages and profit.

Production unit ('Industry')	Value of goods produced	less Goods purchased	equals Value added		of which			Total income
					Wages	Rent	Profit	
Farmers	80	—	80		40	30	10	80
Flour miller	400	80 (wheat)	320		200	25	95	320
Baker	1,000	400 (flour)	600		400	110	90	600
Totals	1,480	480	1,000		640	165	195	1,000
	This total includes wheat three times and flour twice; it exaggerates national product	This 'nets out' the double and treble counting	Leaving the value of output or *national product*					This total is *national income*

Figure 8a and b Inter-industry payments

typical *primary* producers – the term frequently applied to those responsible for the output of raw materials like grains or minerals. The
flour-milling firm itself represents the manufacturing or processing stage,
and those engaged in such production are known as *secondary* industries.
These would also include the baker or the biscuit manufacturer who
makes the products finally eaten by the consumers; we distinguish industries producing goods for sale to other industries (producer or capital
goods) from those making consumer goods.

Production invariably requires that goods and people be moved
around: that people communicate with each other; that warehouses and
retail shops exist; and that there are facilities for making payments,
borrowing money and advertising products. In short, there is a great deal
of economic activity which produces services of all kinds. This forms the
tertiary sector of the economy.

Although this grouping of economic activity into three sectors is often
used, it can give the misleading impression that it describes a typical
sequence of events: primary production (of basic materials) being followed by processing and manufacturing (smelting, milling, pressing,
assembly), followed by distribution and consumption. In the real world
there is a much more complex network of producers and producing units
buying goods and services from each other and selling goods and services
to other businesses or to consumers, and all using the facilities provided
by government.

We can begin to move from the individual firm towards the level of
'industry' and 'sector' by extending our previous example of the flour
miller backwards to primary producers and forwards to consumer goods
industries – see Figure 8a. It can be seen that the output of the farmers
(wheat valued at 80) becomes the input for the flour miller, to which
further value of 320 is added in the course in processing it into flour. In
turn the flour (valued at 400) is an input for the baker, who enhances its
value to 1,000 by transforming it into bread. The relationship in the
three industries between their value added and the payments made in
wages, rent and profit is shown in Figure 8b.

So here we have a picture of a very simple little economy which serves
as a basis for understanding the economy as a whole. First of all it shows
us that what each stage of production – i.e. each industry – contributes to
the final output is measured by the 'value' it added to the goods it buys
and processes. This as we now know is the same as the money paid out to
the factors of production used at each stage: the incomes earned. Add all

these together and we have the 'national income' of our mini-economy.

Can we also add up the value of the goods produced, so as to get a corresponding figure for 'national product'? If we were to add the values of the wheat and flour together we should be counting the wheat twice; once as wheat, and then again in the form of flour. Similarly with the flour and the bread. What our economy eventually produces is bread, so we should ignore all the intermediate stages and simply take the value of 'goods for final use or consumption' as our measure of national product. Alternatively we could 'net out' (subtract) the intermediate goods at each stage, which would leave us with 'value added'. It will be seen that the sum of the 'values added' at each stage is the same as the value of the bread, the good which is finally consumed.

Notice that national income and national product are identical – an important equivalence which we shall take up again when we describe the national product and the national income of the UK at a later stage.

In reality, all these producers, and the industries which they represent in this simple model economy, would be purchasing inputs from a wide range of other producers as well. The farmers would be buying fuel for their tractors, fertilizer and seed dressings, and even buying products from other farmers – seed, perhaps. The miller and baker would be buying fuel, power, sacks and bags, paying for transport services and telephone calls and using the financial services of banks. Any real economy is a very complex web of transactions. This line of thought will be pursued further in the section on input–output below, where we shall illustrate the flows between industries in an 'input–output matrix'. But before we can do that we must discuss the definition and classification of industries.

THE CLASSIFICATION OF INDUSTRIES

The complications of the real world soon begin to emerge when we try to classify and group similar types of economic activity into *industries* rather than simply thousands of producers. This may not be immediately obvious. The 'shipbuilding industry', the 'car industry' and the 'leather industry' all conjure up fairly precise images because of their association with familiar and well-known products. But even here there are questions. The car industry makes cars. Does the leather industry make leather or does it use it as its main material?

In practice it is not at all easy to define an 'industry', and that is because there is no single consistent basis for such a definition. Some, such as the chemical industry and the steel industry, are defined by the *material they make*. Others, such as the textile industry, use a range of materials such as wool, cotton and synthetic fibres and weave or knit them into fabric; *process and product* define the industry rather than the raw material. Agriculture might be defined on the basis of *where it operates*, rather than what it does or what it produces. The 'service industries' are particularly hard to classify; the usual basis is the function they serve, but recent developments in information technology are blurring the distinction between, for example, printing and publishing (which are usually grouped with pulp and paper), postal and telecommunications services, and business services.

As a well-known American economist, Kenneth Boulding, has put it, it may be that 'the concept of an "industry", which in economics corresponds somewhat to that of a species in biology, is a classification which exists more in conversation than reality'.

The statisticians who grapple with these difficulties are constrained by the availability of information, and by the need to produce figures which are comparable with those published by other countries. As a result of their efforts we now at least have a 'standard classification' in common and international use. It is a decimal system; the economy is divided into ten major groups, called *divisions*:

0 Agriculture, forestry, fisheries
1 Energy and water supply
2 Extraction of minerals and ores other than fuels; manufacture of metals, mineral products and chemicals
3 Metal goods, engineering and vehicles industries
4 Other manufacturing industries

} Manufacturing industries

5 Construction
6 Distribution, hotel and catering, repair
7 Transport and communications
8 Financial services
9 Other (principally government) services

You can see the traces of a primary (0 and 1), secondary (2, 3 and 4) and tertiary (5–9) basis for the classification, and also some of its problems. Division 6 has little in the way of common characteristics, for example.

The next level of detail is the *class*, and below that again comes the *group* of similar activities – *activity* being the finest subdivision in the system. We can show how it works by looking at Division 2 in more detail. Class 21 covers the extraction of metalliferous ores, and then comes Class 22, metal manufacturing. This is subdivided into:

Group   221   Iron and steel industry
            222   Steel tubes
            223   Steel forming (forging, pressing, rolling, etc.)
then 224   Non-ferrous metals, subdivided in its turn into:
            Activity 2245   Aluminium
                     2246   Copper, brass, etc.
                     2247   Other non-ferrous metals

Information about individual firms, plants and organizations is collected from a variety of sources, principally a periodic Census of Production, and the information is then sorted out and classified in the way described.

Division 2 illustrates some of the problems inherent in any classification. Essentially it is made up of basic industries, extracting, refining and processing raw material to supply other parts of the economy. For example, Classes 23 and 24 comprise the extraction of sand, gravel and clay (231), and the manufacture of bricks, tiles, cement, etc. (241, 242). Group 247, however, is glass and glassware – producing sheet glass for the building industry, safety glass for car windscreens, glass bottles and jars, glass fibre for reinforcement and insulation, and the glasses and tumblers on our tables; in short, a range of products destined for very varied uses, but all made of glass. Class 25, the chemical industry, shows a similar range from very basic industrial chemicals at one extreme to soap and toilet preparations at the other.

INPUT–OUTPUT

When we described in Figures 8a and 8b the way in which a firm's accounts illustrate its purchases of goods and services from other industries, and its purchases of factor services, we emphasized that the simple wheat-flour-bread chain which we used as an example was very much too simple. A large number of inputs were omitted. Farmers would be buying fertilizer and tractor fuel from the oil-refining and chemical industries, and seed from other farmers, i.e. from their own industry. The flour miller would need power, and sacks and bags for his own product; the baker's ovens need fuel. All would require the services of the transport and distributive industries, the banks, telecommunications and so on.

It would be possible in principle to identify the source of each individual purchase of goods or services, and to subdivide the output of the firm by the destination of each consignment sold. After sifting right through the year's financial records one might end up with something like the following:

FM Flour Millers Ltd

Purchases from:		Sales to:		
Firm A	8,000	Firm W	Firm X	Firm Y
Firm B	7,000	15,000	12,000	11,000 etc.
Firm C	3,000			
Firm D	4,000			
etc.				
etc.				
Total purchases	25,000	45,000 Total sales		

The next step is to group all these individual firms into their respective industries and then to add together the figures for every firm in the flour-milling industry. We would then have:

(1) All the goods and services purchased by the flour-milling industry during a particular year, classified by the industry of origin.
(2) The destination, industry by industry, of all the flour and other products produced by the flour-milling industry.
(3) The total input to the flour-milling industry, adding its purchases of factors to its purchases of goods and services itemized in (1).
(4) The total output of the industry, obtained by adding any sales for final consumption to the sum of sales to other industries itemized in (2).

Repeat this exercise, industry by industry, and you would end up with a very detailed but also very vivid and useful picture of the UK economy. The labour of computation is of course very considerable, so that in

Table 3.1. A simplified input/output matrix

(Sales by commodity group) OUTPUT FROM ↓	1 Agriculture	2 Coal, oil, gas	3 Electricity and water	4 Iron, steel, other metals	5 Other basic materials	6 Mechanical/electrical manufactures	7 Transport equipment
1 Agriculture, etc.	19	—	—	—	•	—	—
2 Coal, oil, gas	•	36	27	8	14	5	3
3 Electricity and water	1	2	2	3	6	4	2
4 Iron, steel, other metals	•	2	•	16	3	34	8
5 Other basic materials	5	1	1	3	38	8	3
6 Mechanical/electrical manufactures	1	5	4	8	8	57	23
7 Transport equipment	•	•	•	1	•	•	9
8 Other manufactures	21	2	1	1	11	10	6
9 Construction	1	4	4	•	•	1	•
10 Distribution, hotels, etc.	6	3	3	12	6	20	6
11 Transport and communications	1	5	1	3	10	10	4
12 Financial and other services	7	2	4	4	14	17	5
13 Public services, dwellings							
14 Total domestic inputs	65	62	48	56	111	172	70
15 Imported goods and services	5	51	7	20	31	43	21
16 Labour, } factor inputs	14	30	17	20	40	120	50
17 Capital, land }	25	78	14	−2	20	29	3
18 Total input	106	221	89	99	208	373	148

INPUT TO → (Purchases by industry group)

Note: * = less than £50 million.

onomy, 1979 (£ hundreds of million)

10	11	12	13	14	15	16	17	18	19	20
								Components of final demand		
Distribution, hotels, etc.	Transport and communications	Financial and other services	Public services, dwellings	Total intermediate demand	Total final demand	Consumption (C)	General government consumption (G)	Gross fixed capital formation (I)	Exports	Total output
2	—	—		86	19	12	1	—	7	106
6	10	2		121	97	34	8	3	51	217
8	2	1		37	41	30	5	•	5	78
—	1	•		71	27	•	•	—	27	98
2	1	4		118	82	13	9	4	57	200
6	6	2		146	226	15	19	74	117	371
3	7	2		23	114	5	21	39	49	137
39	6	13		211	295	190	14	14	77	506
5	1	10		89	195	31	13	150	2	284
16	6	7		115	346	286	13	15	32	461
33	13	25		129	117	44	9	8	55	246
41	18	49		197	190	91	34	18	47	386
					336	115	221	—	—	336
160	69	116	—	1,343	2,084					3,427
11	33	7	—	331	215	130	16	59	12	546
164	95	202	228	1,151						1,151
77	41	46	107	528						528
433	241	386	336	3,427	2,480	1,171	383	389	551	5,907

practice it is only carried out at intervals, usually in conjunction with the periodic Census of Industry.

The first such table, known as an input–output table or matrix, constructed for the UK economy was prepared in connection with the 'national plan' launched in the early 1960s. The latest available version refers to the year 1979 and was published by HMSO in 1983. In it the economy was subdivided into one hundred 'industry groups', based on the standard industrial classification we have already discussed. In order to be able to print such a table, which in its original version occupies several large pages of very small print, we have condensed these hundred headings into thirteen, and omitted some other detail, to obtain Table 3.1.

Let us try to get a clearer idea of what the numbers mean (they are all in units of £100 million and have been rounded) by looking first at a *column* of the table. The columns are headed 'purchases by industry group', or 'input to', and we have chosen column 4 as a relatively simple example. It is labelled 'iron, steel, other metals' and is a condensation of columns 10 to 13 of the original 100 × 100 matrix (group 11 being by far the most important):

10 Extraction of metalliferous ores and metals
11 Iron and steel and steel products
12 Aluminium and aluminium alloys
13 Other non-ferrous metals

The entries in column 4 indicate how much this industry purchased from all other industry groups listed down the left-hand margin of the table under the heading 'sales by commodity group'. The slight variation in wording is irrelevant. As might be expected, the purchases *by* the steel industry *from* the agricultural industry (row 1) were negligible, but it purchased £800 million worth of goods from 'coal, oil and gas', row 2. This would have been coke for blast-furnaces, oil and gas for heating furnaces for refining metals and so on.

The largest entry in the column, however, occurs at the intersection with its own row, row 4. The industry appears to be buying a lot of its own products! The figure of £1,600 million is also the largest entry in row 4; the steel industry seems to be the largest purchaser and user of steel, and to be taking in its own washing, as the saying goes. But a moment's reflection will remind us that an industry is a collection of units engaged in similar (but not always identical) operations and using similar (but not identical) materials. Inevitably these units trade extensively with each other. Some are specialist suppliers to the other firms in the industry. Some assemble the parts made by others. In virtually every case the entry on the diagonal at the intersection of row and column is a large one.

All industries have to distribute their products to their customers, which in turn implies the use of transport services. Hence the relatively large entries in rows 10 and 11.

We can think of the entries in column 4 as being like the list of ingredients in a recipe. In this case, they indicate what was used in 1979 in order to produce our steel and other metals.

These were what the industry group produced in 1979, and the entries in row 4 will show us where it all went. We noted that a lot went back into the industry for further processing: for example, steel ingots for rolling into strips, sheets, plates or sections. Most of the output, however, went into the very large and heterogeneous group of metal-using manufacturing industries which we have condensed into column 6.

At this stage it seems necessary to explain why column 13 and row 13 are empty. This is column/row 100 in the original table, headed 'public administration, etc., domestic service, dwellings'. Dwellings, whether we own them or rent them, give us a service (or flow of satisfaction), but neither this nor domestic service could be an input into any industry group. Although many of the services provided by government *are* used by industries, it would be difficult to identify the flows because the services are neither measured nor paid for, and are very widely diffused. Imagine trying to work out where the service of maintaining the motorway network would end up! The *output* of group 13 is therefore assumed to appear only as 'final demand', and not to form part of any intermediate input to other industries.

Looking now at column 13, we realize that sales by other industries, notably group 9, 'construction', would be an addition to our stock of houses, and would therefore appear under the column 'gross fixed capital formation' in 'final demand', not in column 13. Sales by other industries to central and local government appear mainly in the column headed 'general government consumption', again a part of final demand. So there are no sales by other industries to column 13; row and column are blank.

All the transactions which took place *between* industries in 1979 can therefore be thought of as being contained in the space above row 13 and to the left of column 13. They are added, both down and across, in row

Table 3.2. The car industry complex, 1979 (£ million)

Output from ↓ \ Input to →	1 Steel and other metals	2 Metal castings, forgings, etc.	3 Engineers' tools	4 Power transmission and other mechanical equipment	5 Electrical wiring and equipment	6 Vehicle industry	7 Total	8 Total intermediate demand	9 Col. 7 as % of col. 8	10 Col. 6 as % of col. 8
1 Steel and other metals	1,535	1,001	64	331	331	737	3,668	6,929	53	11
2 Metal castings, forgings, etc.	180	378	14	428	172	1,132	2,304	4,736	49	24
3 Engineer's tools	41	23	15	24	10	36	149	396	38	9
4 Power transmission and other mechanical equipment	75	37	4	504	77	465	1,162	2,656	44	18
5 Electrical wiring and equipment	78	9	1	117	140	184	529	1,994	26	9
6 Vehicle industry						596				
7 Asbestos, glass, rubber, paint, etc.						488		4,633		11
8 Total	1,909	1,448	98	1,404	730	3,638				
9 Total manufactured inputs	2,544	1,925	121	1,747	1,091	4,214				
10 Row 8 as % of row 9	75	75	81	80	67	86				

and column 14, which are called 'total domestic inputs' and 'total intermediate demand' respectively. This 'space' is in effect an enlarged view of 'what went on inside the box' (Figure 7), and the remainder of the input–output table is concerned with the flows into the box (factor services and imports) and with the destinations of goods and services which emerged from it for final consumption.

Before we complete our study of Table 3.1 let us continue our discussion of inter-firm transactions by looking at an industry that in many ways typifies the decline of manufacturing which we have already identified as one of our themes. Let us look at the motor-vehicle industry. Figure 2 showed how during recent years the West Midlands has suffered increasingly high levels of unemployment, the result of a dramatic decline in manufacturing employment in the region. Motor vehicles were the dominant industry, not only as a major employer but also because so many other firms in the region were engaged in manufacturing products which directly or indirectly served its requirements. This kind of inter-dependence is brought out most vividly by the use of an input–output matrix, and since we cannot print the full detailed matrix, we have set out a 'mini-matrix' concerned with the vehicle industry in Table 3.2.

The explanation should begin with column 6, 'vehicle industry', so called because it is the sum of three columns of the 100 × 100 table, namely items 34 'agricultural machinery and tractors', 52 'motor vehicles and parts' and 55 'other vehicles' – of which 52 is by far the most important. The rows 1 to 7 contain the industry groups which together supplied the bulk of the vehicle industry's inputs; as the table shows, they accounted for 86% of its 1979 purchases. So any decline in the prosperity of the vehicle industry will adversely affect these supplying industries.

Yet if we simply ask 'what proportion of the output of, say, metal castings and forgings is bought by the vehicle industry?' the answer (24%) scarcely constitutes 'dependence', though it is clearly a significant proportion. It is the fact that this sector of manufacturing industry is part of a complex which is crucial, and this becomes clear only when we fill in the rest of the matrix. When we recognize that this industry is also a supplier to, and purchaser from, all the other industries linked to the vehicle industry then the true extent of the dependency of the metal-using industries of the West Midlands becomes apparent. Between a third and a half of their output is affected, rather than a tenth or a fifth. When we see, for example, in Table 3.3 that the output of the motor-vehicle industry fell by a third between 1979 and 1985 we can now appreciate the consequential effects on the whole complex of industries which formed the manufacturing heartland of Britain, and understand why a region noted until recently for its prosperity is now one of the worst affected by unemployment.

Let us now return to complete our study of Table 3.1. After the total of domestic inputs (row 14) we find in column 4 an entry of £2,000 million of imported goods and services. These are *not* subdivided. We do not know whether this represents iron ore, crude steel or refined metal and alloys, or any of the other goods and services which the industry uses.

The original source of all the data in such tables is the recorded transac-tions of firms, based on the prices at which they buy and sell. Most of these will contain an element of tax (such as VAT or excise duty) or subsidy (notably farm products). The statisticians need to know the extent of this, and a number of other details as well, but since we do not we have omitted it. This omission explains, in part, why rows and columns do not always add up to the totals shown, which are taken from the original tables.

Still going down column 4, we come to the input of factor services: labour, land and capital. The column total thus gives us an estimate of the value of all the inputs purchased by an industry group: intermediate purchases from other domestic industries; imported goods and services; and factor services. This total *should* correspond to the value of the industry's total output, since the entry in row 17 which we have labelled 'capital, land' includes the 'gross margin' between sales and purchases. In most cases the agreement is fairly close, and the reader will appreciate that the inherent inaccuracies will not always cancel out.

Finally let us look briefly at the right-hand end of the rows, taking row 4 again as an example. The sum of all the sales to other industries in column 14 is called 'intermediate demand', to contrast with sales to ultimate consumers, which are 'final demand', column 15. Columns 14 and 15 together make up the total output of the group, column 20. 'Final demand' is conventionally subdivided into personal or household consumption (column 16), where it will be seen that (as might be expected) there is a very small entry. Households use metal products, not the raw material. The same is true of government (column 17) and capital formation (column 18). If this seems odd, remember that steel and similar products will show up as buildings, machine tools, ships or aircraft only *after* they have been processed by other industries. So almost the whole of 'final demand' for this group of products consists of exports.

The extent to which we have had to compress the original table means that many interesting details are lost, but there is still much to be learned about the structure of the UK economy from Table 3.1. Remember that the row entries show where the output goes, while the column entries tell us where the inputs come from. Agricultural output, not surprisingly, goes mainly into the food and drink processing industry (part of 8), with smaller quantities used within the industry itself (e.g. grain grown for animal feed) or going directly, as fresh produce, into final consumption. The output of coal (row 2) is almost all used to generate electricity, with the iron and steel industry using the only other large quantity in the form of coke for its blast furnaces. Oil (also row 2) has to be refined before it is used, which partly explains the very large entry in the diagonal box – crude oil into refineries. It is also a raw material for the chemical industry (column 5), and the life-blood of the transport industry (column 11); but oil and its products, petrol and diesel fuel, are used in considerable amounts by almost every other sector, and by household consumers.

As one would expect, the output of the metal-producing industries (row 4) is used by the metal-using industries (columns 6 and 7), while 'other minerals and their products' (part of row 5), i.e. such things as sand and gravel, bricks and cement, go mainly into the construction industry, column 9. The chemical industry, which is the other main component of row 5, is another whose products are used by a wide range of other industries; notice the inputs to agriculture (fertilizers) and other manufacture, column 8. This consists of such things as artificial fibres (ethylene, nylon, etc.), rubber and plastics.

The large input to agriculture from other manufactures (row 8) is from the food industries and consists of animal feeding stuffs, many of which are by-products. Otherwise most of the output of these industries goes straight into final consumption, in part via column 10, distribution, hotels, restaurants and catering services.

Virtually everything that is produced has to be transported and distributed from its maker to its users, so that one would expect an input from transport services (row 11) and distribution (row 10) in every column. This is true of the communications services (row 11) as well. The penultimate row in the table, row 12, contains rather a mixture. The original 100 × 100 table identifies 'banking, finance, insurance, business services' – services which every other sector will use. With these we have included 'owning and dealing in real estate', 'other services' and 'printing and publishing', some of whose output would appear under final consumption by households and government. Again the end result is a significant input from this sector to all the columns in the table.

A table like this will also show the sectors which use a lot of imported goods and services, relative to their inputs from domestic industries. Notice, for example, column 2, 'coal, oil and gas', which imported almost as much as its domestic purchases; but remember that this was 1979, before North Sea oil came into full production. Exports from this industry group, even so, were equal to its imports. By contrast the construction industry imports only one-tenth of what it purchases from domestic sources, which explains why it has been singled out as a good industry to stimulate through increased government spending; it would increase domestic activity without greatly increasing our import bill.

The main lesson to be learned from such a table is that the conventional 'primary, secondary and tertiary' classification is misleading – developed industrial economies are much more complex than that. If, however, it would be useful to distinguish those industries whose output is consumed mainly by other industries (those which make 'producers' goods', in other words) then the relationship between column 14 headed 'total intermediate demand' and column 15 headed 'total final demand' may be used. Agriculture, row 1, sells over 80% of its output to other industries and could really be said to be a primary producer. Other manufacturing industries (row 8), by contrast, sell nearly 60% of their output as final demand, domestically or overseas. Of the services, only row 10 'hotels, catering and distribution', which gets the goods into the shops and on to the shelves, is mainly serving *consumers*. Other services are as much services to producers as to consumers and are in no sense 'tertiary' if tertiary is supposed to mean 'at the end of the chain of production'.

An input–output table is a very useful tool for the economic planner, because it can be used to calculate the effects, industry by industry, of a growth in final demand. It is not enough to say: 'In five years' time, with more people with higher incomes, I estimate that we shall need a 20% increase in the output of the food industry.' Such an increase requires a corresponding increase in the output of the agricultural sector; this in turn makes greater demands on the chemical industry for fertilizers; the chemical industry must expand; this means a greater demand for oil products ... and so on. In its developed form an input–output model enables the planner to calculate all these secondary effects, and to identify possible bottlenecks which might prevent the achievement of output targets.

The first input–output table describing the British economy was produced as part of the national planning exercise initiated by the government in the early 1960s. During the course of this it was clear that an up-to-date picture of the structure of the economy was essential if the consequence of the targeted 4% annual growth in GDP were to be worked out industry by industry. Planning is now out of favour, so it is perhaps not surprising that the 1979 input–output table which we used as a basis for describing the internal structure of the economy is the latest available.

THE COMPOSITION OF OUTPUT

Before we leave Table 3.1 let us take a final look at column 15, which shows the contribution which each of our thirteen industry groups makes

Table 3.3. Industry share of gross domestic product (%) and growth/decline in output (index 1980 = 100)

Industry	% of GDP			Index of output (1980 = 100)				
	1975	1980	1984	1975	1979	1980	1981	1985
0 Agriculture, forestry and fishing	2.7	2.2	2.1	82	90	100	103	117
1 Coal and coke[a]	1.7	1.5	0.8	110	98	100	97	67
Oil and gas extraction	0.0	4.4	} 7.6	—	99	100	110	150
Oil processing	0.8	0.5		104	114	100	93	99
Other energy and water	2.9	3.1	2.6	89	102	100	100	106
Total energy and water	5.3	9.5	11.0	55	101	100	104	120
2 Metals	1.7	0.9	0.9	123	132	100	106	113
Other minerals/products	1.4	1.5	1.3	110	111	100	89	94
Chemicals	} 2.5	{ 2.4	} 2.7	91	111	100	100	120
Artificial fibres		{ 0.1		136	137	100	85	74
3 Metal goods n.e.s.	2.0	1.6	} 4.4	123	121	100	92	99
Mechanical engineering	4.1	3.8		121	109	100	89	93
Electrical engineering	3.4	3.4	3.6	95	102	100	94	131
Motor vehicles and parts	2.1	1.5	1.3	115	116	100	83	86
Other transport equipment	1.2	1.4	1.3	100	92	100	104	95
4 Food manufacture	2.3	2.4	} 3.4	93	100	100	99	104
Drink and tobacco	1.2	1.2		91	101	100	97	95
Textiles	1.3	0.9	} 1.6	126	121	100	92	98
Clothing and footwear	1.3	1.0		109	115	100	93	106
Paper, print, publishing	2.4	2.4	} 4.4	95	108	100	95	99
All other manufacture	2.5	2.1		103	116	100	91	99
Total manufacturing (2–4)	29.2	26.6	24.8	105	110	100	94	104
5 Construction	6.7	6.3	6.2	100	106	100	90	100
Total production and construction (1–5)	41.2	42.4	42.1	94	107	100	96	107
6 Distribution, etc.	12.6	12.8	12.9	98	108	100	98	112
7 Transport	5.6	4.6	4.4	98	104	100	99	106
Communications	2.7	2.6	2.6	83	97	100	105	123
8 Banking, finance, etc.	10.6	11.6	13.2	77	95	100	105	145
9 Public administration	7.7	6.9	} 21.8	99	99	100	100	99
Education, health, etc.	9.5	8.7		90	99	100	101	105
Other services	5.3	6.1		81	95	100	99	111
Ownership of dwellings	5.9	6.2	5.9	91	99	100	102	106
Total services (6–9)[b]	56.2	55.4	55.2	91	100	100	101	113
Gross domestic product	100	100	100	92	103	100	99	111

Notes: [a] Affected by strikes. [b] Adjustment omitted.

Table 3.4. UK food production as % of total supplies

Product	1973–5	1985
Meat	80	90
Eggs	97	97
Milk	100	100
Cheese	62	67
Butter	14	64
Sugar (refined)	29	55
Wheat	61	103
Potatoes	94	89

to the total output of the economy. It also shows that our groups varied greatly in size and importance. The bottom right-hand corner of an input–output table is in fact an alternative way of setting out the 'national accounts'. The sum of 'payments to factors' £1,679 hundred million in Table 3.1 corresponds to an 'income-based' estimate of gross domestic product. The actual figure for 1979 was £1,714 – quite close! Total final demand, which is equivalent to total expenditure on goods and services, is £2,480 in the table. Imported goods and services must be subtracted (£546), which gives £1,934 as an expenditure-based estimate of gross domestic product. The corresponding figure in the latest national accounts is £1,964 – again very close. These topics are dealt with at greater length in the chapters which follow, and are mentioned here only to establish the links between the two approaches.

In practice the question 'who produces what?' is answered in a slightly different way, in that the industries and sectors of the economy are classified according to the standard which we discussed in the section on the classification of industries above. We are interested in the relative contribution of our major industries, and particularly in the way that their relative contribution has changed over the years, so Table 3.3 uses index numbers and percentages.

The first point to emerge from consideration of Table 3.3 is the very small contribution of agriculture. Despite steady growth in agricultural productivity (per hectare and per worker), and although the UK has in the process become increasingly self-sufficient in food as can be seen from Table 3.4, agriculture is a surprisingly negligible contributor to British domestic output.

Remarkably large, in contrast, is the contribution made by the 'energy' industries, notably oil and gas. 'King Coal' has made some recovery

Table 3.5. Output classified by users (index 1980 = 100)

Output and users	% of total 1980 output[a]	Index of output (1980 = 100)			
		1974	1979	1983	1985
Consumer goods, total, of which:	24	107.5	108.3	98.9	103.7
Cars, etc.	1.1	166.4	120.7	98.4	99.5
Other durable goods	3.7	124.3	116.5	95.8	103.1
Clothing, footwear, etc.	4.0	108.6	113.7	96.9	104.6
Food, drink, tobacco	9.0	96.2	100.9	100.7	101.4
Other	6.6	102.3	108.4	99.5	107.2
Intermediate goods, total, of which:	51	86.3	107.9	107.5	112.6
Energy	25.3	49.1	100.5	116.3	120.7
Materials	26.0	119.9	115.1	99.0	104.6
Investment or capital goods, total, of which:	24	110.2	104.8	92.9	103.2
Electrical equipment	5.7	89.7	97.5	109.3	136.7
Transport equpment	11.2	109.8	104.1	88.1	89.9
Other	11.2	124.1	108.9	88.1	95.9

Note: [a] Percentage of output of 'all industries' (heads 1–5).

from the strike-hit level of 1984 but remains far less significant for the time being than oil.

'Manufacturing' – heads 2–4 inclusive in the standard classification – which we think of as the basic characteristic of an industrial nation, in fact contributes only a quarter of our GDP. The 'service' industries – distribution, transport, communications and finance (heads 6–8) – now account for no less than 34% of the total. Head 9, which is mainly government-supplied services such as health and education, raises the service contribution to over 55%. It is this sort of statistic that leads to the suggestion that Britain is becoming a 'post-industrial society'.

The pattern of output is not static. The expansion and contraction of individual industries and activities are best illustrated by using index numbers as in Table 3.3.

Gross domestic product in total has risen from a low point in 1975 to a level some 20% higher in 1985, interrupted by further recession in 1980–1. This is not a spectacular rate. Within the overall growth, the massive expansion of oil and gas extraction stands out sharply. Coal as a secondary source of energy has declined. Manufacturing now accounts for 4% less of the total than the 29% it contributed in 1975. Absolute declines are to be seen in metals (mainly steel), artificial fibres, a group of 'metal-bashing' industries (especially motor-vehicle manufacture) and textiles. Chemicals and electric/electronic engineering have been growth areas.

In the service sector, the contribution of government services has changed little as a percentage of GDP. The growth has been in communications and banking and finance. Taken together with the statistics on manufacturing, here is preliminary evidence that the UK economy is undergoing 'deindustrialization' – a term which we shall be defining and discussing in more detail later.

Table 3.5 offers another way of classifying industries, based on the *users* of their output. Thus many products such as food and clothing are consumed by households; others form the new capital equipment purchased by firms.

This table shows that despite a very considerable growth in consumption expenditures, the output of our domestic industries has fallen – the difference being made up by imported consumer goods, especially cars and other consumer durables. The situation on the investment or capital goods front is even worse; in what should be the vital sector for an industrial nation, we see another overall decline, despite some growth in electrical goods. It is the growth of energy – North Sea oil and gas – which has tended to mask the evidence of contraction elsewhere.

We shall continue further with the change of viewpoint taken in Table 3.5, from the sources of output to its *destinations*, in Chapter 4.

4

££££££££££££££££££££

The Destinations of Output

Another glance at Figure 7 is needed before going further on this general tour of the economy. We have so far lingered for a while to examine the *stock* of resources – land, labour and capital – which provides the basic wherewithal for economic activity. We then moved on to see how 'firms' (grouped into 'industries') combined those resources and were involved in complex relations between themselves to create a *flow* of production. Now we proceed again, this time to see the *uses* to which output is directed.

If Chapter 3 described what goes on in the box labelled 'firms' in Figure 7, this chapter will describe what happens to the flow of goods and services which emerges from the box. Remember that 'firms' is just a convenient term for 'productive organizations' of all kinds. In particular it includes those parts of central and local government which produce goods and services such as health and education. Where, then, do these goods and services finally end up? They have three broad destinations: in consumption, in capital formation and in foreign trade.

We must also remember how these flows of goods and services are measured. Money – the price paid for each unit of output – is the only common measure, and the physical flow of goods and services out of the box is measured by summing up the flow of payment into the box, i.e. the *expenditure* on the product. All the official data which we shall be introducing in the next few pages have this heading: 'expenditure on gross domestic product'. Where goods and services have no price, such as the treatment of patients by the National Health Service or the teaching of children in state schools, the *cost* of providing the service is taken as a substitute for the expenditure on it.

CONSUMPTION

The largest portion of output by far is that which is bought and consumed by individuals, or more usually by families, since it is the family or household which is the most common consuming unit. The consumption of some output takes place *as it is produced*. This is particularly true of many services. For example, a haircut is 'consumed' at the same time that the hairdresser is 'producing' the service that is being bought. More frequently, consumption takes place after goods have passed through a chain of distribution to take them from the factory floor to the shops and showrooms which are the outlets where individuals and families finally buy them.

Many of these, like the items crammed into a typical supermarket trolley, will be consumed (sometimes literally eaten) almost immediately. Others will be used over a much longer time span. Television sets and washing-machines are examples of goods that are intended to give satisfaction over a lengthy period of time; they are therefore known as consumer durables. The motor car is probably the most expensive of those that families now generally possess. It is even possible for certain services to be 'stored' in some material form. Prince Esterhazy enjoyed the services of Haydn and a string orchestra. If we wish to enjoy a similar pleasure we may go to a concert (a service) or may buy a recording and play it on hi-fi equipment – an embodiment of a service in the form of a material good.

The majority of the goods and services produced end up in this way, purchased and consumed by private households. This major flow we call 'consumption', or 'C'. In 1985 such consumption accounted for some 47% of the total volume of expenditure.

CAPITAL FORMATION

As we discussed in Chapter 3, there are some industries which sell the bulk of their output to other industries. For example, sand, gravel, bricks and cement go mainly to the construction industry, where they are used to build roads and bridges, offices, factories and houses. These are not the things which ordinary families generally buy, any more than heavy trucks or blast-furnaces or machine tools. They are 'capital goods', bought by business firms or perhaps by the government. Even houses, which *are* bought by individual families, are such an expensive and long-lasting asset that the statisticians include them with capital goods rather than in 'consumption'. But the distinction is not always clear-cut; your domestic freezer counts as consumption, but the identical piece of equipment bought by your butcher or grocer would be counted as capital equipment, because it will be used as an aid to production (in this case of the service, distribution) rather than to facilitate consumption. The distinction is based on the criterion: who buys it, and for what purpose?'

This part of the flow of goods and services will be used to increase the stock of capital in the economy, or to replace part of the existing stock which is worn out or obsolete. It is therefore called 'gross fixed capital formation'. When an allowance is made for the capital which is used up during the same period – what the accountant calls 'depreciation' – we get 'net fixed capital formation'.

There is a further element to be included under this heading. The year begins with quite a lot of goods ready to be sold or used. The shelves in the supermarket are not empty on 2 January, and all the other shops in the high street are well stocked. Factories have stocks of raw materials and 'work in progress', as it is called. And the same is true a year later, on 31 December. These stocks are run down and replenished every week of the year, but there is no reason why the quantity at the end of the year should be the same as it was at the beginning of the year. There might be more; stocks, or inventories as the Americans call them, could have risen. Or stocks could have been run down.

If part of the initial stock was used up during the year and not replaced, it will seem as if more goods and services have been used than were produced during the year, and the books will not balance. Conversely if stocks were built up, production would exceed use. So the statisticians calculate 'value of the physical increase in stocks and work in progress' during the year. The physical increase is stressed because at a time of inflation stocks will increase in money value. Since we are concerned with the flow of *goods*, we have to correct for this. The correction is called 'stock appreciation' in the official tables, to distinguish it from the physical increase in stocks.

So we have three distinct components in this second 'destination' for the flow of goods and services which our economy produces. First, fixed capital formation, carried out by business firms and governments; second, new houses, additions to the housing stock of the country; and third, the change in the quantity of stocks and work in progress. When this third element is included the category as a whole is called 'investment', symbol 'I'.

This use of the word 'investment' by economists is an endless source of confusion. In economics it means very precisely those goods and services which are used to increase the fixed capital of a country, or to increase the working inventories of businesses. In everyday speech it usually refers to putting money into a bank or building society, or to the purchase of stocks and shares, i.e. putting money to a profitable use. Try to remember that in this book 'investment' always refers to goods and services, and if it has a £ or $ sign attached, that money is only a measure of quantity.

The reader is by this time probably wondering why the outflow of goods and services is being subdivided and classified in this particular, even peculiar, fashion. We are really dividing the *purchasers* of the goods and services into groups, rather than the goods themselves, because each group can be expected to behave in a different but characteristic way. One most important purchaser of output is the government – important not only because of its size and importance, but also because it can decide to increase or decrease its spending at will. Local as well as central government is included, and the symbol 'G' stands for the flow of goods and services into all levels of government.

Here too a good deal of confusion can arise if we are not careful about definitions. The relevant column in an official set of statistics will be headed 'government consumption' (or 'general government consumption', to include central and local), with the words 'of goods and services' implied. This is not, as we shall see, the same thing as 'government spending'. Governments, of course, are much involved in the creation and maintenance of capital – the 'social overhead capital' which we have already mentioned, for example. This element in their use of goods and services is capital formation, rather than consumption, and is usually separately identified.

THE FOREIGN SECTOR

After all these difficulties of definition, it is perhaps a relief to come to the last of the possible destinations for the annual flow of output. Some of the goods we produce are sold to buyers in other countries, and some of the services we provide are used and paid for by foreigners. Together these form the 'exports from the United Kingdom', for which we use the symbol 'X'. This is a vitally important sector for the British economy. Almost a third of our domestic product is exported, and almost a third of our domestic spending is on imported goods and services.

Table 4.1. Imports and exports of goods and services, 1985

Category	Exports (£ billion)	(%)	Imports (£ billion)	(%)	Balance (£ billion)
Food and raw materials	7.1	7	13.3	14	(−)6.2
Oil	16.1	16	7.9	10	(+)8.2
Manufactures, inc. semi-finished	52.3	51	55.3	56	(−)3.0
Other goods	2.6	3	3.6	4	(−)1.0
Services	24.6	24	18.4	19	(+)5.9
Total goods and services	102.3	100	98.6	100	(+)3.7

Foreign trade has always been very significant to the UK economy. For well over a hundred years we have imported much of our food and many of our raw materials, and we have paid for these imports by exporting manufactures and services, especially trade-related services such as shipping, insurance and banking. The one exception to this rule was the export of coal, but this declined between the two world wars.

In recent years there has been a marked shift in the pattern of imports and exports as a result of the discovery and exploitation of North Sea oil. Oil has ceased to figure prominently among our imports, and instead we have become an important oil exporter, as Table 4.1 shows.

The visible balance on oil changed from − £3.1 in 1975 to + £8.2 billion in 1985, and this change was offset to a considerable extent by a parallel deterioration in the visible balance on finished manufactures from + £3.2 billion to − £3.1 billion. Oil has recently accounted for 20% of our exports, and finished manufactures for 41%, whereas in 1975 the corresponding figures were 3.8% and 52%.

Trade in services, part of 'invisible' imports and exports, provides around a quarter of total exports and a fifth of total imports. The positive balance on invisibles has traditionally offset the negative balance on visible trade.

There have also been changes in the direction of these trade flows. Trade with the countries which now make up the European Community has increased in importance and now accounts for nearly half of our trade in goods. Exports to 'other developed countries' such as Japan and Australia, to the oil-exporting countries and to the Eastern bloc and the Third World have decreased in quantity, as have our imports from the oil exporters in the Middle East.

Enough has now been said to give a general idea of the foreign trade sector. We shall be returning to look at foreign trade and payments in the detail which the subject deserves in Chapters 8 and 17.

THE TOTALS

Total expenditures (in £ billion) by each category of users in 1985 was as follows:

			(£ billion)
C	=	consumption by households, or personal consumption	213
G	=	general government consumption	74
I	=	investment (capital formation and changes in stocks)	111
X	=	exports	102
		Total final expenditure	450

This, however, ignores the fact that there is an imported component in most if not all the goods and services produced in the UK, and that some of the expenditure will represent the direct use of foreign goods and services – as, for example, when we fly on a foreign airline to enjoy a holiday in Spain. So we must subtract the value of imports, which in 1985 was £99 billion, which leaves £352 billion as an estimate of the gross *domestic* product. This (and other similar estimates of the size of the economy) is usually symbolized by 'Y'.

One last complication. At the end of Chapter 3 we summed up our description of the structure of the economy by listing the output of each sector, from agriculture, through energy and manufacturing, to government services. The total (for 1985) was £303 billion, whereas we have just estimated the same flow – 'what comes out of the box' – at £352 billion. This difference is explained by the fact that our total expenditure is derived from 'quantity × price', and the 'price' will often include an element of tax, such as VAT or excise duty. Or it may be artificially reduced by a subsidy, a negative tax. When allowance is made for this, expenditure becomes £352 billion less £49 billion, or £303 billion. The larger figure is an estimate of GDP 'at market price'; the smaller an estimate 'at factor cost'.

5

The National Income

We have been looking so far at the flow of *goods and services* through the economic system produced by using a flow of economic resources. There is also, as we saw, a corresponding flow in the *opposite* direction: of payments to the owners of the factors of production in return for their services. It is this flow that we now explain, before seeing how the various totals can be set out in the form of 'national accounts'.

THE CIRCULAR FLOW OF PAYMENTS

We have already briefly mentioned 'returns to resources' in Chapter 2, pages 37–8 where we estimated the payments to labour at £225.2 billion in 1985, the return to land at £23.2 billion and the return to capital at £60.3 billion. This total (£309 billion, in round figures) has been adjusted, principally to allow for a rise in the *value* (as opposed to the quantity) of stocks, which would otherwise exaggerate the incomes of their owners. The adjusted total was £306 billion.

Of this, £6 billion went to factors owned by governments, leaving £300 billion as the gross income of the 'owners of factors'. These individuals can be assembled into a category of 'households', and they play a dual role in the economy as suppliers of factor services and as consumers of goods.

The government levies a wide range of taxes on income, of which income tax is only the largest and best known. Profits are taxed separately, and the connection between National Insurance contributions and benefits is so tenuous that this too is best regarded as a tax on income. In total, in 1985, £87 billion was taken by government.

What it takes with the one hand, however, it gives with the other, and almost all of us are receivers as well as payers. Payments by the govern-

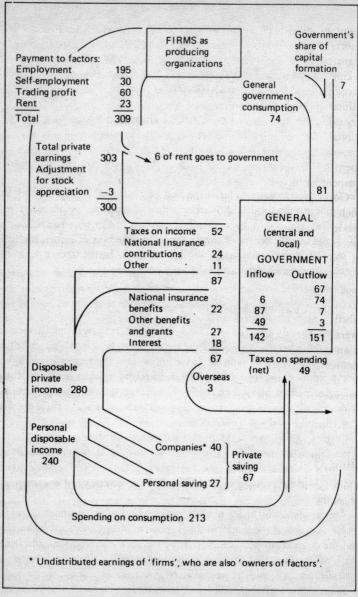

Figure 9 What happens to the flow of incomes

ment to individuals in the form of pensions, benefits and grants – in short, as supplements to income – came to £67 billion in 1985. The net transfers *to* the government were £20 billion. What was left after all the taking and giving was £280 billion, which is called 'disposable income' in recognition of the fact that recipients can dispose of it as they wish. £40 billion of this accrues to firms rather than to individuals or households, because 'firms' are also owners of factors, especially the factors land and capital. We can think of this as undistributed profits, because *personal* disposable income totals £240 billion. Of this income, £213 billion was spent on consumption, as we have already noted, leaving £27 billion unspent, or 'saved'.

Governments do not only tax incomes, however. A wide range of taxes such as VAT and excise duties are added to the prices of the goods and services we buy, though sometimes the price is reduced by a negative tax, called a subsidy. The net effect of this was that the government took in £49 billion in indirect taxes.

We have now introduced government, both central and local, as a modifier of the flow of incomes, as well as a consumer of goods and services. When we look at the flow of payments into and out of the box labelled 'general government' in Figure 9, we see that there was an overall deficit – an excess of outflow over inflow – of £9 billion. (There is an outflow of £3 billion to overseas recipients, which we have not mentioned above.)

The only flows which escape consideration when we look at the 'income' side of the circular flow are the payments for imports and exports. When these are included we have all the information we need to make up a set of 'national accounts'.

THE NATIONAL ACCOUNTS

The staff of the Central Statistical Office who compile all these figures have two main lines of attack. They can obtain data about *incomes*, primarily from the Inland Revenue Department, and they can get data about *expenditure* from such sources as the Household Expenditure Survey, from the government itself in respect of its own spending and from firms about expenditure on capital formation. Import and export statistics are in many ways the easiest to collect, and the most comprehensive and accurate.

In terms of our first 'flow' diagram (Figure 7) they attempt to measure

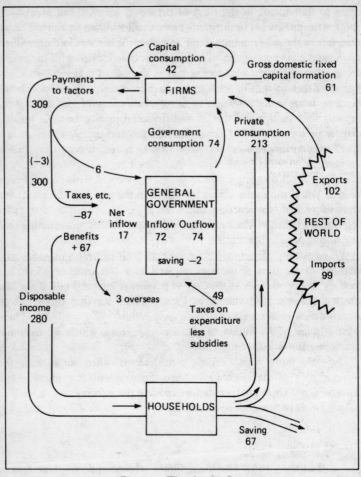

Figure 10 The circular flow

the flow of payments for the use of resources (the flow going left out of the box labelled 'firms') and the flow into the box, which is the flow of expenditure on the goods and services produced by the firms. We have already examined what happens to the income flow in some detail using Figure 9, and we can complete the picture by adding the remaining expenditure flows which we discussed in Chapter 4. When we do so we

The National Income

Table 5.1. Gross domestic product, 1985 (income-based)

	£ billion	
Factor incomes:		
from employment	195.4 ⎫	225.2
from self-employment	29.9 ⎭	
Trading profit of companies, etc.	60.3	
Rents, etc.	23.2	(Note: royalties are treated as taxes)
Total domestic incomes	308.8	
less Adjustment for stock appreciation	(−)3.0	
Gross domestic product, income-based	305.7	
Gross domestic product, expenditure-based	302.5	'at factor cost'
Residual error	3.3	

Table 5.2. Gross domestic product, 1985 (expenditure-based)

	£ billion	
Consumption	213.2	
General government consumption	74.0	
Gross domestic capital formation	60.1	
Value of physical increase in stocks, etc.	0.5	
Total domestic expenditure	347.9	
Exports	102.3	
Total final expenditure	450.2	
less Expenditure on imports	(−)98.6	
Gross domestic product at market prices	351.6	
Adjustment to factor cost	(−)49.1	of which taxes 56.8 and subsidies 7.7
Gross domestic product at factor cost (expenditure-based)	302.5	

have a version of a model of the economy which is deservedly famous in economics under the name of 'the circular flow of income and product'. It is illustrated in Figure 10, and it serves at one and the same time as a method of describing the economy and as the basis for theories about how the economy works. This is the topic of Chapter 6, in which we ask what determines the size of the various flows. Why does domestic product or national income fluctuate, sometimes falling, as in the 1930s, and sometimes steadily growing bigger year by year as in the happy 1960s?

To return to the statisticians, attempting to estimate the magnitude of these flows: they should find that after they have made various adjustments (some of which, like the adjustment for stock appreciation, we have already noted) the income and expenditure estimates give the same total. But they never do. There is always a residual error, and this is one reason why it is difficult to put numbers into a circular flow diagram like Figure 10. We have already drawn attention to the imprecision of *all* economic data in the Preface, but having issued this warning let us look at the estimate of gross domestic product obtained from measuring the flow of income. We have inserted almost all the necessary figures in Figure 9.

At the end of the section on 'the totals' in Chapter 4 (page 66) we totalled up all the expenditure flows, so all we need do here is set out the detail of the expenditure-based estimate of the gross domestic product – Table 5.2.

There are two points to keep in mind from what we have discussed so far. First, all these figures are estimates, and different estimates yield different totals, despite the best efforts of the statisticians. Second, note the difference between estimates 'at market prices' and estimates 'at factor cost', the difference being the removal of the taxes and subsidies from the former to obtain the latter.

There are, however, some more aspects of the national accounts which we must look at. The first of these is again a consequence of the fact that we live in a fairly open international economy. This means that some of the factors of production which contribute to our domestic product are owned by foreigners, and this is particularly true of property in the form of fixed capital. Much of the capital equipment which helps to produce oil from the North Sea is owned by United States citizens, the large US-based multinationals like Esso, for example. A lot of foreign capital is involved in the UK-based but US-owned motor-car industry, Ford and Vauxhall (General Motors) being prominent, even dominant.

Table 5.3. Expenditure on gross domestic product, 1985

	(£ billion at current factor cost)
Consumption	176.3
General government consumption	69.5
Gross domestic capital formation	56.5
Exports	98.7
less Imports	(−)98.6[a]
Gross domestic product at factor cost	302.5
Now let us deal with the adjustment discussed below:	
Gross domestic product at market prices	351.6
Net property income from abroad	3.4
Gross national product at market prices	355.0
Factor cost adjustment	(−)49.1
Gross national product at factor cost	305.9
Capital consumption	(−)41.8
Net national product at factor cost = national income	264.0

Note: [a] Imports are valued at landed prices, so that no adjustment is needed.

It is not one-way traffic, however, because British nationals own a great deal of property overseas from which they derive an income. So the accountants include an item called 'net property income from abroad' which for the United Kingdom is a plus or positive entry; we earn more income from abroad than foreign nationals earn here. This converts gross domestic product into what is called 'gross national product'. For some reason it is the latter which has entered into most people's consciousness, often in the abbreviated form of GNP. Fortunately the difference between the two measures is small (£3.4 billion in 1985, i.e. well within the overall range of error), and it does not often matter which phrase we use or which figure we quote.

The second issue concerns capital. When we talked about capital and investment we recognized that in the course of producing each year's output some of our stock of capital was used up. Part of our national product has to be earmarked to replace that capital if our economy is to continue to produce at its present level. Neither a nation, nor a company, nor a family can live off its capital indefinitely – one of the few cases, incidentally, when the 'family' analogy is true; usually it is wrong or misleading.

The statisticians recognize this by estimating the value of the capital which was used up, or wore out, during the course of the year. Accountants call this 'depreciation' and calculate it in various ways, but the figure they put down often bears a closer relationship to the tax allowances available than it does to the state of the capital equipment. 'Capital consumption' is not easy to estimate, but when it is subtracted from gross domestic or gross national product we get 'net domestic or national product'. Net national product is also called 'national income', because it tells us what income we as a nation have available after we have maintained our stock of capital.

As well as applying the 'factor cost' adjustment to the total gross domestic product, it is possible to adjust each separate component of expenditure on gross domestic product to obtain a table headed 'at current factor cost'. Such a table for 1985 is Table 5.3.

6

ℓℓℓℓℓℓℓℓℓℓℓℓℓℓℓℓℓℓℓ

The Economy at Work

So far we have traced the general flow of goods and services through the economic system and the corresponding financial flows of income and expenditure that result from such economic activity. We have seen how firms use the economic resources of land, labour and capital to create an output which is then either consumed or invested in capital formation. We have also given some indication of how this pattern is complicated by the activities of government and by the existence of a foreign trade sector. And on the payments side, it has become clear that the process of production in turn generates a flow of incomes to the owners of economic resources: wages and salaries, rents, interest and profits. Once again, it is a flow that may be interrupted by the action of government or the existence of trade with the outside world.

But the account to date has essentially been a description of the flows through the economy during a particular period of time. In this chapter we move to the next stage of setting it in motion and watching a working model. For example, instead of taking the size of output and income as given, we shall be asking: what determines their level? Why should they rise or fall from year to year? What happens if there is a variation in any of the various components? Why, in other words, do *changes* take place?

SPENDING AND SAVING

A good starting-point is the 'disposable income' we introduced in Chapter 5. This, it will be recalled, accrued to the households in the model and amounted to some £280 billion in 1985. This was the income available to them *after* the flow had been intercepted by government – taxing on the one hand, but paying out benefits on the other. It must also be remembered that 'households' are defined as the 'suppliers of factors'.

Their income as suppliers therefore includes the profits of private and public corporations, and it is customary and sensible in discussions about what income earners do with their earnings to distinguish between the earnings or incomes of private households and the earnings of business corporations.

In both cases there is an important choice to be made: between spending the income or saving a part of it. However, the reasons for saving, and the type of spending, are likely to be different. Let us take the ordinary households first.

Many households 'save' a proportion of their weekly or monthly incomes with the intention of spending the money later, perhaps on a holiday, or at Christmas. All this does is redistribute their spending over the year, and what we are concerned with here is the accumulation of unspent income at the end of the year.

This kind of saving might be intended to finance, or to help finance, a very large item of future expenditure, often a house or a flat, but perhaps also expensive consumer durable items such as furniture or a car. People also save so as to enjoy a higher income in the future, probably after retirement, or to guard against a sudden loss of family income due to illness, accident or death.

A very large proportion of this kind of saving is called 'contractual', because it involves payments into a fund, or the payments of regular premiums to an insurance company. Much of it these days is 'saving' after expenditure has taken place, and it consists of the repayment of a mortgage loan or a hire purchase advance. It is saving none the less, since saving simply means 'income not spent'.

The question, then, is how households decide what proportion of their incomes will be used for current spending – 'consumption expenditure' as we have termed it – and how much will be saved. Since John Maynard Keynes wrote his *General Theory of Employment, Interest and Money* in 1936, it has been held that the amount saved depends on the level of income received. Poor families save relatively little of their incomes; some perhaps even overspend and go into debt. Rich families can, and do, save a relatively high proportion of their incomes. In aggregate, therefore, a fraction of disposable income will be saved, and this fraction has varied between a low savings ratio of 11.1% in 1985 to an unusually high 15% in 1980.

Generally, however, it has been a fairly stable proportion, so that we can reasonably expect that an increase in disposable income of, say,

Table 6.1. Savings ratio, 1975–85

	1975	1976	1977	1978	1979	1980	1981	1982	1983	1984	1985
Personal disposable income (index 1980 = 100)	88.9	88.4	87.4	93.5	98.7	100.0	97.6	97.8	100.1	102.2	110.6
Savings ratio (%)	12.8	12.1	11.6	12.7	13.5	15.0	13.1	12.7	11.3	11.7	11.1

£1 billion will result in about £125 million more saving and £825 million more consumption expenditures.

Many people still seem to think that an increase in the rate of interest will increase the amount saved. However, the evidence suggests that changes in interest rates might affect the form in which savings are held, but not the proportion of income which is saved. Less will be held in cash or in a current account, and more will go into the Post Office or a building society when interest rates are high, but the total volume of saving will not be greatly influenced.

Strictly we should distinguish between the proportion of an *addition* to income that is saved (the 'marginal propensity to save') and the proportion of total income that is saved (the 'average propensity to save'). For our present purposes, though, it is sufficient to think of spending and saving as given fractions of disposable income.

What about the 'capital-owning' and 'profit-receiving' element in the 'household' box? Some profits are distributed to the owners of capital in the form of dividend payments, and become the kind of personal income we have just discussed. What is left is called 'retained earnings' or 'undistributed profits'; and it is the management of the firm which decides how this should be used. One option is to save all or part, and to add it to the reserves of money held by the organization. The alternative is to spend it on new capital assets, such as buildings, machinery and equipment.

The actual flows into and out of the 'firms' or the business sector of the economy in 1985 show that there was a balance of income over current spending of about £42.8 billion. In addition, the personal sector saved about £26.1 billion, and total saving amounted to the £67.68 billion shown in Figure 10.

The important point about saving is that it represents a 'leakage' from the circular flow of income. By definition, it is an act of not spending – and if that is the end of the story, then it will form a withdrawal from the circular flow which will not therefore return to producers. If that is what happens, then firms will subsequently be able to hire less factors of production than previously, thereby reducing incomes.

Saving *as such* therefore exercises a *downward* pressure on the level of income in the circular flow. But that assumes that there are no offsetting forces at work. In practice, there will also be 'injections' into the circular flow to take into account, and the main one of these is investment.

INVESTMENT

As well as the demand for the output of firms for the purpose of consumption there is demand for 'capital' goods of one kind or another – goods which will be used in the process of production. This is shown in the top right of Figure 10 as the item 'gross domestic fixed capital formation', and in 1985 it totalled some £61 billion. Of this total, £11.9 billion represented housing, £20.2 billion plant and machinery, £14.8 billion 'other building and works' and £5.9 billion vehicles, ships and aircraft. Another way of dividing it is to note that general government and public corporations accounted for £16.0 billion or 30% of the total, and private firms spent some £33 billion on capital goods.

We shall discuss the government element in connection with general government expenditure in a later section. What decides the level of private spending on new capital equipment? Keynes, as usual, had an answer, placing great emphasis on what he termed 'animal spirits'. By this he meant to imply that the level of spending depended a great deal on the prevailing degree of optimism about the future level of sales and profits; on 'business confidence', to use another much-used expression. This implies that it is a changeable, unpredictable and volatile element in spending, and amongst its components is one – the increase or decrease in the volume of stocks and work in progress – which is especially prone to large swings.

1984 and 1985 happened to be years in which change was very small, but a glance back over the past few years shows increases of £2.6, £2.2 and £2.5 billion in 1977, 1978 and 1979, followed by decreases of £2.9, £2.6 and £1.1 billion in 1980, 1981 and 1982. 1979 to 1980 therefore represents an overall reduction of £5.4 billion, 2% of total domestic expenditure. In 1980 firms clearly expected a fall in sales, and responded by running down the stocks they held as quickly as they could.

In general, as we have already suggested, investment or capital formation should be thought of as an *injection* into the circular flow: spending additional to that on consumption which therefore has the effect of increasing the capacity of firms to hire factors of production. Its impact is therefore the opposite of saving, in *raising* the level of incomes in the economy. But, as Figure 10 indicates, there are further elements yet to take into account which will help to determine whether the level of income in the circular flow is tending to rise or fall. One of these is what is happening in the foreign trade sector.

IMPORTS AND EXPORTS

Figure 10 shows the flow of expenditure on imports going out of the economy and the inward flow of spending by foreign buyers of British goods and services. It is just a coincidence that in 1984 the two were more or less equal at the (rounded) figure of £92 billion. In 1985 there was a net inflow of £3 billion, exports being £102 billion and imports £99 billion. There have also been many years in which Britain has spent more overseas than foreigners have spent on British goods and services.

The level of foreign expenditure on British exports will depend, other things being equal, on the level of economic activity in the rest of the world. Spending on imported goods and services similarly depends on the level of income in Britain, and it is possible to make predictions about how much of every pound will be spent on imports.

Spending on imported goods and services as a proportion of total domestic expenditure has risen slowly but fairly steadily from 22.5% in 1971 to 28% in 1984 and 1985. (Exports have also increased during this period, but a worrying fact is that the volume of imported manufactures has been rising twice as quickly as the volume of exports of manufactures.)

What this means is that out of any given increase in disposable income a proportion, currently just under 30%, will *not* result in an increase in spending on domestically produced goods and services; it will be spent on imports. This represents a second 'leakage' out of the circular flow, in addition to that part of disposable income which is saved. Exports, the purchase of British goods and services by foreigners, form a second element of injection of spending, which will increase the demand for the output of firms.

From what has been said so far it will be clear that if total expenditure and the level of income in the circular flow are to be maintained, these leakages (into saving and imports) must be offset by inflows or injections of spending on capital formation and on exports.

The last complication to take into account is the activities of government and how they affect the circular flow.

GOVERNMENT AND THE CIRCULAR FLOW

Government is the final component of our working model of the economy, and it has a dual role: as a spender itself, and in influencing others' expenditure. In Figures 9 and 10 it has a box of its own, labelled 'general government', and it can be seen that there are flows of spending going into and out of it.

Remembering that both central and local governments (though not usually the public corporations) are included, we should note that they supply factors on a small scale, and earn an income, most of which is rent paid to local authorities. The great part of their income, however, is the result of taxing other people's incomes, or their expenditures, thus influencing at one and the same time their disposable income and the prices of the goods and services they buy.

The expenditures of government which are included in 'capital formation' have already been mentioned briefly. The important point here is that governments have a good deal of discretion about the level, and the timing, of their capital spending. If for any reason they wish to reduce their spending, then capital expenditure is the usual choice, because it is easy to delay or defer it. Current expenditures are less easy to change, because much of the spending reflects a legal obligation to provide a service – children's education being an obvious example. Even so, there is room for manoeuvre, if only by modifying the rate of increase in spending from year to year. More details about government expenditures can be found in Chapters 16 and 19.

The share of total expenditure on goods and services which is attributable to government has in fact remained virtually constant at 17% since 1975. If spending on capital formation is added in, the percentage, which was 21% in 1975, had shrunk to 19% in 1980 and 18% in 1985.

When we come to examine the impact of government on the circular flow, we are on the borderline between simply explaining how the economy works and policy issues about what could be done to make it work better. If we look again at the left-hand side of Figure 9 or 10, we see that government takes away a very considerable part of the initial income accruing to factors. Since it then restores (though not necessarily to the same people or organizations) most of what it has taken away, a similarly large proportion of disposable income consists of payments (transfer payments, remember, not payments for factor services) from government.

This complex system provides the government with a great deal of control over the level of disposable income, and therefore over the level of spending. If you think of the flow of factor incomes as travelling down a pipe, then you can imagine the government as opening and closing a valve which diverts some of the flow into its reservoir of income (taxation is the final leakage from the circular flow), and then, through a second valve, allowing a greater or lesser amount to flow back into the stream of disposable income (an injection like investment or exports).

Governments can take such decisions for a variety of reasons. A government might, for example, raise taxes on tobacco or alcoholic drinks for reasons of public health, or raise the allowances paid to the parents of small children in response to public concern about family poverty. Whatever its motives and reasons, it cannot avoid affecting some elements in the circular flow of income and expenditure. And since the ideas of Keynes became part of the conventional wisdom, i.e. since 1945, governments have consciously varied the level of taxation and spending *in order* to influence the level of economic activity. So when we look at the performance of the British economy over the past few years in Chapter 9 we shall look at the levels of government spending, and at the changes in disposable income, to see just how they influenced output and employment.

THE WORKING MODEL

Any or all of the flows of expenditure can change, therefore. Some changes will be spontaneous or autonomous; for example, consumers' tastes might change in such a way that they bought more domestically produced goods and fewer imported goods. Firms might take a gloomy view of future sales prospects and cut back on stocks and output. Other changes will be overt and deliberate, as when the government decides to expand its programme of road construction, or to increase the size of national insurance contributions.

The best way of understanding how the economy works is to begin with one such change and trace its consequences. Let us suppose that for reasons which do not concern us households begin to save more, i.e. to spend a smaller proportion of their aggregate incomes. The first effect shows up in the shops in the high street at the end of the week or the month. It is noticed that the shelves and the stock-rooms are fuller than usual, and the takings are lower. The next order to the wholesaler or to the depot will be smaller than the last.

In turn the wholesalers, or the purchasing departments, reduce their next orders to the manufacturers. Their production plans for the next month or quarter are revised downwards; less overtime will be worked; some workers may be laid off or go on short time; orders for raw materials will be cut. In Chapter 3 we looked at the very complex network of connections between industries, so it will be clear how such a reduction in spending by one industry would ramify throughout the economy.

We have now reached the stage where employment has fallen, and the income of some of those still employed has been reduced. Spending, being closely linked to income, will therefore fall again, and we could go round the circle once more. Now, however, many people will have been affected by the drop in spending, and a more gloomy view of the future will have spread. Plans for expansion and for re-equipment will be postponed; in short, capital formation will fall, other sections of industry will experience a drop in demand, and a general recession will come about. All because people decided to save more – which is usually thought to be a virtuous thing to do!

When will the decline stop? When incomes fall to a level at which it is not possible to save more or, more probably, when some other element of expenditure increases to offset the fall in consumer spending. The Keynesian remedy would be a compensatory increase in public spending, or some government action such as a tax cut, or a fall in interest rates, which would stimulate someone else's spending.

It is more usual to consider the effect of a *rise* in spending, perhaps caused by business firms investing more in new capital goods. This would lead to increased employment and higher incomes in the capital goods industries, and part of that increase in income would be spent on consumption. The high street shops would now see empty shelves and gaps in the stock-room, and would raise their orders accordingly. Firms expand their output and employ more workers, and so a secondary wave of increased spending spreads through the economy.

When will this come to an end? Sooner or later the economy will reach the stage where it is using all its available resources of land, labour and capital equipment, a stage at which it cannot produce any more no matter what the demand may be. Two things can happen now; all or part of the unsatisfied demand will be met by an increased flow of imports, or the available goods and services will be taken by those who are able and willing to pay more for them, i.e. prices will rise.

In reality the economy will not suddenly reach 'full employment'. Shortages, bottlenecks, increased imports, selective price increases and longer waiting-lists all combine to choke off some of the expansion. But as we noted right at the beginning of this book a high level of demand, and a close approximation to full employment, *was* sustained for twenty years or more from 1945.

One very important idea emerges from this consideration of 'What would happen if . . .?' *Any* increase or decrease in expenditure will produce secondary increases or decreases as its effects spread through the economy or (thinking of our diagram) circulate round the circular flow several times. This is known as the 'multiplier' effect, and its importance is that it allows the government to exert a greater impact than at first seems possible.

A second important idea to carry away from this discussion is that while Figure 10 represents a snapshot of the economy at a particular point of time, we have now begun to see how the model actually *works*. The structure of the real economy and its capacity to produce are constantly altering. The several sub-flows we have identified – consumption, exports, government expenditure, capital formation and so on – are also changing in magnitude all the time. The economy is exposed to external shocks – a rise in oil prices or a recession in the USA, perhaps – the effects of which will influence internal spending flows. Whatever the government does, for whatever reasons, is likely to affect the distribution of income and the level of somebody's spending. The collective optimism or pessimism of businesses will have a profound effect, especially on capital formation and the growth of stocks. Some sectors of the economy like housing and automobiles tend towards a 'cycle' of expansion and contraction. For example, for a few more years a larger number of new families than normal will be being formed, as the late 1960s babies marry and set up home.

In short, everything in the economy affects everything else. It is dynamic, mobile, interactive, and our tables and diagrams cannot illustrate this as vividly as we would wish them to.

7

Jobs, Prices, Growth and Distribution

We have now reached the stage of seeing how the main elements *within* the economy interact, and shall return in Chapter 8 to relationships with other economies in the form of foreign trade and payments. For now, however, with the advantage of a framework into which to fit them, we shall look again in a little more detail at those topics which we identified right at the beginning as of major concern. These were employment (or rather the lack of employment), the rapid rise of prices, the uneven distribution of the national income and the capacity of the economy to produce goods and services ('economic growth' if the capacity is expanding, which it has not always done in recent years).

The working model of the economy which we have been building up is aimed at showing how broadly the levels of *income and output* are determined in an economy. What it does not tell us about is how many jobs will be generated or the general price level at which all this economic activity will take place. We must also look at the changes which have taken place in the *composition* of the total domestic product, and the way in which the economy can *increase* its total output of goods and services over the years. Finally, there is the question of how the benefits of production are *distributed* between the members of the society.

EMPLOYMENT

Perhaps the most dramatic change that has taken place in the British economy during recent years has been the reversion to levels of unemployment not experienced since the 1930s. Between the wars unemployment averaged some 14%, and the period between 1945 and 1970 must be regarded as a remarkable episode in British economic history in that unemployment during those years never rose above 3%. There was then a rise to a level of about 5%, with a further rapid deterioration from 1980 onwards. By 1981 there were 2 million out of work; by 1985 the 3 million mark had been passed, 13% of the work-force.

Measuring unemployment

Calculating just how many are unemployed is itself a matter of controversy, so let us first look at the way in which the official total is arrived at. The employment figures which appear monthly are based on the records held by the unemployment benefit offices and therefore cover only those *registered* as unemployed. Changes in the benefit rules can therefore affect the total; for example, a change in 1983 removed 162,000 men aged 59 and over; they became 'retired' rather than 'unemployed'.

The annual Labour Force Survey, on the other hand, is a survey of a sample of 57,000 households (about 1 in 350), and everyone over 16 in these households is questioned about their employment status. It therefore covers those who did not register as unemployed.

An analysis of the Labour Force Survey in the spring of 1984 estimated the total population over 16 years old at 42,593,000. Of this total 23,343,000 were employed or self-employed on a full- or part-time basis, and 2,627,000 were registered as unemployed, seeking work and available for work. There is a similar category of unemployed people who for some reason, such as sickness, were not immediately available for work. These 278,000 are added to the other unemployed to give a total of 2,905,000. Employed and unemployed together make up the work-force or 'economically active' population, so that the unemployed formed 11% when this survey was undertaken.

The remainder of the over-16s are classed as 'economically inactive', or not part of the work-force, and this group comprises pensioners, students and the severely disabled, who total some 9 million. Of the remainder, some are fully occupied by home and family and content to remain so, but the Labour Force Survey identified 2,555,000 people who would like a job, even though they were not actively seeking work. Those who are not entitled to unemployment benefit have little incentive to register as unemployed, especially if they perceive the chances of getting a job as remote, and so there is a debate about the 'real' number of unemployed, and the extent to which the official figure underestimates it. Presumably not all the 2,555,000 should be counted as unemployed members of the genuinely active labour force, but some undoubtedly are. They are known as 'discouraged' because they believed that there were no jobs available. Some had looked for work in the weeks previous to the survey (350,000); others had not looked (250,000). These figures suggest that at least 600,000 people might be added to the total. To offset this, however, are the unknown and presumably unknowable number of people who, though registered as unemployed and claiming benefit, are really already working, even if only on a part-time basis. A figure of 7% (210,000) has been suggested.

Causes of unemployment

There are many types of unemployment and therefore a variety of causes. All we shall do now is outline an important area of debate about what is probably the *main* element in the total.

In the final section of Chapter 6 it was suggested that an initial change in any of the components of aggregate expenditure would have a consequent *multiplier* effect, leading to magnified effect on the overall levels of incomes and output and hence, so it was assumed, employment. In essence, this was what is called a 'Keynesian' approach to the question of how the amount of employment is determined, and what causes unemployment to occur. The acceptance by the majority of economists (and governments throughout the Western world) of the basic argument contained in *The General Theory of Employment, Interest and Money* by J. M. Keynes was so widespread as to earn the title of the 'Keynesian revolution' for the two decades following its publication in 1936.

The essential Keynesian proposition was that employment depended on spending: that only if total demand in the economy reached a level sufficient to buy all the output which they could produce would workers and other resources be fully employed. Or, to put it the other way round, the major cause of general unemployment in an economy is that the amount of spending is inadequate to absorb the output of goods and services produced with full employment. It is caused by *demand deficiency*.

Unfortunately, according to Keynes, such a situation is all too likely in an unregulated economy. The basic reason is that decisions to spend and decisions to produce are often taken by separate groups in the economy, acting from different motives. At any given income level the possibility of spending and production plans precisely matching is therefore extremely remote.

On the one hand, as we have seen, spending is planned by three broad groups: private individuals and firms; government; and foreigners (through their demand for our exports). The spending which they hope to do may be either on goods and services to be currently consumed or on investment (capital formation). Output, on the other hand, will be made up of domestic production, by private firms and public enterprises, plus imports; once again, we can make a broad distinction between the production of goods for immediate consumption, and output of capital goods like plant and machinery. We therefore have:

planned spending = planned consumption + planned capital formation;
and:

planned production = planned output of consumer goods + planned output of capital goods.

However, since we are talking about plans, what the various elements *intend* to do, there is no obvious reason why any of these quantities should exactly match. Demand and supply plans are, by and large, formulated independently, and it would be a matter of luck if 'planned spending' just equalled 'planned production', 'planned consumption' just equalled 'planned output of consumer goods', or 'planned capital formation' precisely coincided with 'planned output of capital goods'. But what happens if they do not?

We have already traced the effects of such a discrepancy in our brief account of the multiplier process. If supply plans for the coming year remained unchanged but, for example, households decide to save more, then the amount of intended spending would fall short. There is no reason why producers should realize this until they try to sell their output. Demand deficiency will then show itself initially in an unwanted and unintended accumulation of stocks; in other words, the immediate result is that producers, in effect, supplement the overall demand themselves by 'buying' some of their own output. Once they recognize what is happening, they will start to cut back on output – not only to what they think will be the new level of demand, but also to allow for the surplus stocks which have been built up unintentionally and which will have to be worked off.

The final outcome of supply plans exceeding demand plans is therefore a *fall in income and employment*. In the opposite situation, when demand plans happen to be greater than intended output, the effect will be to *increase* incomes and employment.

For full employment, there would have to be a quite fortuitous correspondence between spending and output plans. The major contribution which Keynes seemed to have made to economic thinking was to stress that there were no forces within an unregulated economy which would automatically ensure that full employment was achieved. His policy conclusion was an unpalatable one for those brought up to believe that the economy was best left to run freely along its own course: if full employment was to be achieved, then governments would have to intervene and *manage* the level of total spending so that demand could be established at the appropriate level. Anticipated shortfalls in spending could be made up by governments either stimulating demand from the private sector (through, for example, tax cuts) or *themselves* undertaking additional spending.

However, as with most matters in economics, there is an alternative view about what determines the level of employment. It is, in fact, the body of thinking against which Keynes was reacting, and which has staged a remarkable come-back in recent years among some economists and those responsible for economic policy-making over the past decade. This is the belief that the level of employment in an economy essentially depends on the prevailing *wage rate*. Broadly we may expect that the higher the wage rate, the greater will be the number of people seeking work, but the fewer will be the number that firms are prepared to employ.

Setting aside the niceties about how precisely it should be defined, unemployment is a situation in which the amount of labour offered for hire is in excess of that which firms are prepared to take on. The reason, so it is argued, is obvious. Workers must be pricing themselves out of jobs.

If a glut of strawberries causes quantities to lie unsold on a market stall, then the stallholder will recognize that the only solution is to lower their price, and thus, 'clear' the market. If only wages were as flexible as the price of strawberries then the 'labour market' would similarly clear itself. But the activities of trade unions in particular *prevent* the necessary adjustment from taking place, and unemployment can consequently persist.

The divide between economists about the causes of unemployment has, as we shall see in Part III, been reflected in major shifts of economic policy. Recent governments have rejected the idea that it is possible for them to reduce unemployment by increased spending, and have instead concentrated on trying to remove the 'stickiness' in the labour market which they see as the main problem. There is a similar and related disagreement about what determines the general price level at which an economy operates.

THE PRICE LEVEL

So far we have been looking at what determines *real* quantities in the economy like output and the quantity of work available. It is possible for all this activity to take place at a variety of price levels. In fact, since 1934 we have been accustomed in the UK to the general price level *rising* year after year: the process of inflation. But before asking whether inflation matters or what causes the economy to operate at one price level or another, we must first decide just what is meant by 'the price level'.

The measurement of inflation

Finding a measure for the general or average level of prices poses difficulties in much the same way as does the measure of unemployment. Price increases affect ordinary people week by week and month by month, as the bills increase and the monthly shopping costs more. The corres-

Table 7.1. Index of retail prices

Category of expenditure	Average annual price change (%)						Weights	
	'71–6	'76–80	'80–1	'81–2	'82–3	'83–4	1984	1961
Food	17.4	12.5	8.4	7.9	3.2	5.6	201	350
Alcoholic drink	11.6	13.2	16.9	11.4	7.5	5.8	75	71
Tobacco	12.0	14.1	23.5	15.4	6.7	10.9	36	80
Housing	13.3	17.1	18.1	12.6	2.5	9.2	149	87
Fuel and light	16.4	14.4	21.3	14.0	7.4	2.9	65	55
Durable household goods	11.0	11.9	4.8	2.8	2.7	2.5	69	66
Clothing and footwear	11.9	10.2	1.4	1.1	2.0	−0.1	70	106
Transport and vehicles	14.6	14.8	11.7	6.5	6.6	2.3	158	68
Miscellaneous goods	13.1	14.5	8.6	8.3	6.1	5.5	76	59
Services	14.9	13.3	14.5	10.2	3.4	4.2	65	58
Meals bought and consumed outside home	17.0	16.5	9.7	7.5	6.5	7.4	36	a
All items excl. housing	16.0	13.3	10.9	7.9	4.9	4.3	851	913
All items	14.5	13.8	11.9	8.6	4.6	5.0	1,000	1,000

Note: a Included for the first time in 1968.

ponding measure of the change in average prices is the Retail Price Index or RPI, which we have already encountered in Chapter 1. A periodic survey of the spending of a sample of households in the UK is carried out by the Central Statistical Office, and from this Family Expenditure Survey it estimates the proportion of spending which goes on food, on clothing, on travel, on drinks and tobacco, on housing (rent or mortgage repayments) and so on. This information enables the statistician to construct a picture of the spending pattern of an average household and provides the 'weights' to be used in the construction of the index.

Some of these items may reflect the government's taxation and pricing policies. For example, alcoholic drink and tobacco prices reflect the level of taxation rather than the costs of manufacture, and housing costs reflect interest rates (mortgages) and the rents set by local government. It is interesting to see how the pattern of spending has changed since 1961. 'Transport and vehicles', which reflects the cost of running a car, has become a much more important item, as has housing; while food, tobacco and clothing are less important.

The problem, of course, is that the average household, like the average person with an average family and an average income, does not exist. Different families have different spending patterns and will be affected differently by the same changes in prices. The statisticians do calculate special indexes for special groups such as pensioners, however.

Prices in the shops are collected by a team of inspectors literally shopping around and obtaining a range of prices for typical items in different parts of the country. These shop prices, however, are the end result of a long chain of transactions. For example, they include taxes such as VAT and excise duty, and the RPI is quite sensitive to tax changes and changes in mortgage interest rates. We can get behind this by consulting an index of wholesale prices. We can go a stage further back still, and start looking at the prices of manufacturers' inputs – costs of labour and raw materials, for example. This often provides a 'preview' of the changes in retail prices six or twelve months ahead.

The most general index of all is the so-called GDP deflator which we have already glanced at. This tells us how much of the change in GDP is a real change in the quantity of goods and services produced, and how much is simply a reflection of changes in the prices of goods and services. Similar deflators are calculated for the major components of GDP, so that if one wishes one can find an indicator of the changes in the prices of exports, imports, goods used by the government, consumer goods and so on.

Finally we can turn any of these indexes upside down, and so find out not how much more a particular basketful of goods now costs, but how much less a £5 note will buy. Series showing the purchasing power of £1, compared with a chosen base year, are available – and politicians use them with telling effect.

In Figure 4 we have used the Retail Price Index and the GDP deflator to illustrate how the price level has risen since 1970. By using the *rate* of increase we can identify the two major periods of very rapid inflation around 1975 and 1980. Notice, however, that the bottom of this diagram is 'no change' or 0% increase in prices since last year. The price level never went down, and indeed the rate of increase during these years never fell below 5% – and at 5% prices will double every fourteen years. Such inflation means that prices are five times higher than they were in 1970. Or, if you prefer, the 1970 £1 note, now a £1 coin, buys 20 pence worth of goods in 1984.

Helped by the fall in oil prices, the annual increase in the RPI did in fact fall to 4.2% in the first quarter of 1986, and to 2.5% in the second quarter, but by the third quarter it had begun to rise again.

Theories of inflation

Economists have put forward several hypotheses about what it is that causes prices to rise. For much of the post-war period, the argument was between those who chiefly ascribed inflation to 'demand pull' and those who emphasized 'cost push' as the prime cause. More recently, an older theory, that 'too much money' is the reason why inflation occurs, has been resurrected and has dominated the thinking of economic policy-makers. Here we will just briefly outline the three explanations.

(1) *Demand-pull inflation* has already been touched upon incidentally in our introduction to the idea of the multiplier (Chapter 6, page 83). In the same way that there may be a *shortfall* of spending below that necessary to purchase full employment output, it is also possible that spending plans may be too high. In this case, there is 'excess demand' in the economy. As consumers, firms, government and foreigners try to fulfil their spending plans they are faced with output that cannot be further increased because resources are already fully employed. Sellers take advantage of the situation and increase their prices.

In effect, this is the multiplier working itself out in *monetary* terms, since it is no longer possible for real output to rise in response to higher demand. Clearly it is when the economy is operating at or very close to full employment that demand-pull inflation is likely to occur. This, as we have seen, was the norm for the immediately post-war decades, and it is not surprising therefore that many economists saw inflation as a by-product of the determination of governments to maintain demand at a high level – with the concomitant danger of periodically overshooting.

(2) *Cost-push* theorists, on the other hand, usually take as their starting-point the fact that firms set their prices on the basis of their costs of production plus a mark-up for profit. Inflation is therefore likely to occur when one or more elements of their costs have risen.

Since wages form a large proportion of costs in many industries, it is inevitable that blame should frequently be placed on wage rises in excess of productivity increases as the prime mover in the inflationary process. Powerful trade unions have been singled out as the villain of the piece as being able to force through such pay increases, which firms have then passed on to the consumer. This they were able to do with impunity so long as the government was determined to underwrite full employment by creating the necessary level of demand.

But wages are not the only cost, and the upward pressure on prices can come from other sources. In particular there is the possibility of a rise in the cost of materials, so that inflation can be 'imported'. And government may itself be responsible for raising costs through, for example, increases in indirect taxes or a rise in interest rates.

(3) *'Too much money'* is the oldest theory of inflation, which in recent years has enjoyed a new lease of life in the guise of 'monetarism'. For monetarists, the fall in the value of money which inflation entails is explained quite simply by there being an excess supply of it in the economy. Generally they go on to blame governments for that situation since it is they who are ultimately responsible for the 'supply of money' in existence. Governments, they claim, have frequently been unwilling to finance their expenditure through raising the necessary funds through taxation. Instead, through their borrowing activities they have, in effect, 'resorted to the printing presses' in creating new money to pay for their programmes.

Whichever of these, or whatever combination of these or other causes, starts inflation, the process of inflation is likely to take a similar form. Once prices have risen, for whatever reason, wages and salaries are likely to respond as employees try to defend their standards of living. But wages form a large proportion of the costs of most goods and services, so that prices rise again, reflecting those cost increases. This interaction between costs (predominantly wage costs) and prices has been called the 'wage–price spiral', and the word 'spiral' indicates that each response takes place at a higher price level than the one before, leading to a steady increase in prices.

Another element common to all three theories of inflation is the importance of expectations. Once inflation has taken hold, pay claims and price increases will begin to take into account the anticipation of *future* inflation; and to the extent that such expectations become inbuilt, they will tend to be self-justifying and help to bring about the expected inflation.

Does inflation matter?

Inflation has been a constant source of worry, even during the years up to the late 1960s when it generally amounted to no more than about a 2% or 3% a year rise in the Retail Price Index. But it was not until the 1970s when inflation began to accelerate sharply that the evils of rising prices began to loom so large that the elimination of inflation supplanted the maintenance of full employment as the paramount economic priority.

So what are these evils? Why do we worry about price increases? In many countries, particularly in Latin America, but also Israel, rates of inflation of 100% or more have been experienced year after year, and everyone adjusts. Wages rise month by month in line with prices; all the numbers get bigger, but no one seems any the worse for it, and it is easy to knock off two zeros from time to time. So why worry?

In part it is precisely because we have *not* had experience of inflation and do not have automatic indexing right across the economy. In particular those whose incomes are fixed in terms of money, or who are dependent on past savings, will find their real incomes reduced as prices rise. More generally, those who are able to keep their incomes a little ahead of inflation, and those who can find an inflation-proof home for their savings, will gain at the expense of those who cannot do so. It is in recognition of the *unfairness* of the effects of inflation that in recent years pensions and other allowances have been adjusted periodically.

Inflation is also widely believed to discourage saving, despite the fact that recent episodes of rapid inflation seem to have led to an increase in the proportion of incomes saved. Perhaps this is another example of lack of experience of inflation – with people trying to maintain the purchasing power of their savings, eroded by the fall in the value of money, by adding to them as far as they could. It does seem true that inflation will alter the *pattern* of assets which savers try to accumulate, as they seek a hedge against inflation. Property, land, old-master paintings, porcelain figures and gold are preferred to bank or building society deposits and to government securities.

£100 lent in 1970 would have to have increased to around £500 if it was to have kept its original purchasing power, let alone earn a positive return to the lender. Not many forms of investment provide this sort of return (except, to repeat, where the system is designed to cope with permanent inflation), so in general it is true to say that lenders lose and debtors gain from inflation.

What everyone fears is runaway inflation, when money loses its value so quickly that no one will willingly hold it. Money is exchanged for goods as soon as possible and eventually ceases to be acceptable at all; sellers want goods, not money, in exchange for what they are selling; we are back to barter, and the economy has broken down. Past savings are worthless, and the only thing to do is to wipe the slate clean, as it were, and start again. Such experiences affected many people in Central Europe during the 1920s and bit deep into their memories. One reason why West Germany has had a lower rate of inflation in recent years than most other European countries is surely the lingering memory of the inflation just after the First World War.

So far we have been considering inflation within a country, but most economies are open, exchanging goods and services on a large scale. The effect on external competitiveness of inflation consistently higher than that experienced in rival economies is a matter we shall be considering in Chapter 8. Later still, in Part III, we shall be returning to the policy implications and impact of the various theories that we have just outlined.

ECONOMIC GROWTH

Economic growth is the process by which an economy's capability for production is expanded over the years. Sometimes, the term 'growth rate' is used loosely to refer to *any* rise in output that takes place. But such an increase may be from a starting-point where the economy is operating at a level well below its capacity, with high unemployment. Strictly, economic growth refers to an expansion of that capacity, rather than simply taking up the slack. It is a rise in what is known as its 'productive potential'.

Table 7.2. UK gross domestic capital formation

	('70	'71	'72	'73	'74	'75	'76	'77	'78	'79	'80	'81	'82	'83	'84	'85)
							(£ billion at constant 1980 prices)									
Gross domestic capital formation	40	41	41	43	42	42	42	41	43	44	42	38	40	42	45	46
Capital consumption	19	20	21	22	22	23	24	25	26	27	28	29	30	30	31	32
Net capital formation	21	21	20	21	20	19	18	16	17	17	14	9	10	12	14	14
As % of GDP	11	11	10	10	9	9	8	7	7	7	6	4	4	5	6	6

So how does an economy grow? The discussions so far will suggest some answers. It may increase the quantity of economic resources which are the basis of production. Or it may improve their quality and the efficiency with which they are combined, i.e. increase the productivity of the factors of production.

Natural resources are not easily increased, although occasionally a dramatic addition may be made as in the case of Britain's discovery of North Sea oil and gas. Many would argue that this afforded the UK an excellent chance of increasing its rate of economic growth – an opportunity which, in the event, it has failed to seize. But generally the factor of land is relatively fixed in quantity. Much the same may be said of labour to the extent that it depends on population growth, which has been very slow everywhere in the developed industrial world in recent years. (As we have seen in Chapter 2, the size of the work-force can be affected also by changes in the *age distribution* of the population; this caused an increase in the early 1980s due to an unusually large number of new entrants and relatively few retirements.)

The factor of *capital* is the most readily increased in quantity. But if the stock of capital is to be increased, economic resources must be directed into the production of machinery, transport, equipment, power generation, motorways and factory buildings. These resources cannot be used to produce goods and services for personal (or government) consumption. In short, consumption must be restrained, or savings increased, if resources are to be made available for increasing the stock of capital.

In this respect the story of the past few years is a grim one. The output of the 'investment goods industries' – those which make capital equipment – shrank from 110.2 in 1974 to 100 in 1980, the base year, to a low of 91.3 in 1981, and it had risen only to 97.1 in 1984. Some capital goods, of course, will be imported; and one index of Britain's relative industrial decline is the proportion of its machine tools which are imported from Japan, West Germany, Switzerland and the USA. So let us look at gross domestic capital formation, and at capital consumption, which together give us some indication of the growth in our stock of capital equipment – Table 7.2.

A more important question, however, is where the investment took place, and what effect it had on the quality, i.e. the productivity, of the capital stock. British government policy has always included incentives for capital investment, but they have been general rather than selective. Such differences as have existed were directed towards depressed regions, rather than growth industries in prosperous areas; and it is only recently that special assistance has been given to, for example, research, development and investment in micro-electronics and information technology. Critics of Britain's performance point to the long-term strategic help and guidance of the Japanese Ministry of Trade and Industry, or the long-term finance available from West German banks to their country's industrialists.

A breakdown of gross domestic fixed capital formation for 1984 was provided in Tables 2.8, 2.9 and 2.10 on pages 33 and 34 of Chapter 2. These figures showed that net investment in manufacturing industry and in the construction industry was actually negative in 1984. While it is probable that any new machines will be more productive than the old ones they replace, so that even if net investment were zero the capacity of the economy might yet increase, these are worrying figures. The trend away from manufacturing into the 'service' sectors of distribution, banking and financial services is evidenced by the figures for employment – and here again by the data on capital investment. To the extent that economic growth does take place, it will continue the trend of change in the composition of output which we noted in Chapter 3. Taking the year 1980 as the base (100), the sectors showing the greatest growth between 1980 and 1985 have been:

Oil and gas extraction	150
Banking, finance, etc.	145
Electrical and electronic engineering	131
Communications	123
Chemicals	120

Those showing decline in output over the same five-year period were:

Coal and coke	67
Artificial fibres	74
Motor vehicles and parts	86
Construction	90
Mechanical engineering	93
Other transport equipment	95

Manufacturing industry by 1984 was the source of only 24.8% of the gross domestic product, compared with 29.2% in 1975. If the 'energy-producing' industries are added in, the proportion rises to 36% – more or less the same as in 1975, since the rise of oil offsets the decline in manufacturing.

There is evidence not only that Britain lags behind major competitors in the quantity and quality of its capital investment, but also that similar capital equipment in the UK produces less than it does in other countries. This might be attributable to the quality of the work-force – both on the shop-floor and in the boardroom – with which it is combined. There are those who claim that Britain is investing inadequately in *human* capital, and that standards of technical and management education leave much to be desired.

United States commentators, for example, have written scathingly of British managers as characterized by 'their amateurism and their frequent acceptance of business as second choice when they fail to qualify for a civil service career. They tend to retain the civil service as their model and settle into a trustee role of gentlemanly responsibility that hardly conduces to rapid innovation.' Labour, according to the same critics, has a 'proletarian spirit which seems conservative even by standards of a traditional society'.

The often superior performance of US and Japanese subsidiaries operating in the UK would seem to afford some support for the view that attitudes play an important role in the growth process. But it is not easy to quantify.

In any case, it is foolish to think of economic growth as an end in itself. What matters are those considerations concealed by the growth index: the composition of the increased output, the costs involved in producing it and how the benefits are distributed. It is to this last question that we now turn.

THE DISTRIBUTION OF INCOME

We can look at the distribution of national income in three ways: the shares going to the various factors of production; how it is shared between individuals and households; and the geographical spread between the

Table 7.3. Gross domestic product by category of income (%)

	1983	1984	1985
Income from employment	68.5	64.4	63.3
Income from self-employment	8.9	9.5	9.7
	74.4	73.9	73.0
Gross trading profits of companies	14.1	15.5	17.2
Gross trading surplus of public corporations	3.7	3.0	2.4
	17.8	18.5	19.6
Rent	6.9	6.8	6.7
Imputed charge for capital consumption	0.9	0.9	0.9

Table 7.4. Household income and its redistribution, 1983 (£ per year)

Average per household	Bottom fifth	Next fifth	Middle fifth	Next fifth	Top fifth	All
Original income	120	2,580	6,880	10,570	18,640	7,760
plus Benefits in cash	3,020	2,260	1,100	730	600	1,540
Gross income	3,140	4,840	7,980	11,300	19,240	9,300
less Income tax and NIC	10	410	1,410	2,340	4,510	1,740
Disposable income	3,130	4,420	6,570	8,960	14,730	7,560
less Indirect taxes	850	1,270	1,860	2,280	3,380	1,930
plus Benefits in kind						
Education	360	370	650	710	780	580
National Health Service	750	700	660	620	620	670
Travel subsidies	50	70	60	70	120	70
Housing subsidies	130	80	70	50	20	70
Other[a]	50	30	30	30	20	30
Final income	3,630	4,400	6,190	8,160	12,920	7,060

Note: [a] Rail travel subsidy, option mortgage and life insurance premium relief, which is received by households.

Table 7.5. Percentage share of income groups

	Bottom fifth	Next fifth	Middle fifth	Next fifth	Top fifth
Original income					
1976	0.8	9.4	18.8	26.6	44.4
1981	0.6	8.1	18.0	26.9	46.4
1983	0.3	6.7	17.7	27.2	48.0
Disposable income					
1976	7.0	12.6	18.2	24.1	38.1
1981	6.7	12.1	17.7	24.1	39.4
1983	6.9	11.9	17.6	24.0	39.6
Final income					
1976	7.4	12.7	18.0	24.0	37.9
1981	7.1	12.4	17.9	24.0	38.6
1983	6.9	12.2	17.6	24.0	39.3

regions of the UK. Chapter 5 began with a discussion of the payments made by firms to the owners of the factors of production which they hired, and we illustrated the way in which this flow of incomes was modified by the taxes and benefits taken and given away by government in Figure 9. The share of income going to each factor – the 'functional distribution of income' as it is called – is set out again in Table 7.3 for convenience.

The table makes it clear that the lion's share of income accrues to the factor labour, which gets about three-quarters of national income. The remaining quarter is income from property, of which capital takes three-quarters and land the rest.

Although income from ownership of property is a relatively small proportion of total incomes, it plays a very important part in influencing the overall pattern of income distribution. This is because property is itself very unevenly distributed; by far the greater part of all the income-generating wealth in the country is owned by a small number of people, whose incomes are correspondingly large.

Table 7.4 shows the average incomes of those in the bottom fifth through to the top fifth of households. It can be seen that the poorest 20% had a negligible 'original income' and depended almost entirely on welfare benefits paid in cash. The top 20% had a gross income before tax over six times as large as the poorest group. But this relatively broad-brush treatment conceals the true extremity of inequality, since the upper fifth of income earners is a group which contains some who are receiving a *very* large income from property, but also a majority who would think of themselves as earning a relatively modest salary.

While the effect of taxes (shown in the lower half of the table) moderates the gap between the groups substantially, it is interesting to see that the higher-income households manage to secure disproportionate benefits from publicly provided health and education.

The next set of figures, in Table 7.5, shows the percentage of total income which is received by households which fall into each fifth when ranked in order of original income, disposable income and final income, as defined in Table 7.4. This table shows that 'original income', whether from wages and salaries or from property, is very unevenly distributed, and that the distribution became more uneven over the seven years to 1983.

In 1983 the top 20% of households took almost half the total income, while the bottom 20% (a group dominated by pensioners and one-parent families) got only three-thousandths! Direct taxation and the payment of cash benefits by the state evened things up to some extent; the poorest 20% now got nearly 7% of total incomes, and the richest 20% just under 40%. Many people are surprised to find that 'benefits in kind' provided by the Welfare State do very little to increase equality of final income. In practice they are enjoyed by all income groups, and the better-off actually gain slightly more than the worse-off (£1,560 compared with £1,340).

Thus income distribution between individuals or households can be illustrated in two ways. As in Table 7.4 we can rank income earners or households from the poorest to the richest, and show the income earned by each unit. Or as in Table 7.5 we can show the percentage of total income earned by each group of units.

The first approach offers the basis for what is perhaps one of the most striking pictures of income inequality, painted by the Dutch economist Jan Pen in his 'parade of dwarfs' (J. Pen, *Income Distribution*, London, Allen Lane/Penguin Press, 1971). Pen asks us to think of ourselves as average people with average incomes and of average height. We are then invited to watch a parade, in which all the income earners (except ourselves) take part. The parade is organized in such a way that the poorest people are in the front, and the richest at the end, and *their heights are proportionate to their incomes*. What do we see? A parade of dwarfs! The procession goes on and on, and it is a very long time, only fifteen minutes before the close of the hour-long ceremony, before we begin to look the marchers in the eye. Then, right towards the end, we suddenly find

Table 7.6. Regional distribution of incomes, 1982–3 averages

	Average household income/ week	Percentage of households in income group				
		under £75	£75–£149	£150–£224	£225–£299	over £300
N. Ireland	£145	32	32	18	11	7
North	£159	29	26	22	14	10
Yorks/Humberside	£163	26	27	23	13	11
Wales	£166	22	29	26	14	10
Scotland	£168	28	25	21	13	13
United Kingdom ave.	£182	22	25	23	15	15
South-East	£210	17	23	22	17	21

(Remaining English regions with ± 5% of UK average.)

ourselves looking up at giants the size of houses and office blocks – the relatively few people with very large incomes have arrived. As we said earlier, most of their large incomes are derived from their ownership of property.

Many of the households in the 'top fifth' in Table 7.4 include more than one bread-winner, so that it is not easy to move from household income to individual earnings. But £20,000 a year is £400 per week, which is considerably more than the typical weekly earnings of professional and lower management employees. Average male earnings in 1982–3 were around £140 per week or £7,300 a year, so that a household with one earner of an average wage would fall into the middle fifth of the income range.

Who, then, are the bottom 40%? Many of these are households dependent on pension or benefit payments, but a surprisingly large number of people in employment earned £100 a week or less in 1982. A household dependent on one such income would certainly be at the lower margin of the 'middle fifth', if not below it, and would receive supplements to its earned income in one form or another.

Among these low-paid workers are the expected ones: roadsweepers, caretakers, hospital porters, shop assistants and so on. But farm workers and farm machinery operators, whose work requires a wide range of skills, are also there, along with butchers and gardeners. Men in these traditionally low-paid jobs earn about two-thirds of the average wage, and the surprising thing is that the same was true of their great-grandfathers; the *pattern* of distribution seems to change very slowly.

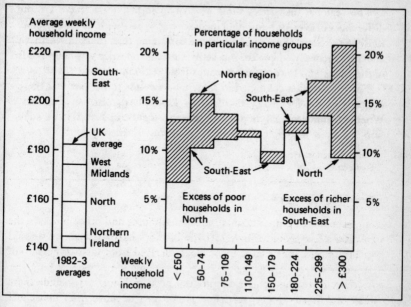

Figure 11 The regional differential

A final distinction must be made between male and female earnings, since women are paid (by and large) only two-thirds as much as men in similar jobs. A household in which the sole bread-winner is a woman can therefore expect to be very poor indeed. A widely accepted definition of 'low pay' is two-thirds of average male earnings, and on this criterion well over half of all full-time women workers are low-paid. We have already noted the fact that a large proportion of women workers are in fact part-time employees earning correspondingly less.

The last aspect of income distribution to be considered is the unequal spread of incomes throughout the country. The readily available data are for the broad regions into which the UK is divided, but we should not forget that the 'rich' regions contain areas of very low incomes. Greater London has areas of very high unemployment, and areas where employment is notoriously ill-rewarded, such as the clothing trades. The North-West and Scotland have their prosperous commuter belts and their high-technology industries. Table 7.6 picks out the extremes, which are illustrated in Figure 11.

The regional disparities show up in two forms. First, there are the differences in average household incomes per week – with, at the extreme, those in the South-East receiving some 50% more than those in Northern Ireland. Secondly, there are markedly varied proportions of households in the upper and lower income groups from region to region.

The information contained in these tables points to the fact that there is considerable inequality of different kinds in the British economy. When we come to analyse policy and performance in Part III, we shall find that these inequalities have been widening in recent years.

8

UK International Payments

We have now reached the final stage in this account of the basic economic mechanism in the United Kingdom. Nearly everything that has been said so far has related to activities taking place within Britain itself. But in fact we are deeply enmeshed in the international economy, as was briefly indicated in Chapter 4's section on 'the foreign sector' (page 64).

Our trade, investment and other relations with the outside world entail a vast number of transactions which involve payments being made between residents of Britain and non-residents. The nature of those payments and the accounts that are kept of them are the first topic for consideration in this chapter. The second topic, exchange rates, is closely related because nearly all such transactions involve the use of foreign currencies.

THE BALANCE OF PAYMENTS

Britain is very heavily engaged in overseas trade (or more strictly 'foreign' trade, since we should remember that we do have a land border with one other national economy, Eire). In 1985, for example, we exported merchandise worth £78 billion and imported over £80 billion worth; in other words, over 20% of the goods we produced were exported, and we spent 23% of our total domestic expenditure on imported goods.

The flows of money corresponding to these two flows of goods constitute the first item in what is called the balance of payments, which is simply a record of all the *money* transactions between our economy and others over the course of a year. However, the term is frequently used rather loosely, and its various connotations need to be clarified. What we have looked at so far is just the inflow of payments for our exports of *merchandise* set against the outflow of payments for our imports of *mer-*

chandise. This is termed the 'visible balance' or the balance of trade. This is the first subtotal in the balance of payments accounts for 1985 set out in Table 8.1 on page 109.

It would be a remarkable coincidence if the balance of trade actually did *balance*, since exporting and importing are generally undertaken by different groups acting in independent ignorance of what the others are doing. In 1980 there was a positive balance, unusual for the UK. This was mainly the result of a sharp recession in 1979–81, which depressed spending on imports as much as it depressed spending on domestically produced goods, combined with more buoyant exports, now including oil.

The negative balance of £2,111 million in 1985 is more typical of the UK, where it is usual for a deficit on merchandise trade to be offset by a positive balance on a second set of flows. These arise from 'invisible' imports and exports – invisible in the sense that although no transfer of goods takes place, certain transactions have the same end result, namely the creation of credits and debits between economies.

Many of these take the form of payments for a variety of *services*, like tourism, shipping and aviation, banking and insurance. For example, Britons taking holidays in Spain create invisible imports; it is as though they were importing goods from that country. A foreign shipper using Lloyd's insurance, on the other hand, would be an invisible export. In Table 8.1 the export and import of services such as these have been listed separately as item 2, so that the sum of items 1 and 2 – the export and import of goods and services – matches up with our earlier discussions in the context of the circular flow.

But also included are some pure flows of money. One of these we have already met under the name 'net property income from abroad', which when added to gross domestic product converted it into gross national product. It consists of flows of profits, interest and dividends, etc. derived from capital owned by UK residents in foreign countries, offset by similar payments made to foreign owners of capital located in the UK. An example is the profit sent back to the USA by Ford, Vauxhall/Bedford or Esso, offset by dividends paid to British holders of shares in IBM or Siemens. This has provided a positive balance in most years, and one which has risen sharply as a result of recent large flows of investment from the UK to foreign countries. It is identified as item 3 in Table 8.1, and certain other current transfers of money (such as government foreign aid and payments to and from the European Community) form item 4.

Bringing all these components (items 2, 3 and 4) together yields inflows

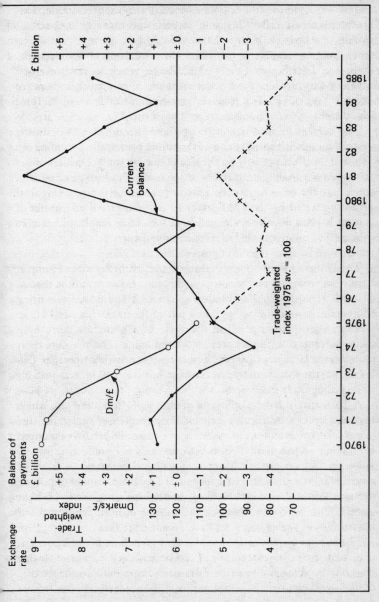

Figure 12 Exchange rate and current balance of payments

and outflows, similar to the flows associated with exports and imports of goods, which are called 'invisible' imports and exports. In the case of Britain, the invisible balance has invariably been positive, i.e. we earn more from the export of invisibles than we pay out for imports of invisibles. Together with the visible balance, which we saw was usually negative, this provides what is known as the current balance – 'current' because it is distinguished from the long-term capital flows which constitute the next element in the balance of payments.

The current balance is plotted in Figure 12, which shows its steep descent into deficit in 1973 and 1974, caused principally by the oil price rise, and its effect not only on the size of our import bill but also (via its impact on our trading partners) on the volume of exports. The sustained squeeze of the economy by the Labour government, culminating in the pressure exerted by the IMF, reduced the import bill and turned the current balance positive again, and from then on a combination of credit squeeze and oil exports led to a succession of current account surpluses which were far from typical of post-war Britain.

The flows of money shown in the next part of the balance of payments have been separated out because they represent changes in the stocks of Britain's external assets and liabilities. Items 5 and 6 in Table 8.1 are short-term flows of money into and out of the banks here and abroad, seeking security from a fall in the value of a particular currency, or taking advantage of differences in interest rates. The net outflow has often been a large negative item and has led to crisis measures; as Table 8.1 shows, the volume of transactions can be very large indeed, matching or exceeding trade in services.

A particularly large outflow in recent years has been 'investment overseas by UK residents', item 7. Foreigners may undertake *direct* investment by setting up subsidiaries in Britain, or *portfolio* investment in purchasing shares in British companies. This would constitute an inflow of foreign capital. More commonly in recent years, since the abolition of government restrictions on the export of capital to purchase overseas assets, it is the outflow of capital which has been very much larger. This, of course, bears fruit subsequently in the form of the inward flow of profits which we have already discussed.

The current account surpluses of recent years have been large enough to offset these net outward flows of capital; and the UK's external assets have increased markedly, particularly since restrictions on the export of capital were removed.

Table 8.1. UK balance of payments, 1985 (£ billion)

Item/category	Credit or inflow	Debit or outflow	Balances
Current transactions			
1 Export (+) and import (−) of goods	78	80	(−) 2.1
2 Export (+) and import (−) of services	24	18	(+) 5.8
Subtotal: exports/imports of foods and services (X and M in National Accounts)	102	99	(+) 3.7
3 Interest, profits and dividends	53	50	(+) 3.4
4 Transfers	3	7	
Subtotal: items 2–4 or 'invisible imports/exports'	81	75	(+) 5.7
TOTAL current account	159	155	(+) 3.6
Capital transactions			
5 UK banks' lending (−) and borrowing (+) in sterling and foreign currencies	30	22	(+) 7.7
6 Private sector lending (−) and borrowing (+) to/from banks abroad	2	4	(−) 1.3
Subtotal: items 5 + 6	32	26	(+) 6.4
7 Investment overseas by UK (−) and overseas investment in UK (+):			
Direct	3	7	(−) 3.9
Portfolio	7	18	(−) 11.1
Total	10	26	(−) 15.1
8 Changes in other external assets/ liabilities (net)	3		(+) 3.2
Subtotal: items 7 + 8	14	26	(−) 11.9
TOTAL capital account	46	51	(−) 5.5
9 Changes to official reserves: increase (−), decrease (+)			(−) 1.8
		Current account balance	+ 3.6
		Capital account balance	− 5.5
		'Balancing item'	+ 3.7
			+ 1.8
		Changes in reserves	− 1.8

In putting together the current and capital balances we must note the existence of the mysterious 'balancing item'. It would be more honest to call this 'errors and omissions', because it simply tells us what is necessary to 'balance the books' after all the identifiable flows have been accounted for. If for example we look at the current and capital balance for 1985, the net outflow was £3,602 million minus £5,538 million, which equals £1,936 million. This outflow has to be financed in some way or another; the money must come from somewhere. It comes from the balances maintained by the government (in practice the Bank of England) precisely for the purpose of evening out the fluctuations in the amounts flowing in and flowing out. When the accounts are closed at the end of the year they might show that the Bank has provided more money than it has taken in (a net outflow from this account) or that the account has grown as a result of a net inflow.

The Bank knows quite precisely how much went in and out of the account during the year. The item indicating this is shown in Table 8.1 as item 9 'changes to official reserves' or 'official financing' and is perhaps the most reliable figure in the whole balance of payments. But it rarely matches the overall balance of recorded current and capital transactions as it might be expected to. The difference, therefore, represents un-recorded or wrongly recorded flows of money. Since trade flows and long-term capital flows are generally well-recorded, the missing sums are usually assumed to be short-term money flows.

So the overall negative balance of £1,936 million should have been offset by the same change in official reserves. But in fact in 1985 there was an *addition* to reserves of £1,758 million, leaving a huge 'balancing item' of £3,694 million. It was a plus – an inflow – as indeed it usually is. But whether there was a genuine unrecorded or under-recorded inflow, or whether some of the outflows were over-recorded, we cannot know. What is very clear is that when one compares the balancing item with the recorded surplus we may be forgiven some scepticism about the precision of official statistics.

We should now go back to consider 'official financing' rather more closely. As we said, the government maintains a reserve in order to cope with the ups and downs in the flows of money into and out of the country, in the same way as most of us maintain a bank account which (we hope) evens out the periodic inflow of wage or salary and the constant outflow of payments. The 'reserves', as they are known, consist in part of gold, which has a long history as the ultimate form of money. Gold, however, is a sterile, non-interest-earning asset, though one which in-creased dramatically in money value from 1970 onwards. Most of the reserves are in the form of official accounts in foreign banks, or holdings of short-term foreign government securities, usually in dollars which are the most-used currency in international transactions. The remaining element is represented by the UK's account with the International Monetary Fund, which acts as a bank for central banks like the Bank of England. In the background, but not counted as part of the reserves, is the ability to borrow if necessary. Analogies with individual circumstances are always dangerous in economics, but it might help to understand this rather esoteric subject if we think of gold as the equivalent of cash in one's pocket; of the foreign bank accounts as the equivalent of one's own (positive) current account at the bank; and of the IMF position as the equivalent of unused overdraft facilities, available when needed.

These reserves are small when compared with the magnitude of the annual inward and outward flows of money, so that they cannot cope with a very large or persistent outflow. When such a situation arises, as it did in 1973–4, something has to be done.

EXCHANGE RATES

One of the features which distinguish international from domestic transactions (though by no means the fundamental one) is that participants in international trade generally have different currencies. A United States exporter to Britain will be wanting payment in dollars which can then be spent in the US economy. However, although pounds sterling are of no use to the American who wants to buy goods and services at home, they *are* required by the US *importer* of goods from Britain, who will be prepared to buy sterling for dollars in order to settle British debts in an acceptable form.

There are huge numbers of transactions taking place which involve the sale and purchase of the various currencies of the world. What determines the value of each in terms of the others?

The 'market' on which foreign currencies are bought and sold is itself international, and consists of the major banks in centres such as Tokyo, Hong Kong, Frankfurt, Zurich, London and New York. They are linked by telex and satellite, and the market handles huge flows of transactions and is very sensitive and volatile. The timing is such that soon after the New York market closes at 9.30 p.m. British Summer Time, the Tokyo market opens, at 1.00 the following morning. It stays open until 7.00 a.m., and Hong Kong and Singapore are open longer, so that they overlap with the opening of the London market at 9.30 a.m. Trading is non-stop, in effect. London is still the largest market in terms of volume and variety of transactions in foreign exchange.

Sales and purchases are broadly of two kinds. They may be related to trade and investment. Or they may be speculative or precautionary in nature. Let us begin with the first of these, using the UK and the USA as the example. Assume that the rate of exchange to begin with is such that £1 buys $2.40.

The UK exports whisky to the USA, and the UK exporter will want to be paid in £ sterling. So a US importer has to buy the pounds needed to pay for the whisky, and sells dollars in order to do so. Conversely a British importer of Florida orange juice will have to sell pounds and buy dollars with which to pay the US exporter. For each exchange of goods there is a corresponding exchange of currencies:

- £1 = $2.40.
- UK importer *sells* £100 and *buys* $240 to pay the US exporter for 100 cases of orange juice priced at $2.40 a case.
- US importer *sells* $240 and *buys* £100 to pay for 10 cases of whisky priced at £10 per case.

So 10 cases of Scotch whisky exchange for 100 cases of orange juice (a point to which we shall return), and there are offsetting sales and purchases of £100 and $240.

Demand for Scotch whisky in the US will tend to rise as Thanksgiving and Christmas draw near, whereas more orange juice will be drunk in the UK in the summer; trade shows a seasonal fluctuation. In the spring, perhaps, there are sales of £200 (purchases of $480) to buy the orange juice, offset by purchases of only £100 (sales of $240) to pay for normal imports of whisky. In the autumn, on the other hand, there are sales of $480 (purchases of £200) to buy extra whisky, offset by sales of only £100 (purchases of $240) to pay for normal imports of orange juice.

Look at this situation now from the UK viewpoint. In the spring there is an excess supply of £, and an excess demand for $. One would expect the price of the £ to fall, and the price of the $ to rise. The exchange rate would move away from $2.40 = £1 to something like $2.00 = £1. An excess of imports over exports – a balance of trade deficit – brings about a fall in the value of a country's currency.

In the autumn the situation is reversed. There are now excess sales of dollars, and an insufficient supply of pounds, so the exchange rate would move in the opposite direction towards £1 = $2.80. An excess of exports over imports – a balance of trade surplus – causes the value of a currency to rise.

The Bank of England maintains its Exchange Equalization Account primarily to even out seasonal and cyclical ups and downs in the demand for and the supply of foreign exchange. An excess demand for £ causes no problem; the Bank of England can supply as many £ as the market demands, buying other currencies (for which the $ serves as a symbol) and adding to its reserves. When there is an excess *supply* of £, however, the Bank has to use its limited reserves of foreign currency to buy up the excess. A balance of trade deficit, which brings about the excess supply of £, exerts pressure on a country's reserves if the government tries to resist the downward market movement.

All we have been saying about the purchases and sales of currencies linked to the import and export of goods and services is equally true of investment. A US company wishing to build a new factory in Scotland, or to purchase an existing business there, must buy £ in order to do so, selling $ in the process. (Unless, of course, it has accumulated £ through its operations in the UK, or is willing to borrow £ from UK investors. A great deal of the investment of multinational corporations is financed this way.) A British firm setting up business in Europe must purchase Deutschmarks or French francs, selling £ in the foreign exchange market. The importance of this is that a trade deficit could be offset by an investment surplus; it is the overall balance of *payments* which exerts upward or downward pressures on the value of currencies.

In addition there are financial flows affecting the foreign exchange market which have little or nothing to do with trade or investment. Large and ever-growing amounts of money move around the world, in response to two main influences: the rate of interest they can be made to earn, and their owners' judgements about the likely *future* movements of exchange rates.

Some of the purchases and sales of foreign currencies are purely speculative. People gamble on future prices of currencies just as they do on future prices of shares or wheat or copper. As well-respected a figure as Keynes made, lost and then remade a small fortune through speculation in the uncertain foreign exchange markets of the 1930s. It can be (and is) argued that such activities are benign, or even beneficial, in that they tend to damp down fluctuations in rates. Others say that they accentuate the swings that are taking place.

Many of the movements from one currency to another are made not in anticipation of gain, but to avoid possible losses. The owner or manager of large sums of money, who might for example be the finance director of a large multinational oil company, or the manager of an offshore investment fund, will not wish to be caught holding large amounts of a currency, or securities denominated in a currency, which suddenly loses 10% of its value. So if he senses that, say, the value of the dollar relative to the Deutschmark is going to fall, he will run down his account in his New York bank, transferring most of his money to Frankfurt. He may not even have to go to this trouble, because it is now quite usual to hold dollar accounts in a London bank or yen in a US account. Whatever the mechanism there will be a large sale of dollars and a large purchase of Deutschmarks – an excess supply of dollars on the market and an increased demand for Deutschmarks. The price of dollars falls, and the price of Deutschmarks rises. This result is exactly what the owner of the money expected to happen. Expectations, if they are general, are self-justifying!

Let us return once again to our simple trade example in the context of expectations about a *future* shift in the exchange rate. The UK importer of orange juice is going to *sell* £100 and buy $240. Should he do this now, or perhaps wait until the invoice arrives with the shipment in a few months' time? If he does wait, and the £ drops to $2.00, his orange juice will cost him £1.20 a case; and if he has a contract to sell it or has planned to use it on the basis of £1.00 per case, he will make a heavy loss. So if he has the slightest fear of a fall in the exchange rate, he will buy his dollars early. The exporter of Scotch whisky, who has perhaps contracted to supply at a price of $240 a case, will on the contrary be willing to wait to be paid, on the chance that when he is paid the $240 will yield £120 instead of £100.

So in general imports are paid for early, or even in advance, and payment for exports is deferred as long as possible. There is a lot of selling of £, and very little buying, and the effect is just the same as if there has been a massive outflow of money. These 'leads' and 'lags', as they are called, place yet another strain on the authorities if they are trying to prevent the currency from falling as the market ordains – which can be prevented only by throwing some of their limited reserves of foreign currencies into the pool.

Speculation can thus arise out of the process of trade. And before getting too self-righteous about the evils of speculation, we should remember that very many of us are involved in this business nowadays, because so many of us go abroad for a holiday. Do you buy your pesetas or lire now? Or do you take the chance that by the time you get off the plane the exchange rate will have moved in your favour? Do you 'lead', or do you 'lag', your foreign exchange transactions? You might note, next time you book, whether your travel firm is carrying the exchange risk by giving you a fixed price in £, or whether it is making you carry the risk by imposing a possible surcharge.

For most of the post-war period a system of 'fixed' exchange rates was in force. At a conference held at Bretton Woods in the USA towards the end of the Second World War it was agreed that:

(a) the value of the US dollar would be fixed in terms of gold;
(b) the value of all other major currencies would be fixed in terms of US dollars;
(c) an International Monetary Fund would police the international monetary system, would extend credit to countries in (temporary) balance of payments difficulties and would allow changes in rates of exchange – known as parities – when a permanent imbalance was seen to have developed.

This system broke down in 1971 and was followed by a regime of 'floating' exchange rates, under which the price of a currency in terms of any other currency was allowed freely to respond to the market forces of supply and demand. We discuss the IMF and the other major international institutions later in the book (Chapter 17). This brief summary is simply to explain the difference between the fixed exchange rate system pre-1971 and the floating exchange rate system post-1972, the period with which we are mostly concerned.

Under the original Bretton Woods system of fixed exchange rates countries were required to keep the exchange rate within very narrow limits. A persistent deficit, exerting a constant drain on the reserves, or a sudden large drop in demand or increase in supply of a currency could cause a crisis.

With a floating exchange rate a country may choose to regulate the extent of a particular movement (a 'dirty float') or allow market forces full play.

Returning to our example of UK/US trade, we can see the effect of a currency devaluation or depreciation by considering what happens if the exchange rate falls to £1 = $2.00. We assume that neither the UK price of whisky nor the US price of orange juice changes, but the shift in the exchange rate alters the US price of whisky and the UK price of orange juice:

- £1 = $2.00.
- UK importer must now sell £120 to buy $240 to pay the US exporter for 100 cases of orange juice priced at $2.40 a case.
- US importer sells $200 and buys £100 to pay for 10 cases of Scotch whisky priced at £10 per case.

So it now takes the proceeds of 12 cases of whisky (£120 = $240) to buy 100 cases of orange juice; or, to put it another way, if we export 10 cases of whisky we must make do with 83 cases of orange juice, since that is all we can buy with $200.

This change in the terms on which whisky (or exports in general) exchanges for orange juice (or imports in general) is called a deterioration or a worsening of the 'terms of trade', and it is the usual consequence of a fall – a devaluation – of a country's currency.

Note however another aspect of the fall in the exchange rate. The US importer of Scotch whisky can now sell it in the US at a lower price, since he had to pay only $20 a case instead of $24. The UK importer of orange juice, on the other hand, will have to raise its price to £1.20 a case if he is not going to lose money. Exports get cheaper (in foreign currency) and imports get dearer (in domestic currency) after a devaluation. If all goes well these price changes will stimulate an increase in the volume of exports and a fall in the volume of imports, and will reverse the trade deficit.

INFLATION AND THE EXCHANGE RATE

In an earlier discussion of the price level in Chapter 7 (page 95) we said that *one* of the reasons for worrying about inflation was the effect on trade if a country's prices rose more rapidly than those of its major competitors. We can now elaborate this somewhat by seeing how the exchange rate is linked to the rate of inflation.

As an example, let us take trade in motor cars between West Germany and the UK and assume that we begin with similar cars (Jaguar or BMW) being sold at similar prices in both countries. For example, if the UK price were £10,000, then the German price would be Dm 80,000 at an exchange rate of Dm 8 = £1, as it was in 1972.

This was a period of high inflation, but as usual the UK rate was greater than the West German rate. Applying the actual rates of inflation to car prices in the two countries would have meant that after four years the £10,000 car has risen to £18,400 in the UK, while in West Germany the Dm 80,000 car would cost Dm 101,600.

What happens when these prices are converted using the original exchange rate of Dm 8 to £1? The British car would cost Dm 147,200, and the West German car £12,700. British cars would be unsaleable in West Germany, and the British market would be flooded with cheaper West German imports. At a fixed exchange rate, Britain would have a trade deficit, and West Germany a surplus.

This, of course, was precisely the time when the system of fixed rates broke down. If exchange rates were free to change, the higher UK inflation would drive down the value of the pound in terms of Deutschmarks.

The question is: how far down? Is there a 'correct' rate? In theory the market would operate (other things being equal) to equalize the purchasing power of the two currencies. This idea goes under the name of the 'law of one price', a recognition of the fact that price differences cannot persist within a single market.

By 1976, for example, there would be sales of £ to buy Dm with which to import West German cars, but there would be no offsetting sales of Dm and purchases of £ by West German buyers of British cars. In the foreign exchange market there would be an excess supply of and inadequate demand for £; and an excess demand for and inadequate supply of Dm. The price of the £ in terms of Dm would fall to a level which, in a rough-and-ready way, equalized the price of similar cars in both countries. This exchange rate goes by the name of the 'purchasing power parity' and is the nearest one can get to the 'right' value of a currency. The actual exchange rate in 1976 was Dm 5.14 to £1, while the rate needed to offset the change in car prices which we calculated above would have been Dm 5.52. The pull of high interest rates, and speculation about the direction of future changes in the rate, will usually cause the actual rate to diverge from the PPP rate, so that even within a regime of floating exchange rates it is possible to find 'overvalued' or 'undervalued' currencies.

The moral of this story is that a relatively high rate of inflation – a rate higher than that of a country's major trade rivals – will lead to a decline in the exchange rate and a corresponding deterioration in that country's terms of trade. If the exchange rate is allowed to fall, the country loses through the terms of trade; it has to export more (and therefore consume less) in order to maintain the level of imports. Or, if it is not possible to expand exports, then imports (and consumption) have to be reduced.

If an attempt is made to cure the inflation and stop the exchange rate from falling through a combination of high interest rates and high taxes (a deflationary policy which we discuss later) consumption again must fall. Either way inflation imposes a cost in terms of lower consumption, and it is these external effects of inflation which make price stability, or at least an inflation rate no higher than that in other countries, an objective to be sought.

Our example of the cars has one more thing to show us. The shift of the exchange rate towards the purchasing power parity robs West Germany of the advantages in trade which its lower inflation rate would otherwise bring. So the West German monetary authorities might take steps to prevent the Deutschmark from rising too much. It is always open to them to sell Deutschmarks, and to buy pounds or dollars, and add them to their reserves. If they do so, then West Germany, with a slightly undervalued currency, has an advantage in export markets (represented by the UK in our example), while foreign goods are dearer in West Germany. If the word 'undervalued' is puzzling, remember that at Dm 5.14 the Deutschmark is worth 100/5.14 or 19.5 pence while at Dm 5.52 it is worth 18 pence.

West Germany and Japan have generally been reluctant to revalue (i.e. to increase the value of) their currencies when rates were fixed; when exchange rates floated some of it was 'dirty', in that rates were prevented from rising to a level which would erode their trading advantage. This, as we shall see, has been one of the problems besetting world payments throughout the post-war period. Countries in surplus have been unwilling to share in the adjustment process, preferring the onus to fall almost entirely on those other countries whose deficits in total must be of a precisely matching amount.

9

␣␣␣␣␣␣␣␣␣␣␣␣␣␣␣␣␣␣

The Recent Economic Record

We now have a general picture of the ingredients that make up the economic system and the broad ways in which they interact. It is time to see how the United Kingdom economy has in fact been behaving in recent years – just what has been happening to those main elements of the economic mechanism outlined in Part I so far. By and large we shall concentrate on the record of the 1970s and 1980s.

KEY INDICATORS

There are a number of possible approaches to assessing the performance of the British economy during these years. First we shall summarize the behaviour of four rather crude 'indicators' of how well or how badly the economy has been doing. Then we will examine their combined significance in certain particularly crucial years.

(1) The first of these indicators is illustrated in Figures 3, 4, 12 and 13, which plot the level of *net* national product or national income – an appropriate measure since the net figures show what is available for use *after* the capital stock of the economy has been maintained.

We have already discussed the problem of separating the effect of rising prices from the underlying increase in the volume of goods and services produced. The figures plotted in Figure 13 are therefore in constant (1980) prices. Between 1970 and 1984 the national income increased from £150 billion to £190 billion, i.e. by about 26%, equivalent to an annual rate of growth of 1.7%.

Compared with the performance of the economy between 1945 and 1975 this was not very good. The rate of increase between 1960 and 1970, for example, was 3%. What is more, the diagrams show that there were two periods, 1973–5 and 1979–81, during which national income actually declined. So there are two questions which we will shortly try to answer. Why did these two recessions or depressions take place? And why was growth, when it did occur, relatively sluggish?

(2) In Figure 4 (page 15) we plotted the rate of inflation, a second key economic indicator. The yardsticks chosen are the RPI year-by-year changes and the Index of Total Home Costs (or the GDP deflator), which measures the difference between GDP at current prices and at constant prices. It shows by how much we have to 'deflate' the current price figure to reduce it to the constant price figure and since it deals with GDP 'at factor cost' it is free from the difficulties caused by tax changes in the Retail Price Index.

Four distinct episodes can be detected. From 1970 to 1973 prices rose steadily at 8% to 10%. Historically this was a rapid increase. Then in 1974, and even more between 1974 and 1975, the rate shot upwards, reaching over 25%. The acceleration did not continue, but inflation remained high, between 12% and 15%, during this 1975–9 second period. The third episode is another sharp rise; from 1979 to 1981 the rate of increase climbed briefly to over 20% again. Inflation then began to slow down, and by 1984 the annual rise was down to 5% or less. Chapter 7 examined these changing rates of inflation in more detail.

(3) The third indicator of performance, with which we shall be much concerned, is plotted in Figure 3 (page 13): the changing numbers of unemployed workers. Here too there is a distinct pattern.

With the exception of a small hump in 1972, which reflects the effect of the coal-miners' strike and the resulting three-day week, unemployment during the years 1970 to 1974 was stable around a level of 600,000, equivalent to about 3%. Then it suddenly rose: to 680,000 in 1975 and 1,140,000 in 1976. It stayed at this new higher level, equivalent to 5% of the work-force, right through to 1980. (The method of calculation changed in 1974, and this had the effect of lowering the figures.)

Then from about the middle of 1980 the numbers rose rapidly, exceeding 2 million in 1981 and reaching the 3 million level in 1985. In percentage terms this is 13%, a level unheard of since the 1930s.

(4) These movements within the UK economy reflected changes which were taking place in the international economic system, and were in turn mirrored in the balance of payments and the exchange rate of sterling. Figure 12 (page 107) showed that there was a deepening balance of payments deficit from 1972 to 1976, when it reached crisis levels. After quite violent swings in 1977 and 1978 there was a period of current

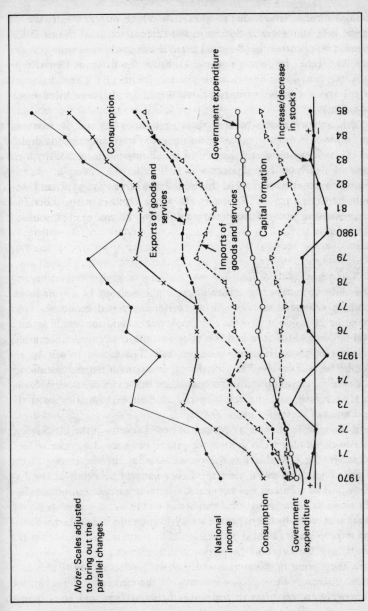

Figure 13 Changes in components of domestic product (constant 1980 prices; scales various)

account surplus, largely due to oil exports at high prices. Meanwhile the period as a whole saw a decline in the external value of the pound in terms of other currencies, despite a sharp rise in its exchange rate between 1977 and 1983. In 1971 £1 would exchange for $2.40 or Dm 8.80; in 1985 the equivalent figures were $1.12 and Dm 3.63. (The dollar fell sharply against other currencies in 1986, and $1.60 is now more representative.)

Although we have separated these various 'indicators' of economic performance in order to make the diagrams less confusing and to simplify the discussions, in the real world they are all interconnected. We can get some idea of how they interact with each other by looking at the two recessions which have marked this period: in the years 1973–5, and then again between 1979–81. Figure 13 shows the changes in the individual components of national income or product, and illustrates the discussion which follows.

THE 1973–5 RECESSION

The early 1970s saw the rather unusual phenomenon of a world-wide boom in economic activity. All the major developed economies were operating at levels at or near full employment, and the resulting high level of demand for food and raw materials meant relatively good prices for most of the developing countries too. The USA, it will be remembered, was involved in a costly war in Vietnam but did not reduce its domestic consumption to accommodate this extra demand. US imports increased, and the resulting rise in their exports stimulated the economies of Western Europe and Japan.

In the middle of 1972, as a result of poor harvests in the USSR and the run-down of the US grain stocks, there was a rapid increase in food prices. In the UK this was the period of what became known as the 'Barber boom', so-called after the Conservative Chancellor of the Exchequer. The economy was stimulated partly by government policies but still more by the removal of a number of controls and restraints on the creation of credit by the banks. Much of this new credit financed speculation in property – a bubble which eventually burst when a number of the new 'fringe' banks found themselves in difficulties.

So there were both external and internal forces tending to drive up prices, especially the prices of imports. At the same time, however, the economy grew very fast in real terms between 1972 and 1973, partly because the 1972 figure was artificially depressed by the miners' strike and the resulting three-day week. The balance of payments went from a healthy surplus in 1971 to a deficit in 1972, but rather than reining back on the expansion the Chancellor allowed the £ to 'float'. (This was the period when the old system of 'fixed' exchange rates began to crumble.) The fall in the exchange rate which followed gave a further boost to the cost of imports, and thus to the rate of inflation.

It was then that the oil-exporting countries, organized into the Organization of Petroleum Exporting Countries (OPEC), administered a major shock to the system. Beginning with a boycott on exports by the Arab producers in response to the outbreak of war with Israel, they increased the price which they charged for their oil until it had quadrupled. The effect on the economies of the oil-importing countries was equivalent to the sudden imposition of a tax, which affected virtually every aspect of their economies because oil as a fuel entered into every productive process. The 'proceeds' of this tax, unlike the proceeds of an internal tax, were not spent; they ended up in the balance of payments surpluses being piled up by the oil exporters.

If the oil exporters had spent these surpluses, by vastly increasing their imports from the industrial world, the shock, though severe, would have been temporary. Most of the major oil exporters, however, had small populations and a very limited capacity immediately to absorb extra imports, so the money piled up in bank accounts in Europe and the USA.

The oil price rise was both inflationary (in pushing up prices) *and* deflationary (in depressing demand). Its effects were compounded by the reactions of the governments of the major industrial nations to the sudden shift of their payments balances into deficit. One after another they raised taxes, raised interest rates and allowed their currencies to float downwards, creating a world-wide recession to follow the world-wide boom.

The internal reaction of the UK economy is clear from Figure 13. There was an immediate fall in the level of stock-building; in 1974 stocks grew by only half as much as in 1973, and they actually fell in 1975. There was a fall in capital formation. Consumers' expenditures were also reduced, and although exports and government spending continued to increase in 1974, the overall result was a drop in GDP – the first for many years.

In 1975 exports fell, consumption fell again, and capital formation stagnated. The growth in government expenditure failed to offset these falls. In fact, the level of spending even began to cause concern, because in relation to the declining GDP it rose sharply, and because 1974 and 1975 were years of severe price inflation – an 18% annual rise by the end of 1974, and 26.5% at its peak in the third quarter of 1975. To those who equated government deficits with an increase in the money supply, and the money supply with the rate of price inflation, the message was clear, and their influence increased from this time onwards.

It could be said with some justice that the 1973–5 recession was caused by international economic events to which a British government could only react passively. Its significance lies in the fact that it was the first post-war reversal of economic growth. People had grown used to steadily rising levels of consumption and public spending, and could not immediately accept the need for decline. Each group tried not only to maintain its real income, but to get the real increase which it had grown used to receiving, with the result that price rises were passed on as greater cost increases, and inflationary forces seemed to have burst free of any restraints. The control of inflation became, after 1975, the over-riding economic objective; the maintenance of full employment, so long at the top of the list, joined economic growth at the bottom.

As Figure 3 (page 13) shows, national income resumed its rise in 1976, but so, very markedly, did the level of unemployment, which increased to the 1,200,000 or 5% level at which it stayed for several years. Five years before, such a level of unemployment would have been thought intolerable. Now attention was focused primarily on the rate of inflation.

Prices continued to rise. In fact the annual rate of increase did not fall below 10% until the beginning of 1978. The government's response was to introduce and maintain a prices-and-incomes policy which was very successful in slowing down wage and price increases until it collapsed in the winter of 1978–9.

A keen eye will have spotted another slight drop in national income in 1977. This had its origins in the growing balance of payments deficit, and the continued fall in the exchange rate. The government felt obliged to borrow in order to offset the drain on its reserves, and did so from the International Monetary Fund. With the loan there came, however, a requirement to restrain the growth in government spending, and to slow down the growth of the money supply – in other words, to deflate. The resulting fall in government expenditure and capital formation explains this pause in growth.

The balance of payments improved dramatically. A huge surplus in 1977 followed the very large deficit in 1976. The value of the £ ceased to fall, and actually rose between 1977 and 1978. In part this was due to North Sea oil; the first shipments were landed in mid-1975, and by 1977 oil imports had fallen markedly. But the success of counter-inflationary policies must have been a significant reason for the renewal of confidence in sterling.

THE 1979–81 RECESSION

The breakdown of the incomes policy in a confusion of disorganization and strikes, particularly in public services, during the winter of 1978–9 probably led to the defeat of the Labour government and to the election of a Conservative government strongly committed to 'monetarism'. We have noted how the IMF had already reinforced the tendency of the Labour government to pay increasing attention to monetary targets and to restrain the growth of public spending. The new government was convinced of the need to carry these policies still further. But its monetarist doctrine also included a commitment to the freedom of markets and the price system, and the first result of this was the formal abandonment of incomes policy.

Although it had committed itself to reduce taxes on incomes, especially at the upper end of the range, its resolve to reduce the government's deficit meant tax increases elsewhere, notably in VAT.

1979 was also a year of further steep rises in oil prices. On the balance of payments front the UK, now an oil exporter, gained from this. In terms of price inflation, however, the effect was as severe as it had been in 1973.

All in all, a government which had declared that the control of inflation was its overriding priority saw the rate of inflation increase dramatically from under 10% to over 20% in the middle of 1980 – very largely as a result of its own actions. Prominent among these was the attempt to control the supply of money; the resulting high levels of interest rates caused yet another rise in the Retail Price Index via mortgage interest rates.

From our standpoint in this chapter, however, we should note the sharp effect that high costs of borrowing and the threat of a credit shortage had on stock-building. This fell, as Figure 13 shows, from an increase of over £2 billion in 1979 to a decrease – an actual run-down of stocks – of nearly £3 billion in 1980. Stocks fell by a further £2½ billion in 1981. Capital formation also fell, and the increase in taxation kept consumers' expenditure down to its 1979 level.

Whatever the government's intentions in trying to control the supply of money, the effect was to bring about a severe deflation of the economy, on top of the already relatively high level of unemployment. Not only did firms respond by running down stocks and postponing investment, but they also prepared for a future of depressed demand by widespread closures of plant and large-scale redundancies among their work-force. Unemployment stayed at around 5% until the middle of 1980, but then started to rise very quickly indeed, passing 10% before the end of 1981.

Not surprisingly with expenditure so much depressed, the level of imports fell, and the balance of payments went strongly into surplus. This helped to finance a large outflow of capital as soon as the last restrictions were lifted. The pound, now a 'petro-currency', rose so much in 1981 that there were complaints that it was destroying Britain's overseas competitiveness.

From 1981 the economy began to expand again, although it did not regain its 1979 level until 1983. This had no visible effect on unemployment, however, which continued to increase and passed 3 million by the end of 1984. The increased demand was met to a considerable extent by imports, helped by the 'strong pound' which made them relatively cheaper, and not by the expansion of domestic production. Manufacturing output continued to fall until 1983, and the drop in manufacturing employment has not yet been reversed.

But eventually the rate of inflation fell back to its mid-1978 low, late in 1982, and continued to decline further, helped in large measure by falling oil and other commodity prices in 1985 and 1986.

So in contrast to 1973–5 the 1979–81 recession was 'internal'. Reduced expenditure and output were the direct consequence of government policies and actions. Whether the depth of the recession and its consequences in terms of unemployment were foreseen is another question.

THE COSTS OF RECESSION: LOST OUTPUT

One way of looking at the 'cost' of a recession is to consider what might have been produced and consumed had the recession not taken place. If, for example, the economy had continued to grow at the average 1970–3 rate of 4%, GDP in 1975 would have been £202 billion (at constant

Table 9.1. The cost of recession: net domestic capital formation (£ billion)

Selected sectors	(Constant 1975 prices) 1971-3 average	1974	1975	(Constant 1980 prices) 1977-9 average	1980	1981	1983-5 average
Oil and gas	0.15	0.56	1.15	1.81	0.84	0.97	0.59 [d]
Manufacturing	1.35	1.42	1.09	1.23	0.24	-1.45	-0.89
Construction	0.11	0.17	0.15	0.10	-0.08	-0.13	-0.03
Transport	0.78	0.57	0.31	0.17	-0.33	-0.99	-0.27
Communications				0.14	0.22	0.06	0.17
Banking and finance [a]	2.21	2.40	1.77	2.94	3.79	3.94	4.72
Other services [b]	2.70	2.42	2.11	2.95	2.53	2.11	3.28
Dwellings	2.83	2.39	2.67	5.45	4.72	3.10	4.14
Total [c]	10.30	10.00	9.30	16.40	13.60	8.80	13.30

Notes: [a] Distribution and other services in earlier period. [b] Social and public services in earlier period. [c] Includes omitted sectors. [d] Oil and gas investment peaked in 1976.

1980 prices) instead of the £184 billion achieved. On this calculation some £18 billion of output was lost; GDP was 10% lower than it might otherwise have been. 4% is, of course, a relatively high growth rate, and might well not have been sustained, so that the figure of £18 billion is the upper limit; £10 billion might be more reasonable.

A similar calculation can be applied to the second of the recessionary episodes. Between 1976 and 1979 GDP at constant factor cost grew at an annual rate of 2.1%. Using this as a measure of 'what might have been' during 1979–81, we arrive at a potential GDP in 1981 of £213 billion, as opposed to the £197 billion recorded, implying a 'loss' of £16 billion at constant 1980 factor cost. To put this large sum in perspective by comparing it with other large sums, it is more or less equal to total public expenditure on education and science, or on defence and overseas aid, during 1981.

So a failure to maintain the growth of the economy is extremely costly. The loss of output is a loss for ever, and one which repeats itself year after subsequent year. Britain might have been a much more relaxed and comfortable country had its GDP been some £25 billion per annum greater in the period since 1979.

Moreover, even when the economy eventually picks up and resumes its upward growth, there is no guarantee that the growth will be as rapid or as vigorous as it was before the recession. There is the danger that, during the course of the set-back, weakening forces may have been at work. For example, particularly in 1980 and 1981, but also in 1974 and

1977, there were marked falls in the volume of capital formation. This meant that the plant, equipment and infrastructure on which future growth of production of goods and services depended were smaller in quantity and probably less modern and up to date than they would otherwise have been. The figures for *net* capital formation set out in Table 9.1 illustrate this point very vividly; the negative figures for net capital investment in manufacturing industry cast serious doubt on whether capacity will be available to sustain continued growth and to re-employ the whole of the presently idle work-force. The consequences of 1973–5 and 1979–81 will be with us for many years to come.

THE COSTS OF RECESSION: UNEMPLOYMENT

The 'cost' of a recession can also be quantified in terms of the unemployment associated with it. There are several aspects to consider: economic, financial and human.

An economic approach is to take the average contribution to GDP per worker (estimated at £7,000 a year in the early 1980s) and to multiply this by the number of 'excess' unemployed. This yields an estimate, once again, of what might have been produced had the recession, and the consequent rise in unemployment, not taken place. The difficulty lies in deciding what should be meant by the 'excess'. In 1984, for example, do you go back to the 1974 figures of unemployed (roughly 600,000) and estimate the 'excess' at 3,000,000 minus 600,000 = 2,400,000? If you do, then the cost is £16.8 billion, very close to our previous figures. If, on the other hand, you believe that a fundamental shift took place in the mid-1970s, so that the 1.2 million unemployed in 1976–80 are the appropriate base, your estimate would be £12.6 billion.

The financial cost to the Exchequer is often calculated by adding to the benefits paid out to the unemployed an estimate of the lost tax revenue – lost because the unemployed are not earning a taxable income and not contributing by spending to the volume of indirect taxation. It has been calculated that, in round terms, the government by the mid-1980s was losing some £5,000 a year for every person unemployed; i.e. its deficit would have been reduced by £9 billion if there were 1.8 million fewer unemployed. In fact, the deficit would have disappeared.

But most important of all is the third interpretation of the costs of recessionary unemployment: the loss of dignity, status, self-respect and economic independence suffered by those who become unemployed.

Table 9.2. Who are the unemployed?

Characteristics	'Stock' of unemployed people			
	1972–5 average		1975–81 average	
	(000)	(%)	(000)	(%)
Unskilled, all ages	400	63	422	40
Skilled, older (45 +)	22	3	214	20
Skilled, young (under 25)	209	33	364	35
Skilled, prime age (25–44)	3	—	45	4
Total	634	100	1,045	100
Of which long-term unemployed:				
Unskilled, all ages	125	95	165	66
Skilled, older (45 +)	7	5	84	33
Skilled, young (under 25)	—	—	2	1
Skilled, prime age (25–44)	—	—	—	—
Total	132	100	251	100

This is inherently impossible to quantify. Even deciding just how many are unemployed in total has become a matter of considerable controversy, with some arguing that the official statistics are 'massaged' to conceal the full extent of the problem, and others claiming that the true level of unemployment is less than the figures suggest. It is abundantly clear, however, that the burden of unemployment is not evenly spread. Particular regions, particular trades or sectors and particular age groups are far more badly affected than others.

The number unemployed on the particular day of each month when the count is taken will include a few who became unemployed the previous day and some who have been unemployed for years. There is a steady flow of people into the 'unemployed' category, and a steady flow off the register into employment. About half the people who lose a job find another within three months, but over the past ten years there have been a growing number of long-term unemployed.

We have some information about the 'stock' or 'pool' of unemployed people. The contrast between the situation of the 600,000-plus of the early 1970s and the 1,200,000-plus of the late 1970s comes out clearly – Table 9.2.

In the early 1970s the unskilled formed the bulk of the unemployed and almost all the long-term unemployed. But by the late 1970s they had

Table 9.3. How long are they unemployed?

Category of person	1963–7	1967–71	1972–5	1975–81
	Outflow from register per week as % of unemployed			
Highly employable[a]	26	21	20	9.6
Poorly employable[b]	2.5	2.6	2.2	1.8
	Average duration of unemployment (weeks)			
Highly employable[a]	3.8	4.7	5.0	10.4
Poorly employable[b]	39	38	45	55

Notes: [a] Skilled, young and prime age. [b] Unskilled and older skilled.
(Young = under 25, prime age = 25–44, older = over 45.)

been joined by relatively large numbers of older and young skilled workers, and many of these older skilled workers found themselves in the 'long-term' category too. Even the 'highly employable' who became unemployed found themselves waiting longer for a new job in the late 1970s, even though few of this group were unemployed for over a year – Table 9.3.

The situation is clearly worse now than in the 1975–81 period, because the major jump in unemployment started in the middle of 1980. The typical unskilled worker and the older skilled worker have every reason to be 'discouraged' while the *average* duration of unemployment is over a year.

Regional differences in rates of unemployment are large. We looked at these in the Introduction and will discuss the regional issue again in Chapter 11 and in Part III. Here it is sufficient to say that – as Figure 3 (page 13) illustrates – it is manufacturing industry which has shed many of its workers, so that male unskilled manual workers form the majority in the unemployment pool. The growth in employment has, by contrast, been in the service industries, where there has been a large increase in female employment, often part-time. There is a mismatch between the type of labour in the unemployment pool and the type of labour sought by employers, and this is made worse by the fact that the manufacturing industries which have shed workers are in the Midlands and North, while the new service industries are predominantly in the South.

The distinction between those lucky enough to have stayed in work and the intolerable numbers who are unable to find gainful employment is perhaps the major division within British society today. The fact that unemployment is so heavily concentrated in certain regions and age groups makes it even more disequalizing in its impact – and potentially explosive in its future implications.

Protagonists of recent economic policies might argue that it is the result of 'rigidities' in the labour market – essentially the fault of labour organized into over-powerful trade unions, having 'priced workers out of jobs'. This is also a matter to which we shall return (see Chapter 13).

Alternatively, unemployment could be seen as the price that has been paid to 'squeeze inflation out of the system'. If so, it is important at least to recognize just how high that price has been and who has borne it, as a prelude to deciding whether it was worth paying.

PART II

THE ECONOMIC STRUCTURE

10

_££££££££££££££££££££_

A Mixed Economy

Britain has a mixed economy. So, for that matter, does every other country in the world. It is the _degree_ of the mix which distinguishes one economic system from another, and in particular the Eastern from the Western bloc.

The 'mix' is partly one of ownership and control. In Britain, the great part of the 'means of production, distribution and exchange' is in private ownership. But there is also a substantial public sector, mainly consisting of the nationalized industries and the provision, by central and local authorities, of a wide range of services like health and education. The two sectors are interdependent as much as competitive, with the private sector in particular relying on the state for the provision of a variety of important inputs. Even where enterprises are privately owned, they may be subject to a range of public controls on their behaviour.

Underlying the private/public division of the economy, although not always coinciding with it, is a further 'mix' of two basically different economic systems for deciding how the nation's resources should be allocated between alternative and competing uses. The first of these is commonly labelled a _command_ system. In this the use of resources is determined by the decision of government or a planning authority, with production of goods and services then organized accordingly. A _market_ method of allocating resources relies in contrast on the outcome of millions of independent decisions by individuals and enterprises.

Since modern economics, dating from Adam Smith in the eighteenth century, was based on an elaboration of the market mechanism, we shall begin by describing the main elements of this mechanism and then analyse cases of 'market failure' which provide a rationale for the superimposition of a command structure.

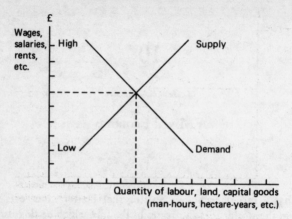

Figure 14a Supply and demand: factors of production

THE MARKET MECHANISM

The mainstream of economic thought, in evolving its theory of the market, has emphasized the role of prices as the key instrument in deciding how resources should be allocated between competing uses. In its fully developed form the economist's 'model' of the market is a beautiful exercise in logical deduction. In explaining it, the starting-point hardly matters since every part is connected to every other, but we shall begin with the production of goods and services.

Producers are concerned to produce at minimum cost, and to sell their product for the best price they can get. 'It is not from the benevolence of butchers and bakers that we get our bread and meat, but from their self-interest,' observed Adam Smith. They hire or buy the factors of production – the land, labour and capital goods – which they need, always with an eye to balancing the price they pay against the extra revenue they will earn from extra output.

Take labour as an example: at the going wage of, say, £100 a week, an extra worker might produce goods worth £200 – and so is hired. The marginal (extra) cost is £100, and the marginal (extra) revenue is £200. A second worker will generally add less additional output (this is the celebrated 'law of diminishing returns'), let us say £150, so is still worth hiring at a wage of £100. A third might add a bare £100 to revenue, just covering the extra cost of hiring but representing the limit to employment

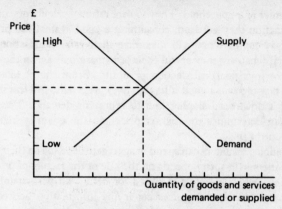

Figure 14b Supply and demand: goods and services

– at which marginal cost equals marginal revenue. This process, multiplied hundreds of thousands of time, determines the demand for labour, and by extension the demand for the other factors of production, in the market model.

In a society like ours, with the institution of private property, the supply of factors comes from their owners. Being a non-slave society we all own our labour, and the richer individuals, including the legal 'individuals' called companies, own land and capital. Sellers too, in the model, are supposed to balance gains and losses: the loss of leisure against the gains of wage income; the gains from renting land against the loss of not having it available for the proprietor's own use. The resulting *supply* of factors meets the *demand* for factors, resulting from their productivity, and together they form the central symbol of economics, the supply and demand diagram – Figure 14a.

More of any factor will be supplied as its price rises, but less will be demanded, so a balance point determines the market price, P, and the quantity bought and sold, Q.

The goods and services produced by firms and individuals form the supply side of a second market, the market for goods and services. Remembering that our producers seek to maximize their revenue, they will produce *more* of a commodity if its (relative) price rises, and less if it falls. The supply of goods can also be represented by an upward-sloping line.

Demand in the goods market comes from consumers, usually thought of as a family or a household. They too are rational calculators, offsetting the satisfaction they get from consuming a good against the price they have to pay for it. They will maximize their *total* satisfaction if they ensure that whatever they spend their last (marginal) £1 on they get the same *extra* (marginal) satisfaction or utility. From this it follows that they will buy more of a good if its (relative) price falls, and less if it rises, implying a downward-sloping line to represent demand. The balance point again determines the market price and the quantity bought and sold – Figure 14b.

How much consumers can spend in aggregate depends on their income, but their income in turn depends on the sale of the factors of production which they own. The circle is closed, or better, all participants in the economy are linked, with prices conveying information between them and influencing their economic decisions. Any change in the system, such as new technology, a new fashion influencing consumer tastes and hence satisfactions, the discovery of a new resource, will result in a change in relative prices, and everyone will react to the price change. The technology of the silicon chip, and the consequent dramatic fall in the cost of computers and similar devices, offers an obvious recent example.

Given a complex system of this kind it is natural to ask whether there is some starting-point – some 'prime mover' – which is not purely arbitrary. This is where ideology and controversy enter the hitherto abstract system. The conventional view is that the consumer – the household – influences the rest of the system.

It is consumers who are 'sovereign'. They know what they want. Their 'tastes' are inbuilt and determine what they are willing to pay, and producers react to the resulting relative prices and adjust their output accordingly. Since the price consumers are willing to pay reflects the utility or satisfaction they gain from spending, the market price from the point of view of demand measures the gains of consumers – collectively the social benefits derived from the consumption of those goods or services. From the supply side, however, the *same* price reflects what it costs the producer to hire resources and to organize the production of the goods and services. Price equals the cost to society of producing the last, extra or marginal unit, *and* the benefits derived from consuming it.

Adam Smith called this 'the workings of an invisible hand', but modern economics demonstrates it quite rigorously and often (in the branch of economics confusingly called 'welfare economics') mathematically. So economists often have a built-in bias in favour of market solutions, although they will admit a few exceptions to the general rule that 'market solutions are best'.

Smith himself would have restricted the activities of the state to external defence, the associated systems of diplomacy and the establishment within the country of a system of law and the means of enforcing it. He was writing, it must be remembered, at a time when 'state' meant a king or an unrepresentative oligarchy, interfering in economic affairs by granting exclusive licences or monopolies, and wasting resources in conspicuous and luxurious spending. A 'minimum state' would not only allow producers to get on with their business: it would also free resources for useful purposes. *Laissez-faire* – 'let us get on with the business of increasing the wealth of the nation' – was in its day a revolutionary slogan.

MARKET FAILURE

In practice, we might be very unwise to rely exclusively on the market as an arbiter of how resources should be used. There are many reasons for this, some more disputable than others. But to begin with we shall look at a type of production which would be very difficult to imagine being left to private activity.

Public goods

Defence and law and order are good examples of a category of goods and services which can be produced only by the state. They are called 'public goods' because once they have been produced anyone can enjoy them. There is no way of enforcing payment for them, and no private individual will produce them. The classic example is that of a lighthouse. Once it is built, and its light is shining, any passing ship can make use of it to fix its position, and the lighthouse owner would find it impossible to collect any payment. Only the state – in this case by imposing compulsory harbour and pilotage dues on all shipping entering or leaving its ports – can do so.

It is interesting that some modern methods of navigation, involving radio transmissions and satellites, need a 'black box' to receive and interpret the signals. The 'black box', or the electronic key to the transmissions, *can* be charged for like any other commodity or service, so these navigation systems can be profitably provided by private enterprise.

What is a 'public good' and what is not is therefore not absolutely clear cut. Roads and bridges are usually seen as 'public', yet the British highway system began as a system of toll roads, and in many countries the motorway system is charged for by its private or public providers.

Merit goods

A second exception – a much more arguable one – goes under the name of 'merit' goods. Here a collective moral judgement is made which overrules the preferences of individual consumers. Goods like heroin and marijuana cannot be produced and sold. Alternatively, the use of certain goods and services is discouraged by high taxes (e.g. on alcohol and cigarettes). Encouragement of the consumption of things which are judged to be 'good' works through free or subsidized provision (milk or orange juice for mothers and children, for example). This is a debatable issue precisely because it involves ethical judgements. There is almost always a conflict between the liberty of the individual to make his or her own judgements and the general welfare of society. Despite Adam Smith, these need not always coincide.

Externalities

The 'virtue' of market solutions stems from the idea that consumers know best and that the sum total of actions to meet their needs represents a collective or social 'best' solution. Private cost is offset against private benefits, and so social cost (the resources used) equals social benefit (the collective satisfactions gained). Regrettably, this is not always true; sometimes there is a divergence between private and social, individual and collectivity. Often this is because something is missing from the private, individual calculation of gain and loss; something 'external' to private calculations nevertheless affects the society as a whole.

The best known of these 'externalities' are water and air pollution, and a current controversy which illustrates the principle very clearly is the deposition of 'acid rain' on the forest, rivers and lakes of Scandinavia. Where does it come from? To a considerable extent from the coal-burning power-stations of the Midlands and North of Britain. The sulphur in the coal is oxidized in the furnace to sulphur dioxide, which combines with moisture in the atmosphere to form a weak acid. The rain which later falls on Norway and Sweden is therefore very dilute but none the less damaging sulphuric or sulphurous acid. Soil and water become less productive; trees and fish suffer.

But the cost (about the existence of which opinions still differ) does not figure in the calculations of the Central Electricity Generating Board. In its books it sees only the price of coal and the value of electricity. Norwegian salmon and trout do not appear. To the CEGB removing the sulphur dioxide would be a cost with no offsetting benefit; in fact the consequent rise in electricity prices would be most unwelcome. Yet if the benefits to Scandinavia could be quantified and *internalized* into the CEGB accounts it might well be well worth while to extract the sulphur.

The significance of external costs and benefits is considerable and lies at the heart of a basic confusion which persists about what is meant by 'economic'. Very commonly this term is used by policy-makers, and interpreted by the general public, in referring to an activity which is *profitable*. But on what basis is profit or loss calculated? It represents the difference between the revenue accruing to an enterprise and the costs which it incurs and it is confined to those revenues and costs which *appear in the firm's own balance sheet*.

This in fact is a measure of *commercial* rather than economic viability. Economics is concerned with the efficient use of resources, and the criterion for whether an activity is 'economic' must therefore take into account *all* costs and benefits, whether they arise internally or externally.

Once this is done, then many economic activities which may be non-commercial (i.e. loss-making for the enterprises concerned) may prove still to be *economic* – in the sense that for the economy as a whole the total gains exceed the total costs incurred. The significance of the divergence between private and social costs and benefits will become clearer when we discuss public enterprise in Chapter 12.

Other defects

Let us look briefly at some other examples of the failure of the market or price system to work for the general good. In the real world, it is very uncommon for an industry either to consist of a large number of small competing firms (which, according to the theory, would make the market work best) or to be dominated by only one seller or buyer, a monopoly or monopsony. It is more likely that markets will be controlled by just a few – oligopoly or oligopsony. In such cases, the solutions in respect of quantities and prices reached by the producers, keen to maximize their gains, will *not* be those which at the same time maximize the satisfactions of consumers. Suppliers will (in general) supply less, at a higher price than the marginal cost of production. The general conclusion that the 'invisible hand' yields a socially desirable solution depends critically on the existence of large numbers of competing buyers and sellers.

It also depends on the assumption that the tastes of consumers are innate, and to be respected. But can consumers really calculate the satisfactions to be obtained from spending an extra £1 or £100? How far in a modern technological world is a consumer able to evaluate the true merits of alternative products? And how far does advertising apply pressure on the consumer rather than inform? The problems of consumer ignorance are compounded when it comes to more fundamental areas such as medicine or health. Does the patient know which doctor, or which treatment, will give the best value for money? Very seldom. Generally, it is only the doctor – the supplier of the service – who has the specialized knowledge, and so the argument for 'marketed' medical treatment breaks down before it really begins.

Finally, there is perhaps the most important reason for doubting that the outcome of unrestricted market forces will be an acceptable one. In expounding the market mechanism, the analogy is frequently used of an economic democracy. Consumers are seen as casting their votes (i.e. incomes) on a range of alternative candidates (goods and services) offered by competing firms. The number of votes they receive determines what quantity of resources firms can lay their hands on when they recast those votes in the markets for the factors of production.

But in economies like that of the UK, income and wealth are very unequally distributed. In terms of the analogy, some of the electorate have very many more votes than others. Yet, when they are cast, the market mechanism is unable to distinguish between the preference expressed by a pound spent from a low-income household and a pound spent by a millionaire. It is therefore no surprise that an inevitable result of 'leaving things to the market' in such circumstances is that the whims of the rich are fully met while the needs of the poor may at the same time be neglected.

After this long discussion about the weaknesses and failures of the market it is worth reaffirming its virtue in conveying a vast amount of information quickly and cheaply. Many of its defects in practice arise, not from the market mechanism itself, but from the parameters (like income distribution) within which it operates. Too often the market is wrongly equated with private enterprise and unfettered capitalism. But in fact it is simply an instrument for allocating resources which is capable of being used under a variety of political and economic systems.

That said, there will also be areas of activity which, as we have seen in the case of public and merit goods, cannot safely be left for market determination. On the other hand, that form of 'planning' which *ignores* rather than manipulates market forces can often be out of touch with consumer requirements and lead to inappropriate types of production. Most countries therefore end up with a sometimes uneasy balance between state ownership and management, state control and direction, state intervention to remedy market failures and a larger or smaller 'private sector' subject only to the broad legal framework within which all economic activity is carried on.

The balance that has been struck in the UK between market and command elements will become clear in the following chapters. It is a balance that has for long periods been largely agreed between the major political parties, a consensus interrupted in particular by the episodes of 1945–50 and, as we shall see in Part III, more recently since 1979.

11

Private Industry

In this chapter we shall try to put some flesh on the bare bones of those producing units that in earlier discussions we have simply referred to as 'firms', with wider groupings along the lines of a 'standard industrial classification'. What forms do they take? What determines their size? Within what market structures do they operate? And how do they behave?

THE NATURE OF THE FIRM

To begin with we shall concentrate on the firms that operate within what is often called the 'private sector' of the economy. When we were describing the overall result of economic activity, using the model of the circular flow of product and income, we chose the word 'firms' as the collective noun covering the productive units within the economy. Here we use the term in a somewhat different sense – as the name of a specific, identifiable organization with a legal identity. The business firm, in short, is one of the institutions within our society, and its principal function is the production of goods and services.

It is very important to distinguish between the firm or enterprise (i.e. the organization as a whole) and the particular units of which it is composed, the 'plants' or the 'establishments' of which it is made up. There are many small firms with only one establishment; the corner shop and the small builder are classic examples. Small firms are also common in the field of services: solicitors, accountants and taxi operators being examples.

These smaller firms often take the legal form of sole traders or proprietors, where a single individual is owner, manager and worker at one and the same time. Or they may be partnerships, in which ownership and responsibility are shared between a few individuals who usually also work in the business. Partnerships are common in the professions; medical, dental and veterinary practices, solicitors and accountants are often legally constituted in this way.

In both cases the capital for the business is provided by the owners, who are also personally liable for its debts. This clearly imposes a limit on size and growth. To overcome this limitation, the idea was conceived in the eighteenth century of 'limited liability'. This entitled a group of people in a 'company' to engage in business or trade, but with their personal liability limited to the capital they had subscribed. The new legal form enabled business to raise more capital easily and cheaply, and so to grow and expand. At the same time the attractions of limited personal liability, and the impact of taxation, persuaded many family businesses and partnerships to adopt the new company status.

Under the most recent legislation (the Companies Act of 1980) companies are of two kinds. The commonest, in terms of numbers, are limited companies or private limited companies. Their common characteristic (apart from their generally small size) is that their shares are not traded on the Stock Exchange. Indeed their frequent origin in a family business often means that there are restrictions on the freedom of the owners to sell their shares. The absence of a ready market for shares makes it difficult to raise new capital by issuing more of them, but otherwise the advantages of continuity, specialization and flexibility make this the normal format for a small business, whether new or long-established.

The companies whose names come into our minds when we think of business are usually p.l.c.s (public limited companies), whose shares *are* traded on the Stock Exchange. This itself imposes some fairly severe restrictions as to size. The extent of the documentation needed to obtain a Stock Exchange quotation, even on the 'unlisted' market, acts as a deterrent to the expanding business seeking to change its status by 'going public', quite apart from the expense. But a p.l.c. does have access to large amounts of capital which it can obtain via a 'rights' issue to its existing shareholders, or through the sale of additional shares. Although there are a few exceptions, the route to growth and expansion is nearly always via a Stock Exchange listing.

The size of an industrial or commercial organization can be, and is, measured in several ways. For example, using the quantity of capital employed gives one 'top ten' ranking, while 'number of employees' yields a slightly different one, as Table 11.1 shows.

Table *11.1*. The 'top ten' UK industrial and commercial companies

Rank	Capital employed (£ billion)	Rank	No. of employees (000s)
1 Electricity Council	36.8	1 British Telecom	238
2 BP	21.0	2 National Coal Board	225
3 British Gas	16.9	3 BAT Industries	186
4 Shell Transport & Trading	15.8	4 Post Office	182
5 British Telecom	10.2	5 British Rail	181
6 BAT Industries	6.4	6 Unilever	175
7 ICI	5.8	7 General Electric (UK)	166
8 Rio Tinto Zinc	5.5	8 Grand Metropolitan	137
9 National Coal Board	4.8	9 Electricity Council	136
10 Shell UK	3.8	10 BP	129

In *The Times 1000*, the source of all these figures on companies, the listing is by annual turnover, so the order changes yet again:

1 BP	6 Electricity Council
2 Shell Transport & Trading	7 Shell UK
3 BAT Industries	8 British Telecom
4 ICI	9 S. & W. Berisford
5 Esso UK	10 British Gas

Some of these companies may be unfamiliar or difficult to identify. BAT Industries used to be the major tobacco firm, but has now diversified into a wide range of other activities. Grand Metropolitan are hotel owners and brewers. S. & W. Berisford are commodity brokers and dealers. Shell, it will be noticed, appears twice, and there is a third manifestation: the Anglo–Dutch parent company which is the world's largest company in terms of sales.

These and other giants which tower over the industrial scene have very large numbers of shareholders (about half a million in ICI, for example). This could create the misleading impression that the shares in these companies are very widely spread. In practice a few large holdings dominate the picture. Prominent among them are those of the insurance companies, pension funds, unit trusts and other financial institutions, which, while they keep a careful eye on the company's progress, rarely intervene in its management. Still less can a very small shareholder exert any influence on the company's affairs. (The contrast with West Germany, where the banks as major investors exercise a good deal of power, or Japan, is worth noting.)

THE SIZE OF FIRMS

The very large firms we have been talking about all comprise a large number of plants or establishments. Marks & Spencer has stores in all major towns, and ICI owns and operates a large number of chemical plants. So are these firms 'large' because they have large plants, or because they have many plants? Or both, perhaps? We must ask why firms have grown larger, and discuss the advantages and disadvantages of large size; in doing so, the distinction between the plant and the enterprise is often critical.

Economies of scale

In many lines of production, the large enterprise enjoys great advantages over its smaller competitors which enable it to achieve substantial reductions in its costs of producton. These are collectively known as the 'economies of scale'.

Many such economies arise from the sheer technological superiority of the large plants. This is most obvious when a very high level of output is required for the most efficient techniques to be deployed at all. However, even when the best equipment can be produced in either large or small versions, the large plant may still gain from the benefits of 'increased dimensions'. This is often simply a matter of geometry. Consider, for instance, an oil tanker. Fundamentally this is a large steel box with a propeller at one end and a rather blunt point at the other. Any ship needs a captain and officers and a crew, but a big oil tanker does not need two captains, or more officers, or even, for the most part, a bigger crew. It does require a bigger engine, and so it uses more fuel, but (assuming similar speeds) the cost of pushing it through the sea is a function of its surface area. This also, to a large extent, decides the initial cost: how many square metres of steel plate does it take to build it? So two aspects of cost – initial capital and fuel consumption – will vary according to the square of the length, while crew costs are virtually independent of size. The quantity of crude oil a tanker can carry, on the other hand, depends on its volume or cubic capacity (arithmetically, the third power of its dimensions).

It is evident that the cost advantages are weighted in favour of transporting crude oil in, for example, one 200 metre tanker rather than in two 100 metre tankers. The two small ships may be slightly cheaper to run, but they carry a great deal less. The 'supertanker' (once it could be successfully engineered and built) rapidly took over from smaller vessels. Its growth is now limited only by the depth of water in the North Sea and the Straits of Malacca.

Similar geometric considerations make one large blast furnace, oil refinery or petrochemical plant more economic than two small ones. Again, only the large plant may be able to afford to *combine* its inputs optimally. Consider, for example, a plant estimating its daily sales at 500 units of a product which results from three successive processes, X, Y and Z. The best equipment in these three processes has the following capacity:

- in process X, 300 units a day;
- in process Y, 400 units a day;
- in process Z, 500 units a day;

The estimated demand of 500 per day means that the plant is large enough to install the best equipment. But demand falls below the level needed for them to be employed in the best *combination*. To produce 500 units per day, the two machines needed for the X and Y processes would have surplus capacity of 100 and 300 units per day respectively. Only machine Z would be fully employed. It is easy to see that the minimum output which allows work at full capacity is 6,000 units per day, using twenty machines in process X, fifteen in Y and twelve in Z.

There are many other similar advantages accruing to the larger plants, and the growth in the size of units has played a significant part in the growth of firms. We have now reached the situation where one unit or one plant can supply a significant proportion of British demand. At the extreme there is the aircraft industry, where the costs of design and tooling have to be spread over several hundred aircraft before a profit is made, and where even the large United States market is too small. It would seem that the world market for civil aircraft is only large enough to support two firms at best.

In several industries one plant of 'minimum efficient size' can produce enough to meet a high proportion of British demand. The list of industries where one plant can supply one-third or more of the domestic demand includes data-processing equipment, steel strip, electric motors, motor cars, washing-machines and similar domestic 'white goods', synthetic fibres, detergents, raw steel, sulphuric acid and machine tools.

New technology has sometimes meant the reversal of this trend favouring the larger unit. With regard to newspapers, for example, recent technical developments in information processing and printing have reduced the minimum plant size considerably, opening up the possibility of an increase in the number of newspapers. The problem now is to create a product sufficiently distinctive to attract readers away from the established papers.

In other areas the trend towards larger plants or larger units continues. Even so, it is clear from the evidence available that the growth in the size of individual plants and the growth in the size of firms or enterprises are two distinct phenomena, requiring different explanations. The share of the 100 largest plants in manufacturing output in Britain has remained remarkably constant at a little over 10% since the 1930s; the share of the 100 largest firms in manufacturing stayed fairly constant at just under 25% until about 1950, but since then has increased steadily to over 40%.

This is in manufacturing, but the same picture is seen in distribution and finance. Firms are growing larger there too, and the small number of very large ones takes an increasing share of the market. Is there a similar process going on? Do large *firms* as well as large plants enjoy economies of scale, and if so, where do they originate?

One source is the ability of a large firm to make full use of the services of highly skilled staff, especially at managerial levels. Whereas in a small firm the works manager may also have to handle personnel problems, and therefore perhaps do neither job very well, in a large firm a full-scale personnel division, staffed by trained experts, can ensure that the firm makes the best possible use of its human resources. Similar arguments can be applied to distribution and sales, especially to advertising. A national advertising campaign, embodying several media, is extremely costly and can be justified only if the cost can be spread over a high level of output.

It is also true that it costs relatively little more to raise £50 million than it does to raise £5 million. It could even cost less, because the sheer size of the borrowing firm makes it a more attractive outlet for lending by the large financial institutions, and it can probably borrow more cheaply than a smaller firm which is seen as more exposed to risk.

TYPES OF MARKET

Discussion of buying and selling economies brings us close to saying that large size creates market power. A large firm is probably the most important buyer in the market, and can therefore insist on quantity discounts, exceptionally high quality standards, guaranteed delivery and so on. The extreme case of 'one buyer' in a market is called monopsony, but the situation does not have to reach this extreme before buyers can extract advantages from their suppliers. Marks & Spencer is well known for its very close control over the manufacturers who supply its clothes, to be sold under the 'St Michael' brand name. In return, of course, its suppliers enjoy the cost advantages from long production runs and the security of an outlet for much, sometimes all, that they produce.

Discussions of market power usually centre around the power of a single seller (a 'monopolist') or a few large sellers (known as 'oligopolists') in a market. A dominant market position enables its possessor to discriminate between different buyers or groups of buyers, 'charging what the traffic will bear', to use a stock phrase. Monopolists are also widely believed to reduce their output below the level which society as a whole would wish, and by so doing earn much larger profits.

We talked above about the 'minimum economic size' of plant, and there is a good deal of evidence to suggest that once this size has been reached then output can be expanded without any significant increase in cost per unit. Once the economies of large-scale operation have been achieved – or, in other words, once the range of output over which unit costs are decreasing has been passed – then 'constant costs' are the rule. The monopolist will then expand output and sales, but by how much? If he is concerned to maximize his total profit, he will expand output to the point where the extra revenue earned from the production and sale of an extra unit just offsets the cost of producing that extra unit. In the economist's jargon, he expands output until marginal revenue equals marginal cost. But he can only sell additional units at an ever-decreasing price, so that while marginal cost does not change (costs are constant) marginal revenue falls as output increases. At the balance point total profit reaches a maximum, and *if* the maximization of profit is his aim, this is the level of output which the monopolist will produce and sell.

It is, however, a smaller level of output than society as a whole would wish. The cost of producing an extra unit of output (which includes a normal level of profit) reflects the quantity of resources used in producing it, i.e. its cost to society. Its value to society is indicated by the price that consumers would be willing to pay for it. The welfare of society would therefore be maximized if output was expanded until the constant marginal cost equals the price or *average* revenue. If (as we explained earlier) demand curves usually slope downwards, this average revenue will always be higher than the *marginal* revenue which the monopolist matches with marginal cost when deciding how much to produce. His output will be lower, and his selling price higher, than those which would be reached in a competitive market. Let price equal marginal cost; that is the economist's recipe for optimal output, and it implies a higher level of output than that which maximizes profit. It is this divergence between the interests of the monopolist and those of society which lies behind the general dislike and distrust of large size.

Before pursuing this topic further we must mention that many writers about the behaviour of business firms – and especially the large firms which are typical of most parts of the economy – would challenge the assumption of 'profit maximizing' as their objective. It often seems that provided that a satisfactory level of profit is achieved, firms, or their managers, feel free to pursue other goals. Prominent among these is growth itself. Prestige in the business world is closely associated with the size of a firm's operations and with the share of the various markets which a firm enjoys; and more mundane issues like salaries and fringe benefits are linked with this as well. So there is a strong built-in drive to expand, or at the very worst to maintain the existing market share. Sales maximization might be a better approximation to the primary objective of business managers.

The negative aspect of this is the fear of being taken over and absorbed into some larger and more powerful organization, a fate which may carry the penalty of redundancy or demotion for the management of a weaker firm.

The conventional criticism of monopoly – restriction of output and excessively high price – loses some, though not by any means all, of its force if large firms are seeking to maximize their market share. One could criticize the apparently excessive spending on advertising, which can make up a significant part of the price of some consumer products. It can be argued that if one firm uses its size and power to obtain supplies or finance at a lower cost, then all that happens is that someone else is paying more than they should; there is no gain to society once the genuine economies of scale have been reaped. It may well be felt that these immense concentrations of economic power should be subjected to some kind of social control, and that the control exerted (in economic theory) by the consumer is ineffective in the absence of genuine choice. Is there anything that can be said in defence of large firms?

The case for large size commonly rests on two arguments. The first of these points out that the British market is open to external competition, and that the existence of only one or two British producers is irrelevant when Japanese and West German and Italian producers also sell their goods here. In part this is a criticism of one of the measures often used to assess the degree of monopoly: the share in total output, or total employment, of the three or five largest firms in the industry. This, it is pointed out, does not mean a similar share of the British market. It is true that on this basis the UK and the USA appear to have a much greater degree of concentration than France or West Germany – though the process of merger and amalgamation has been going on everywhere, and the difference may now be less than the rather dated information available suggests.

The defenders of large size point out that nowadays the relevant market is at least the European market, and in many cases the world market, and that in such a large pond small fish are quickly swallowed up. One of the reasons widely quoted in the early 1970s for encouraging amalgamation and integration was the need for large units when Britain entered the Common Market. Experience seems to show that even if smallness equals weakness, large size does not necessarily mean strength. The British motor car industry has been through a long period of concentration, culminating in the formation of BL, now the Rover Group. Some will say that it is still too small, viewed on a European scale. Others will look for different explanations for its manifest failure to compete successfully in its own British market, let alone the larger European one.

The second argument is that only large firms can afford to spend large sums of money on long-term programmes of research and development, on which we depend for new and improved goods and services. It is true that a relatively few large firms account for a very high proportion of industry's 'R and D' spending, that the cost of even a modest research establishment places it out of the reach of smaller firms and that large firms are credited with the majority of the new products and processes of recent years. Yet the example of agriculture – the industry of small units *par excellence* – shows that successful research and development can be carried out either through state-funded research or through shared facili-

Table 11.2. Share of five largest UK enterprises in output and employment, 1982

Industry	% of industry total contributed by five largest firms	
	Output	Employment
Tobacco	99	98
Artificial fibres	94	92
Motor vehicles	91	89
Cement	88	86
Wire and cables	82	78
Mineral oil processing	64[a]	66
Iron and steel	76	79
Organic oils and fats	77	66
Spirits (distilling)	69	67
Aerospace	75	77
Filament yarn	67	63
Grain milling	68	55
Pharmaceuticals	38	37
Pulp, paper and board	35	41
Wool/worsted textiles	28	26
Foundries	21	20

Note: [a] 80% of output in 1981.

ties paid for by the firms in the industry, of which the Timber Research and Development Association is but one example. An industry of small firms need not necessarily suffer from lack of R and D.

In practice, oil, vehicles and telecommunications are the industries with member firms occupying the top places in the world rankings, although it is not easy to identify the major activity of the very large Japanese organizations known as *sogo shosha*. Most of them originated as trading companies, but they are now financial and manufacturing giants as well. Of the ten largest companies in the world, four are oil-based (Shell, BP, Exxon and Mobil) and five are Japanese conglomerates such as Mitsui and Mitsubishi. Only General Motors of the manufacturing industries pure and simple makes the top ten.

A little further down the list we find Ford at number 11, IBM the computer giant at 13 and Toyota at 16. Sears Roebuck is the largest general merchandiser at 17, and it is followed by AT&T, the largest US telecommunications firm.

Europe reappears with ENI, the large Italian state oil and chemical combine at number 20, and other well-known European companies in the top 40 are:

29 Elf (France) – oil
30 Unilever (Anglo–Dutch) – food and detergents
31 Siemens (W. Germany) – electrical
32 Philips (Dutch) – electrical
35 Volkswagen (W. Germany) – cars
36 Daimler-Benz (W. Germany) – cars and trucks
37 Nestlé (Switzerland) – food and confectionery

CONCENTRATION AND MARKET POWER

The figures in Table 11.2 show the extent to which a few large firms dominate particular industries in the UK. Information is usually provided in respect of the *five* largest firms in an industry, so that individual firms are not identifiable. Where there are fewer than five, the data are absent; and where, as in the case of certain nationalized industries (although some are now privatized), there is only one firm in the industry, the five-firm measure is irrelevant. So there are a handful of industries, where one or a very few firms account for 100% of employment and output, which are not included in Table 11.2.

The industries listed near the foot of the table are typical of a large number of industries in the mechanical/electrical groups where the five largest firms produce about a quarter to a fifth of total output.

It is not easy to see whether concentration has increased in recent years, because of changes in the way in which industries are classified. The broad impression is that the five largest firms have maintained their share of output and employment during the past ten years, but have reduced the number of establishments which they operate, concentrating output in the more efficient.

It is also interesting to observe the impact, as illustrated in Table 11.3, of the number of large foreign enterprises operating in the UK.

Notice that although a very small proportion of the total number of firms and plants in British industry are foreign-owned, foreign firms are very much more important in respect of employment and output; one in seven industrial employees work for foreign firms, producing one-fifth of total output. The foreign firms, as one would expect, are relatively large. It is also noteworthy that although European Community investment has increased during the five-year period, the USA is still by far the most important source of foreign investment in British industry. US firms find Britain a useful base for their European-scale operations.

Table 11.3. Foreign investment in British industry

	Number of enterprises (firms)		Number of establishments (plants)		Employment (000s)		Gross output (£ million)	
	1977	1982	1977	1982	1977	1982	1977	1982
UK total	89,822	90,068	107,691	108,276	6,883	5,778	125,321	165,471
Foreign	1,370	1,522	2,654	2,825	1,014	858	27,963	31,909
% of UK	1.5	1.7	2.5	2.6	14.7	14.8	22.3	19.3
of which EEC	291	340	495	575	137	127	4,871	4,565
% of foreign	21.2	22.3	18.6	20.3	13.5	14.8	17.4	14.3
of which USA	788	827	1,592	1,510	712	568	19,180	21,797
% of foreign	57.5	54.3	60.0	53.5	70.2	66.2	68.6	68.3

The tendency for firms or enterprises to grow in size is not confined to manufacturing industry. A walk through the main shopping centre of any British town will indicate the extent to which retail distribution is dominated by a few firms. And if one knew what lay behind some of the names on the shop fronts, the degree of concentration would be revealed as even greater. It is common practice for a shop to continue to trade under its old name long after it has been taken over by a larger organization.

This concentration is paralleled by similar concentration in distribution and transport. The advantages of large size stem in part from the genuine economies arising from the reduction in duplication of warehouses, distribution networks and stockholding. The ability, using modern methods of data handling and processing, to know exactly how sales are going, plus the ability to reorder and receive goods within a very short time, enables these large chains to operate with minimal stocks.

But the major gain seems to derive from the power that a major buyer can exert on its suppliers: the power of a monopsonist. An organization like Sainsbury, Tesco or Asda can obtain price discounts from its suppliers which would not be available to the traditional corner shop, unless it tried to obtain similar benefits through co-operative purchasing and distribution.

In the world of finance too there has been steady growth in the size of organizations. We are now down to four major banks, and there has been a similar process of amalgamation and take-over among building societies, insurance companies and so on. Are there economies of scale to be reaped here as well?

In one sense the answer must be 'yes', since it is just as easy to carry out a transaction involving millions of pounds as one involving hundreds. It is also true that if an institution is offering one financial service (such as accepting deposits of money or lending money for house purchase) it can just as easily offer some others, such as property insurance, conveyancing or loans for cars. Over the past few years we have seen the banks invading the field of the building societies, and the building societies broadening the range of services which they offer until they begin to resemble banks. If the end point is to be the financial equivalent of the supermarket, then again there will be fewer and larger organizations involved. In part the growth in the size of financial institutions is a response to the growth in the size of firms in manufacturing. The financial requirements of enterprises as large as IBM, Shell and Marks & Spencer can be met only by a financial institution of large size offering a complete range of services and operating world-wide.

One of the most important questions which we face is whether this process of concentration should be controlled or curbed, and if so, how it should be done. We have seen that there are genuine economic gains to be reaped from an increase in the size of plants, and to a lesser extent from growth in the size of enterprises. But there are also losses and dangers, which we shall be looking at in a moment.

Mergers and take-overs have been going on at a rate of about two acquisitions per working day during the past few years. Most of them are small, and it is the large ones which attract attention. Indeed they compel attention, not only because of the occasional scandal which becomes public, but because they are accompanied by a barrage of expensive advertising designed to persuade the owners of the target company to sell, or to retain, their shares. Add to this the costs of the various advisers, and the final bill, whether the attempted take-over is successful or not, can reach tens of millions of pounds. The figures in Table 11.4, list only the price paid and exclude these peripheral expenses.

These figures show that it is the sheer scale of merger and take-over deals rather than their mere number which has significantly increased in recent years. It is not simply large firms absorbing small ones, but marriages (or cannibalism) involving already giant enterprises which now compel attention. The huge sums that are required in such deals may not be 'real money'; most mergers and take-overs are conducted on the basis of an exchange of shares in the new, merged organization for shares in the company absorbed. The 'sellers' obtain new pieces of

Table 11.4. Acquisitions and mergers

Year	Number of acquisitions	Expenditure involved (£ billion)		
		In cash	In shares	Total
1981	452	0.8	0.4	1.1
1982	463	1.3	0.9	2.2
1983	447	1.0	1.3	2.3
1984	568	2.9	2.5	5.5
1985	474	2.9	4.2	7.1
1986 (1st 3 quarters)	433	1.7	9.6	11.3

paper which entitle them to future dividends and are saleable. They hope that the dividends will be higher – which they should be if the merger has some commercial rationale – and that the market value of the new security will be higher than that of those they have sold or exchanged.

The size of total acquisitions and mergers can be gauged by comparing the total expenditure entailed in 1984, for example (£5.5 billion), with the total net capital formation by the private sector in that year, excluding dwellings (£7 billion). Whether such activity is in the public interest and how much of it, for that matter, can be argued to have even a *commercial* justification are matters to which we shall return shortly.

COMPETITION POLICY

Before the Second World War, government attitude towards the growth in the size of firms and increased industrial concentration was one of guarded approval. To secure the advantages of 'rationalization' into larger units seemed in the depressed conditions of the time more important than avoiding the dangers that went with it. But in the post-war years it became clear that many of the restrictive practices which had previously been defensible would not be so in the sellers' market which now existed.

In 1948, already late in the day of industrial integration, the government took its first tentative steps in the direction of curbing monopolistic power. In 1948 the Monopolies Commission was set up, empowered to investigate industries (which were referred to it by the Board of Trade) in which 'one-third of the final output or the processing or export of a good is in the hands of a single firm or two or more firms being interconnected or corporate ... or where the firms are acting in such a way as to prevent or restrict competition'. These were wide terms of reference covering much of British industry. Once it had been referred to an industry, the Commission would undertake an investigation, then producing either a purely factual report or one including recommendations for the removal of practices it considered contrary to the public interest.

This at first sight seems fairly strong medicine. But the Commission's progress was, in the first place, agonizingly slow; only twenty-one cases were investigated by 1956. This was due mainly to the smallness of its membership (ten, later increased to twenty-five) and supporting staff and to its tiny budget. Secondly, its effectiveness was limited by the fact that it had to proceed case by case, with its recommendations confined to the particular industry under scrutiny, rather than being generally applicable. Thirdly, the Commission lacked teeth, with enforcement being the responsibility of a relevant government department – which in most cases disregarded what the Commission had recommended.

In 1955 the Commission published its first general report, on the practice of collective price maintenance, and it resulted in the 1956 Restrictive Practices Act which outlawed the then widespread custom of manufacturers jointly enforcing the retail prices at which their products should be sold. The Act further dealt with agreements between two or more parties which limited freedom in respect of prices, sales or production. All such agreements were to be registered with a Registrar of Restrictive Practices, and by January 1957 the register held some 2,300 agreements. At the initiative of the Registrar, selected agreements were brought before the Restrictive Practices Court, consisting of five judges and up to ten lay members.

It was then up to the parties to the agreement to demonstrate that their practice was positively in the public interest. This had to be argued under one or more of seven 'gateways' as they became known. Two were concerned with consumer protection, three with conditions necessary to ensure fair competition between producers, one where the abandonment of an agreement would lead to serious and persistent unemployment and a seventh covering exports.

The onus lay on defendants to prove that their agreement fell into one or more of these classes. But this in itself was not sufficient. The Registrar would point out any 'detriments' arising from its operation, and a 'tailpiece' of the judgement involved balancing whether, on the whole, the agreement was in the public interest.

Ostensibly the Restrictive Practices Act was highly effective. Although in the early years only a small number of agreements were brought before the court, the result of its judgements was that a large proportion of those remaining on the register were abandoned. However, it became clear that many of these had been replaced by 'open-price agreements'. Instead of overtly colluding in fixing prices and sharing markets, members of an association might merely agree to circulate information about what prices they were charging and where they were selling. Such an exchange coupled with a *tacitly* restrictive approach could escape the scrutiny of the Registrar.

An attempt to close this loophole was made by a 1965 addition to the legislation under which information agreements also became registerable. At the same time, an eighth gateway was introduced whereby it could be argued that an agreement did not materially restrict or discourage competition. The Registrar then made a valiant start in tracking cases of apparently innocuous agreements hiding implicit collusion.

A further danger of the restrictive practices law was that, in adopting a hard line towards agreements *between* parties, it may have encouraged mergers instead. It was partly to meet this possibility that the 1965 Monopolies and Mergers Act was passed. This strengthened the Commission and enabled it to look into the production of services as well as goods – but also into mergers, either actual or proposed, where the assets involved amount to more than a certain value.

Meanwhile government has at times actively *encouraged* the formation of larger enterprises in certain circumstances, in particular so that British firms should enjoy sufficient economies of scale effectively to match foreign competition. Earlier piecemeal steps in this direction (for example, with regard to the cotton, aircraft and shipbuilding industries) were generalized between 1966 and 1971 by an Industrial Reorganization Corporation charged with the catalytic role of identifying and facilitating the merging of companies where clear economic benefits could be expected.

There were thus two strands in government policy towards big business: a quest for increased efficiency, but recognition that where this involved industrial concentration it must be within a framework of extensive government surveillance.

Since 1973 competition has largely been based on the Fair Trading Act, which co-ordinated much of the previous legislation and widened its scope. A new Office of Fair Trading (OFT) was established headed by a Director-General empowered to make references to the Monopolies and Mergers Commission (MMC), as it now became known (in addition to those made by the Secretary of State, who also reserved the right to refer mergers). The Restrictive Practices Court was also brought under the OFT.

The potential area of the MMC has been widened in a number of ways. Now it is a 25% market share which serves as sufficient to justify investigation. New candidates for reference include nationalized as well as private concerns and firms suspected of engaging in anti-competitive behaviour even when not in 'monopoly' positions.

The attitude of British governments towards big business can therefore be best described as one of cautious pragmatism. It has broadly distinguished between market *structure* (how many firms operate in the market, how much power they possess and whether there is a dominant firm) and market *behaviour* (whether they discriminate between their customers or exercise market power). The tendency both in Britain and in Europe has been to concentrate attention on the latter, and to worry less about the size and number of firms. Certainly there has never in Europe been the feeling that monopoly as such must be prevented, with concentrations actually being broken up, as in the USA.

It is a policy which has had some considerable success in modifying at least formal behaviour patterns. And the widening of the net on restrictive practices has led to basic changes in important areas – recently, amongst others, the Stock Exchange, banking and building societies, and parts of the legal profession.

But there is the suspicion, inherently difficult to assess, that some overtly restrictive behaviour has been replaced by much less traceable types of informal collusion. It is extremely difficult to legislate against specific practices, because as soon as one is outlawed another takes its place. So the latest legislation follows the pattern of the European Community legislation, and outlaws practices which have the *effect* of restricting or distorting competition. The Community, of course, is particularly concerned with those which do so across national borders, and its actions against Hoffman La Roche, the Swiss drug company, and against IBM, the US computer giant, suggest that it is more committed to anti-monopoly policies than some of its member governments. Lack of commitment is suggested by the number of MMC recommendations on which British governments have subsequently failed to act. It is interesting that British industry is believed to have felt much more threatened by the probings of the brief-lived Prices Commission looking into company affairs to see whether price rises were justified than by the activities of the Monopolies Commission.

Beyond that, two fundamental doubts remain about the effectiveness of competition policy. The first stems from the fact that a substantial proportion of recent industrial integration has cut across industrial lines – in the formation or the strengthening of massive conglomerate firms with a vast range of output involving many different types of productive activity. Past policy may well have been sensible in not being over-concerned with the growth of enterprises *within* individual industries until they are shown to be exploiting their position. But in mergers and take-overs of the conglomerate form, such is the variety of production within the new enterprises that it is often very difficult to see what significant potential economies of scale might result. Indeed, evidence suggests that mergers often lead to no perceptible improvement in profit rates or other indicators of performance, and may be motivated by other considerations such as *security* of profits or simply the growth of the enterprise as an end in itself. There is thus a strong argument for requiring mergers and intended mergers to demonstrate, along lines similar to the restrictive practices gateways, that they will yield positive public benefits rather than that they are not obviously contrary to the public interest as laid down in the 1973 Act (which, in the mid-1980s, is interpreted narrowly as to whether or not a monopoly would result).

The second great problem is the extent to which the behaviour of multinational corporations, with their potential for intricate 'creative accounting' within their nation-spanning structures, *can* be controlled by a single government or even a wider grouping like the European Community.

MULTINATIONAL CORPORATIONS

We have already noted that a significant proportion of manufacturing output (about one-fifth) is produced by 'foreign' firms – that is firms whose official home base is in another country. A considerable number of British firms operate in foreign countries as well as at home. If we take the 100 largest British firms, then only 12 operate wholly within Britain. The same would be true for West Germany, France, Italy and particularly the USA. Most large firms are 'multinational' in the sense that they operate in two or more countries.

The reasons for this are many, but an important one is the advantage of being close to the market, so that the product can be varied to match local tastes. Proximity to the market also avoids the costs and delays of shipping, freight, customs duties and restrictions and so on. In any case, it is usual for the import duties on finished products to be much higher than the duties on the raw materials, so that a British chocolate manufacturer would find it cheaper to import cocoa and sugar into the USA and to manufacture chocolate there, than to export the finished product from Britain. (This is a hypothetical example; alternatives are to buy all or part of an established US firm, or to agree with a US firm to manufacture under licence.)

Some of the largest firms, however, are 'multinational' in a different sense. Their markets and customers are world-wide and they manufacture, distribute and sell on the same world-wide basis. Their 'home' may be simply where the parent or controlling company is legally registered, which could (for tax and other reasons) be Liechtenstein, Monaco or the Cayman Islands. Or it may be their 'country of origin', the base from which they expanded. But although we think of IBM and General Motors as American, and of Unilever and Shell as British (or, more exactly, Anglo-Dutch), firms as large and diverse as these plan their operations on a global scale in their own interests. In terms of sheer size they are sometimes bigger than the countries in which they operate; they are estimated to control over a quarter of total world output; and their 'inter-firm' shipments of goods from one country to another account for nearly one-third of recorded trade.

The degree of control which any government can exercise over the operations of these multinational giants is very limited, since they always have the option of moving outside its legal jurisdiction.

The two major benefits from being multinational are the ability to *locate* the firm's activities in the best (i.e. the most profitable) places and the ability to move goods and services around within the firm at *prices* which need not match external market prices. The first of these means that it can exploit cheap labour, cheap raw materials, lower interest rates and tax advantages wherever they are to be found. The second enables it to ensure that its profits emerge from the particular process, and in the particular country, which suits it best.

So, for example, a typical multinational in the electronics field might carry out its research and development in the USA or West Germany, where the 'knowledge base' exists and where high-level manpower is relatively cheap and abundant. The advanced manufacturing processes, which require high levels of skill, complex machinery and very high quality, might be located in Japan or Sweden, producing parts which are often of high value and small size, and can be air-freighted around the world quite cheaply. The routine manufacture and assembly, involving connecting up devices, fitting keyboards or video screens, testing and packaging, is increasingly being done in the so-called NICs – the newly industrializing countries – like Brazil, South Korea, Portugal, Turkey, India and parts of South-East Asia. Here labour is cheap but well disciplined, and there are often generous inducements offered to firms which set up an assembly plant and provide employment. The final process – the marketing – returns to a major centre such as New York or London, where the communications, the media facilities, the skills of advertising and the finance are all on tap.

If there are good reasons to do so, it would be quite easy to ensure that the main manufacturing/assembly stage makes a large profit, by letting it buy the components at just above cost, but by requiring the sales/distribution section to buy the finished product from it at a high price. In this way the bulk of the profit emerges (let us say) in Singapore, where the firm happens to have negotiated a five-year 'tax holiday' as part of the inducement to locate there, rather than from the R and D base in the USA or the sales headquarters in London, where profits taxes are high and less easily avoidable. Once the 'holiday' is over, a readjustment of internal 'transfer' prices ensures that from now on the Singapore factory earns less profit.

In the opinion of some economists a major relocation of the world's manufacturing industries is taking place, which explains why manufacturing employment has fallen in almost all the major economies of Europe and North America. Obviously the process is linked with the growth of multinational enterprises; but whether the multinationals *cause* the relocation, or simply respond to changed economic circumstances, is less easy to assess.

THE LOCATION OF INDUSTRY

Turning aside from the huge unanswered questions of controlling multinationals, a more parochial but very important issue is *where* firms choose to site their operation within the UK itself. Conventionally, economic analysis has seen such decisions as the result of a variety of often conflicting pulls: towards sources of raw materials, power, pools of labour and markets. The original location of manufacturing in Britain was mainly dominated by the need to be close to water or coal, and the decreased significance of such factors compared with the advantages of being close to markets was the genesis of the 'regional problem' – a disparity of incomes, employment and generally economic activity between different parts of the country.

It can be argued that market forces will render such a situation self-correcting, with flows of labour and capital tending to reduce regional inequalities. Thus labour will move from high unemployment areas to those where jobs are more easily available. Capital, in contrast, moves in the opposite direction to take advantage of surplus labour, capacity and less-used social amenities in the relatively less prosperous parts of the country.

However, all the evidence suggests that market forces are more likely to accentuate regional disparities rather than to remove them. In fact, labour *has* moved on a substantial scale – in particular, a southward movement away from the traditional regions. But since it is mostly younger workers who are prepared to move, the poorer regions become characterized by an older and less adaptable work-force. Frequently, too, such areas are regarded as having a heritage of labour problems built up during the decline of staple industries. Wage rates in many occupations are negotiated on a national basis so that the price of labour is no lower than elsewhere; social capital (housing, transport and communications, and general amenities) may have been run down in the process of decline. Thus capital, far from moving *to* such regions, instead concentrates in already prosperous parts. The market mechanism produces a *cumulative* widening rather than a narrowing of the gap between regions.

Recognition that this was so led governments since the mid-1930s to pursue positive regional policies aimed at reducing regional disparities, not only on social grounds but for the good economic reason that the problem of regional decline was mirrored in the over-congestion and increased costs incurred in the more prosperous parts.

Such policies have been of the 'carrot-and-stick' variety, with a range of financial inducements to locate in certain areas being coupled with disincentives to site enterprises in others. A great variety of measures have been employed, and there have been an equally bewildering number of changes in the areas designated for their application. Indeed, one of the criticisms of regional policy is the uncertainty engendered by the number of changes which occur. A further criticism is that a good deal of aid has taken the form of general, non-discriminatory programmes which subsidize investment which would have taken place anyway and encourage capital-intensive investments such as oil refineries which provide few jobs and even fewer unskilled jobs.

The problem of reducing regional disparities proved intractable even during that part of the post-war period when the general context was one of national full employment and general prosperity. However, the evidence suggests that it was effective at least in preventing a further deterioration in the situation.

By the 1980s, however, the situation had radically changed. For a while, the regional problem was swamped by the re-emergence of mass unemployment throughout the economy as a whole. But it soon became clear that, as has always been the case, the impact of the downturn was most severe in the already weaker regions, and this has persisted into the mid-1980s. What we are now witnessing is an increasingly sharp division between a belt of prosperity stretching from East Anglia and the South-East through London towards the South-West – and the rest. The gap between them widens year by year, whether it is defined in terms of unemployment, incomes or broader social indicators. Thus, for example, whereas in the South-East the increase in unemployment between 1980 and 1984 was 3.5% below the national average, in the North it was 5.2% above it. Similarly, while the South-East in 1984 enjoyed a level of personal income per head 16% higher than the UK as a whole (in Greater London 25% more), in Wales it was some 14% lower than the UK average, a gap of about 30 points; this could be crudely translated into as much as perhaps £4,000 to £5,000 per household.

At the same time, governments wedded to a market philosophy have markedly reduced the scale of regional assistance and their willingness to interfere with the freedom of enterprises to locate as they deem most appropriate on commercial grounds. Regional and other general aid to industry rose to a peak level of £914 million in 1982 and then fell to an estimated £434 million in 1985–6. Specific assistance to aerospace, motor vehicles, shipbuilding, coal and steel (i.e. expenditure to those industries in which government had a continued involvement) peaked a little earlier, in 1981–2. Much of this 'aid' was in practice aimed at easing the run-down and rationalization of the industries concerned and took the form of redundancy payments. Overall, in real terms, it has been estimated that regional policy spending may have fallen by as much as two-thirds in the decade since 1976.

Currently aid is directed at regions which together contain over a third of the national work-force, divided into 'development' and 'intermediate' areas. Apart from providing a number of factory units and land for industrial building, government aid primarily consists of regional development grants: a 15% contribution towards capital investment, and regional selective assistance to employment-creating projects meeting set criteria. Intermediate areas are eligible only for the latter, development areas for both types of help.

Present policy is to bias the aid towards job creation, and the inclusion of services as well as manufacturing is a recognition that this is where most new jobs will be. There is also an emphasis on small businesses, encouraged through a wide range of schemes of assistance: the removal of perceived obstacles such as lengthy and elaborate planning applications, or requests for statistical information, from which new enterprises should be exempted; the provision of specialized advice by consultants, for which government will pay; and easier access to finance through government guarantees to banks. The number of small businesses is growing; but it is not clear how many of them are at the forefront of new technology, and are destined to grow, and how many are the traditional corner shop or jobbing builder, financed from the redundancy payments of ex-industrial workers.

Within the overall framework, there are also attempts to deal with problems of urban decay in the older declining cities by the creation of small 'enterprise zones', in which very generous assistance is available. It includes exemption from rates, 100% tax allowances for new buildings, exemption from training levies and other 'burdens'. The intention is to stimulate the creation of really new firms, rather than simply influence the location of a new factory or warehouse. The cost, in lost rates and taxes, is considerable, and there is evidence to suggest that many of the 'new' firms continue to be those which have simply crossed the boundary line to take advantage of the concessions.

In addition to that from the British government, there is regional aid from the European Community. Although Britain has taken a substantial proportion of the funds available, they are very small in comparison with the national total. However, because the Community has strongly resisted attempts by member governments to treat its expenditure as a substitute for, rather than a supplement to, national regional spending, it has provided a useful element in diversifying the nature of regional projects and in reinforcing their long-term element.

The shift in emphasis in recent years of regional support recognizes that previous policies were unduly biased towards very large organizations, creating few new jobs and sometimes in receipt of government funds for locating where they would have done anyway. From this point of view it may be sensible that grants for capital investment (which in the past mainly helped the establishment of capital-intensive oil, gas and petrochemical installations on the east coasts of Scotland and Northern England where they would probably have been sited regardless) are now limited to £10,000 per new job, and that service industries have also become eligible. But although it is important that the *quality* of assistance is often more appropriate, it is worrying that its *quantity* in real terms has so sharply declined at a time when the North–South divide has become most acute. Moreover, the switch in emphasis towards the fostering of new small enterprises wherever they are located is likely in practice to lead to a greater increase in 'self-employed' in the prosperous South rather than the depressed North. The same is true of scientific and technological assistance, particularly in connection with the applications of micro-electronics.

The top priority in improving the often desperate plight of the poorer regions must be to raise the *national* level of employment and activity. Given the profound nature of the present regional problem, it is possible that the relative gap may in the first place widen still further although accompanied by an improvement in the absolute prosperity of the weaker areas. It would then become still clearer that there was a need for a higher scale of assistance, for co-ordinating the work of the various regional aid agencies and for stimulating rather than discouraging new initiatives like local enterprise boards – *if* the deep-rooted disparities were genuinely regarded as intolerable.

12

The Public Sector of the Economy

Much recent controversy has resulted from a breakdown of the broad consensus that previously existed about the mix between private and public output that was appropriate for the British economy. Conservative governments since 1979 have energetically pursued policies of privatization and aimed at reducing the degree of government involvement in the economy. The arguments behind this thrust will be deferred to Part III.

For now, we shall examine the extent and form of public provisions of goods and services as it had developed by the end of the 1970s. First, there are the nationalized industries – their origin, nature and record. Second, there is the major contribution made to domestic product which is best described as part of central or local government – the National Health Service, education, the provision of housing and roads and so on.

NATIONALIZED INDUSTRIES

Some enterprises *began* as a part of government: the Post Office being a good example. Where it was evident that a natural monopoly would be more efficient than competing operators duplicating facilities, public control was exercised at an early date, examples being the London Passenger Transport Board and the Central Electricity Board, formed to set up and operate a national distribution 'grid'.

But the main wave of nationalization took place between 1945 and 1950, when the so-called 'commanding heights of the economy' (the phrase was much quoted in the 1940s) were brought into public ownership and management. Coal, airlines, the 'area' electricity production and distribution system, rail and road transport, gas, and iron and steel were the main industries taken into the public sector by the immediate post-war Labour government.

The arguments for state control of iron and steel and road transport were hotly disputed, and the advent of a Conservative government in the 1950s saw the denationalization of these industries.

The return swing of the pendulum resulted in the renationalization of steel and the formation of a National Freight Corporation which (it was hoped) would integrate rail and road freight traffic. Airports were nationalized, and the Post Office became a public corporation instead of a government department.

A third wave of nationalization came during the Labour period of office after 1974. Aerospace, shipbuilding and the ports (the Port of London had been publicly managed since 1908, interestingly) were taken into public ownership and management. Moreover, the government participated in the management (and the profits) of the new North Sea oil industry through the British National Oil Corporation. Public involvement, without complete ownership, was to be extended through the formation of a National Enterprise Board, which was soon involved in the rescue and reorganization of British Leyland. This, like the case of Rolls-Royce, was essentially a salvage operation.

By this time, nationalized industries had become very big business. They included the largest employers in the UK and provided jobs for nearly two million people. The assets of the largest public enterprises were even greater than those of the private enterprise giants. They accounted for some 11% of gross output and annually invested nearly as much as the whole of the private manufacturing sector.

It was a collection of industries sharing remarkably few common characteristics, and the arguments for including them in the public sector differed accordingly. An important consideration was undoubtedly the feeling that some industries were too basic, too fundamentally important, to be left in private operation with profitability as the only criterion. The 'commanding heights of the economy' were to be brought under public control.

Many of these industries were 'natural' monopolies, in which there was room for only one supplier, and in particular one distributor. Although competing railway lines were built at the height of the Victorian mania for railways, it was sensible for one organization to provide rail transport for each region, and perhaps for the whole country. (Before British Railways was formed, there were four major railway companies, and this framework persists in British Rail's regional organization.) The same was true of the distribution of water, electricity and gas and the removal of sewage; what was the sense in the duplication of wires or pipes in each street?

Such monopolies, like any others, must be subject to some measure of control. Left to themselves, they could charge high prices, exploiting their monopoly, and they might fail to serve 'uneconomic', i.e. inaccessible or distant, consumers. But control need not necessarily have implied ownership, and in some countries electricity, rail transport and gas supply are private enterprises subject to public regulation of their activities, especially their pricing.

Coal and steel are different. They fall clearly into the 'commanding heights' category, and their nationalization was in part a reflection of their industrial history, and in part a sense that they were basic in a way that other industries were not. At that time, it is worth remembering, coal was the major source of energy, and steel had provided the sinews of war.

A third set of considerations arose out of questions which transcend the boundaries of particular industries. Transport policy, for example, is a matter of exploiting in the public interest the particular virtues of rail, road, water and airways, and of minimizing their evils such as congestion, noise and pollution. Energy policy considers, or should do, how a country like the United Kingdom could best meet its energy requirements and most efficiently deploy its energy resources, taking a long view. It is much easier to apply these broad policies if some or all of the industries involved are in the public sector, or under public control.

Finally there was a feeling, backed up by a certain amount of evidence, that private industry had failed to invest an adequate amount in new plant and machinery, and that the long-term industrial future of the country could best be secured by a great deal of state intervention: first, to ensure the investment, and second, having made it, to see that it was being properly used. Public ownership was one way in which this could be attempted. Rationalization, redeployment, new investment and new stimulants to effective management lay behind such proposals as the nationalization of the major ports.

Just as we found it difficult to define an industry in Chapter 3, so it is not as easy as might be thought to define the 'public sector' of the economy. The statisticians do, however, separate out a group of enterprises under the name of 'public corporations', and we have already used this category in our discussions of capital investment, for example.

There were forty-nine of these public corporations in existence at the end of 1984, varying greatly in size and importance. The major productive enterprises in the list were:

Bank of England
British Airports Authority (privatization planned)
British Airways Board (privatization planned)
British Broadcasting Corporation
British Gas Corporation (privatized in 1986)
British National Oil Corporation
British Railways Board
British Steel Corporation
British Shipbuilders
Electricity Council
London Regional Transport
National Bus Company (privatization planned)
National Coal Board
Post Office
Regional Water Authorities
Royal Ordnance Factories (privatization in hand)
British Telecommunications was privatized in 1984.

The public corporation was the commonly chosen device for operating a nationalized concern – managed by a board, run by a chief executive and subject to ministerial control. This took two forms: financial control exercised by the Treasury, and industrial policy controlled by the relevant minister. An annual report was submitted to Parliament, to whom the minister, and therefore at one remove the industry, was responsible.

Thus the day-to-day running of public enterprises was to be left to the chairmen of boards and their professional managers, with ministers laying down the broad lines of policy to be pursued. In practice what has occurred is unfortunately close to the opposite. A great deal of political interference has taken place in the running of nationalized industries: interventions, for example, on particular price changes and investment plans to meet the political contingencies of the day. Chairmen of nationalized industries have sometimes been only too vocal in expressing their own views about what in general public enterprise should be aiming to achieve.

The principles on which the nationalized sector should be operated were never very clearly enunciated. From what has been said so far, it can be seen that for the Labour government in the immediate post-war years, nationalization was almost an end in itself. It was justified primarily in the negative terms of avoiding concentration of economic power in private hands and ensuring that, instead of being exploited, consumers and workers would be the main beneficiaries of public enterprise activity. Positive thinking was largely limited to securing the economies of large-scale production; to the possibilities of using public investment as a compensatory device to offset the vagaries of the private sector (helping keep employment at a higher level); and to the broad idea of 'integrated' policies in areas like transport and energy.

How exactly was a nationalized industry supposed to *behave*? Beyond a general injunction that they should be expected to break even taking one year with another, and a general reference to a responsibility to 'further the public interest', little was put forward in the way of policy guidance.

Before dealing with the subsequent development of policy and its effects, it is worth dwelling for a moment on the possible objectives that nationalized industries should be set. There are three very broad alternatives to consider. We could regard them as simply *commercial* enterprises, we could expect them to operate on more sophisticated *economic* principle, or they could be regarded as instruments of a wider *social* framework of policy.

(*a*) *The commercial approach.* Essentially, this consists of telling nationalized industries to ignore the fact that they are part of the public sector and to behave as though they were private concerns. A public enterprise would then be distinguished from its private counterpart only in terms of ownership; its surplus (or deficit) would accrue to (be borne by) taxpayers as a whole rather than a group of shareholders.

This criterion appears to have the merit of straightforward simplicity. Yet even this is doubtful, since private commercial behaviour is itself not simple. In practice, private firms are not exclusively motivated by profit maximization; their objectives are frequently wider and more complex. Consequently, the injunction to a nationalized industry to run itself like a private business does not prescribe a unique course of action; the same profit level, for example, might be attainable with very different output and pricing policies.

However, the main drawback to the commercial approach is its narrowness. It leaves out of account so many considerations to which most people would attach importance. These can be brought into the picture by going on to outline the two alternative policy bases.

(*b*) *The economic approach.* As we explained in Chapter 10, commercial and economic criteria are very often confused. The difference between them is that whereas the commercial criterion considers only private costs and benefits, an economic criterion is one which also takes externalities into account.

Thus, the massive railway closures that took place under the 'Beeching axe' of the 1960s were mostly undertaken by asking of each line or service, 'Does it *pay*?' Similarly, criticism was voiced in official circles of London Transport's low fares policy in the early 1980s on the grounds that it would lose money for the London ratepayer. In both instances, what is ignored are the *external* effects of policy, in particular on non-users of the services. The gains in terms of reduced congestion on the roads, for example, might be so considerable as to yield a positive overall 'economic return'. Admittedly such external costs and benefits are difficult to quantify, but when attempts have been made to do so, as for instance on the investment which took place on the Victoria Line, it is clear that the divergence between commercial and economic rates of return can be very considerable.

Similarly pit closures in the coal industry during the 1980s were frequently made on the basis that costs exceeded revenues and losses were consequently being made. But the *economic* concept of 'cost' involves asking the question, 'What alternative output is being forgone as a result of this economic activity?' Frequently in the case of coal-mines the answer would have been 'very little' or even 'none' – since the capital resources used were highly specific, and the miners made redundant stood little chance of securing employment elsewhere. Clearly, the notion of what is or is not 'economic' will vary with circumstances; if there had been full employment, then there *would* have been output forgone as a result of keeping workers occupied in the coal industry rather than in some alternative and more productive use.

(*c*) *The social approach.* It is also possible to adopt still broader principles of evaluation. What is economically appropriate might at the same time be thought unfair, undesirable or politically inexpedient. Are such considerations to be set aside as irrelevant? Is economics the be-all and end-all? Or should not the public enterprises be used to further social ends such as regional development, the maintenance of traditional communities and a more equitable distribution of income – which might require moderation of a purely economic approach?

Policy in practice

In the event, a clear expression of public enterprise objectives and how they should be achieved has never been formulated. Instead there has been muddle and inconsistency.

To begin with, nationalized industries were left to themselves in grappling with possible conflicts between commercial and public service obligations, resolving them as they saw fit, and with consequent variation in practice from one industry to another. The mounting financial deficits which resulted in many cases finally led government to a re-evaluation of the role of public enterprise in a 1961 White Paper on *The Financial and Economic Obligations of the Nationalized Industries* (Cmnd 1337).

There is substance in the view of one critic at the time who said that the document merely codified the muddle of Whitehall thinking. The approach of the White Paper was basically commercial, setting definite financial targets for the nationalized industries so that surpluses should be at least sufficient to cover deficits over a five-year period. At the same time it was admitted that 'public corporations cannot be regarded only as very large commercial concerns which may be judged mainly on their commercial results; all have, although in varying degrees, wider obligations than commercial concerns in the private sector'. The proposed solution, that these wider obligations should be taken into account in 'fixing the financial standard for each undertaking', did little to resolve the underlying conflict of objectives.

Six years later came another White Paper (1967: *Nationalized Industries, A Review of Economic and Financial Objectives*, Cmnd 3437) which, with some modification in 1978, remains the official policy formulation. The statement showed a much more encouraging awareness that public enterprise objectives cannot be achieved merely by maximizing the financial returns of each industry; significant costs and benefits occur which are outside the financial concern of the industry, and it is the special responsibility of the government to ensure that these 'social' factors are reflected in the industries' planning.

Subject to these considerations, the government's continuing intention is 'to treat the industries as commercial bodies', and 'investment projects must normally show a satisfactory return in commercial terms'. To this end the White Paper recommended more widespread applications of discounted cash flow techniques of project appraisal, generally using an 8% (later 10%) 'test rate' of discount. This figure appears to be that which the government judged comparable with the rate of return in the private sector after allowing for differences in taxation, investment grants and so on. How this private sector rate was derived and why it was appropriate that the public sector should emulate it remain unanswered questions.

Nationalized industries have been bedevilled over the years, not only by lack of clear policy guidelines from above, but by constant ministerial interventions which would have made the consistent application of *any* set of criteria extremely difficult for those responsible for the industries' day-to-day management.

Their investment has been chopped and changed as an element in implementing short-term government management strategy, despite the fact that its scope and importance clearly require long-term planning. At times, prices and incomes have been held down in the public sector as part of counter-inflationary policy; in other cases prices have been put up to increase returns to the Treasury and minimize public borrowing or taxation. Such interventions have created an atmosphere of uncertainty which is hardly conducive to the efficient operation of these major concerns.

In such circumstances it is hardly surprising that nationalization has in many quarters achieved a bad name, or that morale should be low. But it should be emphasized that this has been due less to the record of performance in public enterprises – which has been mixed – than to the absence of overall direction and of public as well as official understanding of what their objectives should have been.

The solution, as seen by governments in the early 1980s, has not been to rethink the nature and workings of public enterprise but rather to embark on wholesale *privatization* – a massive dismantling of the nationalized sector. The arguments for and against such a policy are a major policy issue which we shall postpone until Chapter 19.

GOVERNMENT PROVISION OF SERVICES

What, however, of those parts of the public provision of goods and services which fall outside the conventional meaning of 'nationalized industries'? Quantifying the extent of this is not straightforward. As we saw earlier, there is government spending which includes transfers of income, and 'government expenditure on goods and services' which counts as part of gross domestic product. A second complication is the existence of more than one classification of spending.

Table 12.1. Government expenditure by programme

Programme	£ billion, constant 1983–4 prices						
	1979–80	'80–81	'81–2	'82–3	'83–4	'84–5	'85–6
Social security	29.1	29.6	32.8	34.9	36.3	36.4	37.8
Health and personal social services	16.1	17.3	17.6	17.9	18.3	18.8	18.8
Education, science, arts, libraries	16.5	16.9	16.8	17.0	17.1	16.7	15.8
Housing	8.2	7.0	4.7	3.9	4.3	4.1	3.1
Environmental services	4.9	4.7	4.4	4.6	4.7	4.6	4.1
Transport	5.8	5.8	5.7	5.5	5.3	5.5	5.0
Employment services	1.7	2.3	2.4	2.4	2.7	2.8	2.8
Law and order	4.5	4.7	5.0	5.2	5.5	5.7	5.6
Defence, overseas spending	16.4	15.6	15.8	17.3	18.1	18.9	18.9
Other expenditure on programmes	8.8	9.7	11.3	9.7	8.0	8.0	8.8
Total	111.8	113.5	116.6	118.4	120.3	122.3	120.7
of which							
Local authorities	31.4	30.7	29.7	30.5	33.2	32.7	30.4

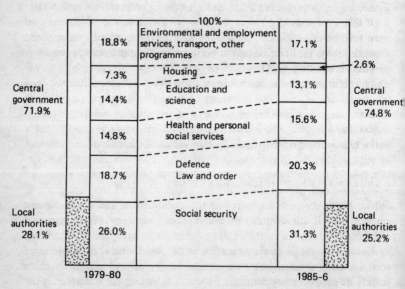

Figure 15 Changes in the pattern of government spending

Some idea of the growth of government spending on various activities may be gained from Table 12.1, which is in constant prices.

Table 12.1 and Figure 15 show the steady rise in spending on social security, brought about by the massive increase in unemployment. They also indicate the way in which other programmes have been cut, or their growth arrested, in order to restrain expansion of total government spending while allowing for increases in expenditure on defence and law and order according to government priorities. The main sufferers have been education and science, and housing.

Social security spending is mostly transfer payments, and together with debt interest it accounts for some 40% of the total. Other programmes, by contrast, use resources to provide goods and services (mainly the latter) which for a variety of reasons are not provided by private industry or by public corporations. Some of these 'providers of services' are very big enterprises indeed. Two stand out: health and education. If their total expenditures were to be equated with 'turnover' in the commercial sense, they would rank third and fourth in the list of industrial and commercial enterprises. In 1984 the health service employed 865,435 people, making it by far the largest single employer in the country. (For comparison, British Telecommunications and the Post Office combined employed 420,682.)

Of this total, over 40,000 were doctors or dentists, just under 400,000 were trained nurses, and other professional staff totalled over 70,000. What did they 'produce'? There is no way of adding up and valuing their output, except by using the cost figures as a substitute for the amount which might have been paid for health services, but some indication can be given. Spells in hospital, which is roughly equivalent to patients treated, came to 5 million in 1984. There were 31 million courses of dental treatment, and 320 million prescriptions were dispensed – a rough guide to the number of people who consulted a doctor. 22 million were treated as out-patients, of whom over half were accident or emergency cases. Whatever measure we use, the government-supplied health services are huge businesses, as are the education services which are described below. One major difference between these organizations and their private counterparts is the level of remuneration of their managers and senior staff!

Most of the spending on education is done by the local authorities. Of the £15,827 million spending recorded for 1983–4, local authorities were responsible for £13,605 million or 86%. The way this money was spent is indicated in Table 12.2.

Table 12.2. Education expenditure, 1983–4

	(£ million)
Schools	
Nursery	67
Primary	3 377
Secondary	4,675
Special	583
	8,702
Further and adult education	2,157
Teacher training	86
Universities	1,497
Other education	656
Meals and milk	519
Youth services	209
Grants and allowances	825[a]
Miscellaneous	459
Capital expenditure	717
Total	15,827

Note: [a] Mainly for higher education.

Table 12.3. Numbers of students, 1983–4

	(000s)
Higher education	
Universities (undergraduates 98.6)	
(postgraduates 11.4)	110
Public sector (polytechnics, etc.)	124
Overseas students	12
Part-time students	103
	349
Further education	
Full-time	223
Day release	117
Part-time day	174
Evening	433
	947
Adult education (enrolment)	1,581
Schools	
Secondary	4,384
Primary	4,655
Special	138
Nursery	95
	9,152

How much education did all this provide? All we can do is count heads, i.e. number the customers for this service, instead of measuring total sales – see Table 12.3.

So here are two massive enterprises producing the services of health and education to be added to the large public corporations or nationalized industries and to the assorted 'quasi-governmental' organizations which provide services like broadcasting (BBC), outdoor recreation (National Parks), timber (Forestry Commission) and so on. Sometimes the precise organizational form is arbitrary and historically accidental.

But why is this heterogeneous collection of enterprises in the public sector at all? We have already outlined the main reasons for state involvement in Chapter 10, and we simply summarize them again here.

First, there is a group of services which must be publicly provided if they are to be provided at all. Prominent among them is external defence, the traditional function of government. It must be provided collectively, and once provided, no one can avoid its protection. For the same reason no one is allowed to opt out of his or her share of its cost, despite a few well-publicized attempts at refusing to pay taxes for nuclear weapons or the Vietnam war. In general, when it is impossible or very difficult to exclude people from the enjoyment of some good or service – when it cannot be 'appropriated' or made into private property – it cannot be produced by private individuals or sold through the market mechanism. If those who use it are to be made to pay for it, then the taxing power of the state has to be used to collect the money.

The second set of reasons for state involvement arises, as we saw, from 'market failure': where market solutions are not impossible but inadequate or inefficient. These are cases where the sum total of decisions made by individuals does not add up to a situation which is regarded as socially desirable. There is a divergence between private costs and benefits and public or social costs and benefits.

Earlier we cited the case of acid rain. Another example is the rate at which we use up non-renewable resources such as oil or gas. Private calculations are conducted within the time span of an individual lifetime at the most, and usually with a much nearer time horizon only a few years ahead. This may lead to a quest for a quick return on investment and a high rate of depletion. Generally, it is only the state which can take a longer view and worry about future generations. For Britain as a nation it might have been better to spin out the life of North Sea oil into the middle of the next century, as some have argued.

Another reason for market failure stems from lack of knowledge on the part of consumers about the goods and services they are buying. This may be particularly acute in the case of medicine and, to a lesser extent, education. Finally, as we have already stressed, a powerful argument for state involvement in many areas of social provision stems from the existing inequality of income and wealth, which creates the rationale for a system of 'free' and universal public provision which has characterized the post-war Welfare State in Britain.

However, throughout this period there has been a contrary view which assumed much greater force after the advent of the Conservative government in 1979. Those who hold it persist in believing that privately owned enterprises operating in a market context will automatically serve the interests of the society while pursuing their own. The 'invisible hand', invoked by Adam Smith to explain how the pursuit of private interest led to the growth of collective well-being, will *still* serve us efficiently, it is believed, if only the state would cease to interfere and would confine its actions to its proper sphere, the provision of law and order and national defence.

To these believers in the working of the market or price system, government intervention is not only unnecessary but also damaging. Resources will be misallocated; the wrong technologies will be chosen; sectional interests will benefit at the expense of the consumers. And so, in recent years, the emphasis has switched to reducing the size of the public sector and to returning the nationalized industries to private ownership. We shall discuss such attempts in Part III.

13

The Labour Market

A 'market', as by now it will be clear, is simply a contact between buyers and sellers. In the sophisticated economies of today, this may be far removed from the colourful hustle and bustle of the traditional market-place.

Just as a number of large firms occupy a dominant position in the markets in which they sell the goods and services they produce, so too in the labour market a small number of major trade unions bargain over wages and conditions of employment, sometimes with a single employer, which is often the government, but more often with representatives of the employers. So, for example, the National Union of Mineworkers and the National Coal Board, and the teachers' unions and their local government employers. This situation, in which two powerful organizations confront one another, bears no relation to the meeting of large numbers of buyers and sellers in a conventional market, but the term 'labour market' persists.

COLLECTIVE BARGAINING

During the early part of the nineteenth century the Combination Acts banned worker associations and gave to individual workers the unwanted right to negotiate their own contracts with individual employers. Wage bargaining was thus made 'free', but hardly fair. The single employer, with greater resources, and particularly when there is less than full employment, will always enjoy greater bargaining strength than the individual worker.

It has been the prime function of trade unions, as they have developed over the subsequent century and a half, to redress that imbalance in bargaining power. Workers have combined to negotiate and act in a concerted fashion on the principle that unity is strength. Sometimes groupings have taken place on the basis of a common craft or skill; in other cases it has been the industry which has defined the membership of certain unions; a third category has been 'general unions', containing a wide variety of workers within their ranks.

The result has been that today relatively few wage contracts are negotiated on an individual basis. In addition to union members whose pay and conditions are predominantly set by national or local union bargaining, there are many non-members whose rates are indirectly the result of union activity. A further slice of the working population (about three and a half million, generally of the lower-paid) makes its wage bargains through state-organized bodies like wages councils. All these are examples of collective bargaining – associations of workers to establish greater bargaining equality with their employers. As we have already mentioned, such bargains are frequently struck with employers who themselves have organized into associations of one kind or another.

The aim of collective bargaining is improvement of working conditions, which could take many forms. In Britain, however, the unions have concentrated most of their efforts in securing increases in money wages. Since wages are costs as well as incomes, it is often argued that most trade union activity is self-defeating; wage increases cause rising prices, which swallow up the money gains and leave workers no better off in real terms than they were before. Or alternatively, pay increases simply result in unemployment of those workers now priced out of the market. To see whether there is truth in such contentions we need to look at the mechanism of wage rises.

A union puts in a wage claim. The employer grants it. How is it paid for? Clearly there are only three possibilities. The first is a reduction in profits. Secondly, profits may be maintained or even simultaneously increased if the higher pay is offset by an increase in productivity (output per worker) – due to either greater effort on the part of the individual worker, better organization by management or greater capital investment per worker. Thirdly, the wage increase may be financed by a higher selling price being set for the product.

Thus wage increases do not necessarily lead to rising prices. If they come from reduced profits or increased productivity, union action will genuinely have improved the real incomes of its members. The further question remains, however: *how many* of its members? If wage increases result in reduced employment, the benefit from trade union activity will be confined to those members lucky enough to avoid redundancy. Lower profits may force marginal firms out of business; improved productivity may replace labour with machines; increased prices may cut the demand for the product. This is particularly likely when a firm in a competitive market is faced with higher wage costs which its rivals do not have to bear.

However, it may be a different story if *all* firms are meeting similar wage pressure and all are passing on some part of their increased costs through higher prices. The typical post-war condition has been one of *generally* rising prices, with the responsiveness of demand to particular price increases correspondingly reduced. We must also remember that the worker has a dual role as factor of production and consumer. On the one hand, wages are *costs*, helping perhaps to push up prices; at the same time, wages are *income*, providing the means to buy the more highly priced output.

The fact remains that wage increases passed on as higher prices mean that the cost of living rises. If some workers get more, the result will be that other unions will put in defensive pay claims on behalf of their members, who are the consumers paying for the initial increase. Prices will consequently rise still further, and this leads to another round of wage bargaining. Is anyone better off?

Trade union activity certainly looks abortive when the wage/price spiral is presented in these terms. However, the analysis skips from the initial wage increase to the end result of the wage round. And real benefits may accrue to many union members in the intervening process. Clearly, the union which is first in the wage round does secure an increase in the real income of its members, at least temporarily. Wages will be higher, and unless the workers spend the whole increase on the product which they themselves produce, they will find that they can buy more for their money. And even the last in the wage queue will be achieving something in at least preventing the fall in real wages which would otherwise occur. There may, secondly, be genuine gains for all of them if there are sections of the working community who, for one reason or another, do not take part in the wage round. Some money wages will have risen, but not all prices. The effect will be a shift in real purchasing power from the relatively fixed income groups to those who are more strongly organized.

Trade unionists are not ignorant of the economic facts of life. But their sectional nature frequently leads to a narrow allegiance. Trade union officials are essentially responsible to their own members. It is not their prime function to improve the lot of workers as a whole or act as custodians of the national interest. The result is that sometimes wage bargaining involves a tacit collusion between workers and employers, and much of it is a competitive struggle between the unions themselves to improve their relative positions.

THE ECONOMIC FUNCTION OF WAGES

In pure economic theory, the market for labour is based on similar principles to any other. In the same way that the price of strawberries is determined by the quantities offered for sale and by consumer willingness to buy them, so wages represent the price which balances the supply and demand for labour.

The underlying assumption that the supply and demand for labour respond to changes in wage rates does not at first sight seem unreasonable. Higher wages may expand the labour supply by either increasing the number prepared to work or inducing those already in jobs to increase their hours.

On the demand side, the amount of labour which a firm employs depends on the net addition which further workers will make to its revenue. How much can be produced depends also on the amount and quality of equipment per worker; if this is assumed constant, then employment of additional workers will ultimately yield only diminishing returns, and it is also probable that, as output increases, the firm will have to cut its price to induce consumers to take up the larger quantities of the product coming on to the market. Broadly, then, a firm will weigh the wage costs of additional workers against the net change in its revenue position which occurs as a result of employing them. Employment will be offered to the point at which this is just equal to the extra wage bill incurred. Other things being equal, we can conclude that the higher the wage rate, the smaller will be the volume of labour that the firm finds it profitable to employ.

Two conclusions of current interest are suggested by such a model. The first is that unemployment is the result of excessively high wage rates, with workers consequently pricing themselves out of jobs. The second is that wage differentials serve as signposts indicating the relative abundance or shortage of labour in various occupations in relation to the strength of consumer demand for the output they are involved in producing.

With regard to unemployment, however, what may be true for one firm need not hold for the economy as a whole. For the individual firm, a lower wage rate might well induce it to employ additional workers since its profitability is thereby enhanced. But, as we have already stressed, wages are incomes as well as costs. If, therefore, wages are cut across the board, firms will find that it is not only their costs which have fallen but also the demand for their goods or services.

As to wages acting as indicators of the shifts in resources dictated by changing consumer preferences, in the real world differentials are likely as much to reflect 'imperfections' in the labour market as these underlying economic pressures. It is trade unions which are frequently cited by some economists as one such imperfection, preventing wages from *falling* when that is what the employment situation would suggest as appropriate. More important, perhaps, are the various barriers which exist to the *mobility* of labour.

Immobility of labour

Old industrial centres decay as new ones emerge. One firm prospers and expands; another fails or is taken over. One range of skills becomes obsolete, while another is in great demand. Wages in such circumstances act, in theory, as signals for labour to flow from one use to another.

For example, increased demand for micro-electronics should lead to higher earnings in that industry, inducing workers to move from declining sectors like shipbuilding and other heavy industries.

In practice, shifts of labour take place only partially and slowly. While capital might flow freely around the world, and from one part of the United Kingdom to another, labour cannot. People are understandably unwilling to tear up all their roots and leave their family, friends and the familiar surroundings of home, even if there *is* work somewhere else. 'Getting on your bike' is not as easy as it sounds.

A major problem is housing. A council tenant from Sheffield or Glasgow would go to the end of a long waiting-list if moving to, say, Reading or Southampton to take a job. A home-owner would find it impossible to sell a property in the North at a price which would buy a similar home in the South, so that the move would mean a bigger, often completely prohibitive mortgage.

Moreover, changing jobs increasingly implies the acquisition of quite different skills, which is not possible for many workers because of age, lack of ability or inadequate retraining opportunities.

British governments have tended in the past to regard these processes and changes as something to which each individual must respond in his or her own way. Given this attitude, it is not surprising that job preservation is an important element in trade union thinking, but unfortunately it often extends to a reluctance to help or co-operate when retraining or redeployment is clearly inevitable. It seems almost as if unions have feared that even to mention redundancy is to invite it, and that to participate in retraining programmes means acquiescing in the loss of membership.

For whatever reason, Britain now has the least well trained and educated industrial work-force among the major industrial powers, and finds itself short of skilled workers in electrical/electronic engineering at a time when over three million workers are unemployed.

Housing and retraining are two of the areas on which policies aimed at the 'supply' side of the labour market should concentrate. 'Supply side' economics has earned a bad name from its focus on 'incentives', which involve sometimes tax cuts but also the removal of minimum wage legislation, security of employment, equal opportunity laws, reductions in unemployment or supplementary benefit and so on. There are plenty of people only too anxious to rejoin the ranks of the employed, who do not need greater incentives, positive or negative. What they might well need is much more generously financed opportunities for acquiring new skills, and help in relocation. These and other policy-oriented matters will be looked at in Part III.

In addition to difficulties in moving from one occupation or area to another, there is a third set of barriers to the movement of labour which remain formidable in the British economy. Such barriers add up to what may be termed 'social immobility'. These are the problems involved in moving from one *class* of job to another. It is obviously extremely difficult for a coal-miner to become a doctor, or to switch from shop work to stockbroking – however great the financial differential between the two types of occupation. It can be argued that the process will take place, but only slowly. The higher earnings of doctors and stockbrokers will induce a greater supply in the future; it may be the children of coal-miners and shop workers who make the upward move. However, all the evidence suggests that class continues to play an important role in the British educational system, and that in higher education the offspring of parents in the lower income groups are proportionately greatly outnumbered by those from a higher socio-economic background.

The result in practice is that the 'labour market' is fragmented into many non-competing groups. Thus, for example, the earnings of car workers and other manual workers in Oxford may well be related by market forces as outlined above, because the emergence of a differential between them *will* lead to a movement from the lower- to the higher-paid occupation. But there is practically zero mobility between those employed in the car industry and academic staff at Oxford University, and therefore no such relationship exists between their pay.

Between the non-competing groups therefore there is ample scope for relativities in pay to be set by social considerations – conventions about what is the 'appropriate' or 'fair' extent that one should earn more than another. Such 'non-economic' criteria are unlikely to command general acceptance, and it is not surprising that there is bitter controversy about the 'proper' rates of pay that should be received by teachers or nurses, or the multiple by which the remuneration of top managers should exceed the pay of those in their employ.

The basic disagreement between the various groups that comprise the work-force about how much each is worth in relation to the others is one of the major stumbling-blocks when governments try to introduce 'incomes policies' of one kind or another. Such policies, as we shall see later, have proved difficult to introduce and implement. One of the problems, at least, is that those affected do not regard the starting-point of the existing distribution of income as fair; they can therefore hardly be expected to support what they see as limitations on their ability to change it in the future.

ARE TRADE UNIONS TOO POWERFUL?

By the 1970s there was a growing view both in government circles and among the general public, including many trade unionists themselves, that trade unions *had* become too powerful, that their leaders were able to exert an unreasonable amount of influence and that some of their traditional rights and freedoms should therefore be curtailed.

With over 13 million members, a considerable income and (in many cases) ample financial reserves, with considerable political support and with a voice through membership of such organizations as the National Economic Development Council, the trade unions were in a strong position to affect the course of economic events. In the 1970s and earlier, it was primarily inflation for which they were held to blame – as the major

Table 13.1. The largest fifteen trade unions, 1980

	Membership (000)
Transport and General Workers	1,887
Amalgamated Engineering Workers	1,444
General and Municipal Workers	916
NALGO	782
National Union of Public Employees	699
Association of Scientific, Technical and Managerial Staffs	491
Shop, Distributive and Allied Workers	450
Electrical/Electronic/Telecommunications and Plumbing	439
National Union of Mineworkers	369[a]
Construction and Allied Trades and Technicians	312
National Union of Teachers	273
Confederation of Health Service Employees	216
Civil and Public Services Association	216
Union of Communication Workers	203
SOGAT '75 (printing trades)	200

Note: [a] Now (1987) considerably lower.

force in the process of 'cost push'. More recently, government has attempted to lay responsibility for unemployment at their door.

Yet it is easy to exaggerate the power of the unions. Their number has shrunk through mergers and amalgamations from 470 in 1975 to 373 in 1985, and the ten largest now have nearly 60% of the total membership. The very small size of most unions can be seen from the fact that the 25 largest have over 80% of the membership; there are 205 unions with under 1,000 members.

Moreover, they are often responsible for very different groups of workers. Some, on the whole the declining ones, represent workers in traditional industries and trades such as mining and engineering. Others look after the interests of government employees. Others, those with the most rapid growth in membership, represent the so-called 'white-collar' workers in the growing service sectors – see Table 13.1.

Admittedly, at the head of some but by no means all of the unions stands the Trades Union Congress. Considerable progress had been made over the years in the formulation of positive TUC policies on the leading economic issues of the day. But it remains a hortatory, advisory and sometimes conciliatory body with little control over the affairs of individual unions. TUC resolutions may sometimes be reflected in unions' policies, but if affiliated unions decide to pursue alternative lines of action there is little that the TUC can do to restrain them.

It is possible to argue therefore that the problem with trade unions is that they are too weak rather than too strong: that it is their inability to speak with a single voice, and the extent to which their sectional interests are competitive, that is the flaw in the British trade union structure compared, for example, to that which exists in West Germany or Scandinavia.

However, the Employment Acts of 1980 and 1982 and the Trades Union Act of 1984 have aimed at a limitation of union power. In particular the need to obtain a majority in a postal ballot of members before a strike can be called, and restrictions on picketing, make it difficult for a union such as the mineworkers to gain the help of the railwaymen or the power-station workers. The activities of wages councils in setting rates, particularly for low-paid workers, has also been weakened.

On top of that, the broad economic context within which unions operate has radically changed. Gone are the days when government was committed to underwrite full employment by creating the appropriate level of demand to ensure that sufficient jobs were available for the whole of the work-force. In the quite different circumstances of mass unemployment, the influence of organized labour in the economy has inevitably been reduced.

Union membership has fallen to around the 11 million mark, with a consequent weakening of unions' financial position. Soaring unemployment naturally made union members more chary of taking industrial action in support of pay claims, and government showed itself determined to resist pressures from key groups of workers as in the bitter and prolonged miners' strike of 1985.

It is interesting therefore to note that by the mid-1980s the earnings of those in work and outside the public sector were rising at some 7% to 8% per annum. With inflation by then reduced to just over 3% this represented a sharp increase in average real incomes for those in private sector employment. This suggests that while sharply rising unemployment may well have a dampening effect on worker expectations of pay increases, the normal pressure to improve their position is resumed as the rate of increase of unemployment slows down. And since it takes two to make a wage bargain, there has been little resistance from those firms which have survived recessionary policies to meeting union claims; indeed, they sometimes themselves bid up wages in an attempt to attract the work-force they require.

INCOMES POLICIES

Throughout the post-war period intermittent attempts have been made by governments to modify the process of free collective bargaining by the imposition of prices and incomes policies. These have been introduced on the assumption that inflation is caused by cost-push pressures, or at least that trade unions are a prime element in the inflationary mechanism.

The rationale of such a policy is very simple. Wages, salaries and profits, which are incomes to their recipients, are also the costs of production which firms must recover in their selling prices. Price stability therefore means that incomes should rise no faster than the consequent increase in costs can be absorbed by greater productivity.

But although every Chancellor since the war has emphasized the need to keep incomes in line with productivity, the history of attempts to introduce incomes policies has been a discouraging one.

It began in the years 1947–50 with a call for wage restraint which resulted in a moderation of demands from unions until, with prices shooting up after the 1949 devaluation, their loyalties to the Labour government became over-strained. It was a decade later, in 1961, that the next attempt was made with the introduction of a 'guiding light' of 2% to 2½% as the safe limit for future annual increases (later raised to 3% to 3½%) and with a National Incomes Commission to consider exceptional cases. The unions, however, refused to have anything to do with the NIC, which was replaced by the Labour government at the end of 1964 with a National Board for Prices and Incomes, adjudicating on variations from a set 'norm', and with the passing of the Prices and Incomes Act in June 1966. This provided for a *zero* norm for wage and price increases for the next six months, to be followed by a further six months of severe restraint. The standstill was to be compulsory. But by 1967 there was a return to an essentially voluntary system – 'norms', 'ceilings' and a 'range' required of both wage and dividend increases.

All were abandoned by an incoming Conservative government which, however, by 1972 had undertaken a volte-face with the imposition of a wages freeze, followed later by a '£1 + 4%' norm and the setting up of a Pay Board and Price Commission to examine individual cases. By November 1973 the policy had been given a statutory basis, with a third phase of 'threshold agreements' between firms and workers whereby 40p became automatically payable for each percentage point rise in the RPI over 7%.

In 1974, with Labour back in power, there was a pledge to continue and intensify a statutory control of prices, combined with a voluntary restraint of incomes, within the framework of a broad 'social contract' under which the government, for its part, was committed to a range of policies which would make the idea of income restraint more acceptable to the trade unions. The policy was maintained for four years, culminating in a particularly severe Stage IV in 1978. Whether because of government persistence or because of the other deflationary measures which accompanied the incomes policies, the rate of inflation fell steadily from its 1975 peak to 7% to 8% in mid-1978. However, breakdown came in the 1978–9 'winter of discontent'. Antagonism was particularly intense among the relatively low-paid workers in the public sector, and the resentment their industrial actions caused among the electorate undoubtedly helped in the defeat of the Labour government in the 1979 election. The incoming Conservative government of 1979, strongly averse to government interference with markets, promptly dismantled the whole thing; and the resulting explosion of wages sent the R P I back up towards 20% in early 1980.

This brief catalogue of events illustrates the extraordinary variety of institutions and criteria that have served as the basis for a succession of incomes policies. What they have had in common is that they were introduced in response to immediate crises and had an essentially transient flavour. So it is not surprising that their impact was generally short-lived in containing pressures which subsequently exploded as restraint was relaxed or broken down.

Prerequisites of an incomes policy

People have come to expect that year by year their money incomes will, or should, be increased – either to catch up with inflation, or to gain an improved standard of living, or to achieve a fairer position *vis-à-vis* others. The first condition of a successful incomes policy is to secure agreement about the *total* permissible rise in incomes. This first requirement therefore presupposes a broad consensus about the economic policies which are being pursued on growth and inflation. But beyond this is the much more difficult issue of how the total should be distributed, between the various groups of wage earners, and between wages and other incomes.

With regard to wages, one possibility is to link increases to productivity rises in different occupations. Thus if productivity rapidly improves in micro-electronics, then workers employed in that industry will receive correspondingly high pay rises; if productivity remains constant in textiles, then textile workers will get no wage increases. Such a system would amount to restoring to the wage mechanism something of its theoretical function as a system of signposts to resources, with higher wages in the expanding industries tending to attract labour from less productive uses.

But since productivity is mainly determined by the amount and quality of capital employed, why should workers in slow-growing industries be prepared to see others receive the full benefits of growth in the economy? A further practical difficulty is that of measuring productivity in many occupations, like teaching and medicine.

In any case, the wage system is not based on pure economic rationality; it also embodies notions of what constitutes a traditional and 'fair' system of differentials (which different groups still, of course, try to modify). Difficulties arise for an incomes policy if it is based on flat rate increases which erode time-hallowed differentials. Percentage rises across the board, on the other hand, raise questions about the equity of the initial starting-points.

On top of this, the sectionalism of British trade unionism presents a problem. Trade union officials are paid to look after their own; they are not watchdogs for the working class as a whole. Each union does the best it can by its members, even if this is at the expense of those in weaker unions or not organized at all.

Moreover, no incomes policy will ever succeed unless *all* incomes are equally subject to limitations, with similar scrutiny being exercised over price increases imposed by at least the major firms in the economy. But earned incomes other than wages are inherently more difficult to regulate because they tend to contain greater elements of fringe benefits, because they are sometimes self-determined and because of the greater job mobility of salaried and professional people. Restraint on 'unearned' income from dividends ignores the increase in future income and share prices which can accrue from profits being ploughed back. Limits imposed on profits as a whole discriminate against the more enterprising concerns and weaken the possibilities of fresh investment.

Simply to list such complications shows the difficulty of implementing and policing an incomes policy, which must have general acceptance if it is to have any hope of success. For governments espousing free market monetarism such a policy is in any event irrelevant. But agreement on income restraint (involving holding back *rises in real wages* rather than actual cuts) would be an essential quid pro quo of any alternative reflationary strategy.

In countries such as Sweden and Austria organized labour participates to a much greater extent in the central economic planning processes, and it is surely not just a coincidence that both have managed lower rates of inflation and lower levels of unemployment than the UK. Their economies have not been, and could not be, immune to world-wide recession and inflation, but they do seem to have coped better. So in its own way does West Germany, where the unions participate in the management of the industries in which their members work, and where the relationships between inflation, employment, wage rates and investment from profits can be understood and influenced during the decision-making process. But these countries which are sometimes held up as exemplars have very different institutions from ours, and a consensual framework about basic economic policy which for the time being at least no longer exists in the UK.

14

Money and Banking

Understanding the nature and role of money in the working of the economy is difficult and confusing not only for non-economists but for the experts and policy-makers as well. Above all, doubt and debate has recently centred on the part which money does or does not play in causing inflation. However, in this chapter we shall confine ourselves to examining the nuts and bolts of the system: the operation and relationships of the financial institutions responsible for creating and handling 'money' or similar assets, and the mechanics of monetary control by the authorities.

THE NATURE AND ROLE OF MONEY

The fundamental importance of money in a developed economy hardly requires emphasis. Economic development entails specialization, and the consequent interdependence of economic units necessitates the use of money – to lubricate the exchange of surpluses as the division of labour becomes more sophisticated, and to facilitate the process of saving and capital accumulation needed for the breakthrough to higher living standards.

Money acts as a link. It is a link between goods *now*, a common denominator in terms of which a vast variety of output can be expressed, and a medium through which exchange transactions can be effected. It is also a link between goods now and goods in the future, allowing comparisons to be made of the value of present consumption and consumption later, and extending the time horizon for economic decisions by the introduction of money contracts relating to lending and borrowing.

'Money is what money does.' In other words, anything qualifies as money which performs the functions of a medium of exchange and a store of value. But what do salt, silver, goats, cigarettes, gold and paper – which have all at times served these purposes – have in common which fits them for the role of money?

First, money must have certain convenience qualities: portability, durability, divisibility and so on (which suggests that goats may not have been very satisfactory!). It must also be relatively scarce, and this scarcity may be either natural, as in the case of precious metals, or artificial, as when the printing of banknotes is concentrated in the hands of state authorities. But what above all entitles something to be called money is that it is *acceptable* as money. It must be widely regarded as a means of settling debts and making future contracts. Money is what people think of as money. Unless they do regard it as money, then no legal sanctions can *make* it money; similarly, a form of money can operate perfectly well without being labelled legal tender.

We have so far implied that money must be something that can be touched or carried about or built up in piles. But money need not be tangible at all. It can take the form of transferable book debts. Suppose X owes Y the sum of £10. This debt may be recorded by both X and Y making entries in their accounts. If Y now incurs a debt of £10 with Z, and Z is prepared to accept as payment of the debt a claim on X, then these book entries are serving as money. The only problem is of establishing credit-worthiness; if Z does not know X and cannot quickly assess X's integrity and resources to meet the claim, Z will clearly not be happy about regarding such a claim as a genuine asset.

Money in practice

Notes and coin are the most obvious form of money in the United Kingdom. These are legal tender up to legislatively stipulated amounts and are generally accepted as a means of payment (a small limitation is the occasional difficulty in persuading an English trader to accept a Scottish banknote). The basis of this acceptability is the fact that they are issued nationally with uniform denominations and physical characteristics by an institution in which there is the highest public confidence, the Bank of England.

This concentration of notes and coinage in the hands of a single institution (Scottish banks continue to issue their own notes, but only to the extent that they are backed by Bank of England notes) is a relatively recent phenomenon. The process of monopolization which began with the Bank Charter Act of 1844, replacing a system of different paper money of only limited regional acceptability, was not completed until some seventy years later.

Parallel with this concentration has been the establishment of a purely paper currency unbacked by precious metals or any similar commodity of alternative value. The 1844 Act limited the quantity of currency which the Bank of England could issue to the value of its stock of gold – into which banknotes would be freely transferable. Paper money was thus used merely as a more convenient method of effecting transactions than the specie which it represented. But the Act also allowed the Bank to issue £14 million of notes unbacked by gold, the so-called 'fiduciary issue'. After this initial breach, the fiduciary element was consistently increased until the break from gold was completed in 1939 with the transfer of the Bank's gold holdings to the Exchange Equalization Account, for use only in international payments.

The 'I promise to pay the bearer on demand the sum of . . .' which, until very recently, used to be printed on Bank of England notes, had therefore no significance whatever. There were surely not many optimists who thought that taking notes to the Bank and demanding payment would have yielded anything more than an equivalent amount of identical currency; but a surprising number of people still seem to cherish the belief that the currency is in some way ultimately backed by gold. The fact is, however, that the Bank of England and its nominal master, the Treasury, are legally empowered to issue any amount of currency they see fit, with the limitation only of *post hoc* approval by Parliament, which is always forthcoming. The acceptability of a paper currency of no intrinsic value ultimately rests on confidence in the monetary authorities' ability to ensure that the system functions smoothly and soundly.

A large proportion of the transactions taking place in the economy do not involve any use of currency at all. Payment by cheque, first popularized in the nineteenth century, is now common practice. Are cheques therefore part of the money supply? They are not. Cheques do not have general acceptability because an individual with plenty of cheques may lack the means to honour them. Cheques are only instruments for drawing money on bank (and, increasingly, building society) accounts.

But since bank accounts are created by customers going to the banks and depositing notes and coin, receiving in exchange IOUs from the bank, will it not be double counting if we include *both* bank deposits and notes and coin in the total money supply? That it would be a great deal more than mere double counting is clear when the amounts are compared. In December 1985, sterling accounts held with banks in the UK were more than £110,000 million. The amount of paper and metal money in existence was very much less: under £13,000 million. Moreover, the bulk of this was already in the hands of the public. Therefore bank deposits not only vastly exceed the notes and coin which the banks hold against them; they also dwarf the *total* currency in circulation. The statistics show that banknotes as well as coin have become the small change of the system and that bank *deposits* form far and away the most important element in the money supply.

For the moment we can therefore regard the UK money supply as consisting mainly of bank deposits only fractionally backed by currency, and a currency which is itself 'backed' by nothing at all. This is a sobering thought for those who still cling to the superstition that the value of a money depends on its connections with precious metals, but perhaps they may take some reassurance from the following account of how this state of affairs has come about.

HOW MONEY IS CREATED

The discrepancy between total bank deposits and the amount of currency suggests that banking business is being conducted on rather reprehensible lines. What would happen if all bank depositors suddenly took it into their heads to go along to their banks and demand encashment of their deposits in notes and coins? Before we go on to discuss the British banking system in particular, it may be helpful to see in general, by use of a simple model, how bank deposits can come to exceed cash reserves.

Let us suppose that the public initially holds wealth in two forms, currency and government bonds.

Stage I

Public
£500 *currency*
£2,000 *bonds*

If people now feel that keeping such large amounts of currency or cash is both unprofitable and unsafe, they may decide to keep no more than £400 under the bed or up the chimney, and to deposit £100 with a bank for safe keeping. A bank, like any other enterprise, can draw up a balance sheet of matching assets and liabilities. Its assets are now the £100 of currency, and its corresponding liability is £100 of bank deposits (which to depositors are assets withdrawable at any time).

Stage II

Bank		Public
Assets	Liabilities	
£100 currency	£100 deposits	£400 currency
		£2,000 bonds
		£100 deposits

Nothing very significant has happened by Stage II. The public has merely exchanged £100 cash for £100 bank deposits (which it regards as being as good as currency), and bank deposits are still backed 100% by currency.

However, this is by no means the end of the story. Through experience, the banker realizes that the cash deposited by and large remains idle. Although deposits are constantly being withdrawn, they are replenished by fresh deposits from those firms and individuals who receive payments as a result of the original withdrawals. Inflows roughly match outflows, and the bank discovers that only a small proportion of its cash reserves are, in fact, ever required to meet any excess of withdrawals over deposits. It may find, for example, that 10% of its cash holdings are all that it needs to keep in its till to meet day-to-day demands, and that the remaining 90% continuously lies idle in the bank vaults.

By its next move, there is an evolution from mere 'cloakroom banking' as the bank uses the idle £90 to buy assets which it thinks will be easily resaleable should there ever be a 'run on the bank' by depositors. If it buys £90 of government bonds (from the public), then Stage III will look like this:

Stage III

Bank		Public
Assets	Liabilities	
£10 currency	£100 deposits	£490 currency
£90 bonds		£1,910 bonds
		£100 deposits

Bank deposits still stand at £100, but only 10% are now backed by cash reserves, government bonds being held against the remainder. But Stage III is not likely to be a position of equilibrium. We assumed to begin with that the bank began operations because the public did not like holding more than £400 in cash. If this feeling persists, then the public, which now finds its cash holdings inflated by the sale of bonds, will redeposit £90 with the bank.

The bank, which in Stage III released its unused cash by buying
bonds, finds in Stage IV that the public has redeposited the excess of
£90 cash which it does not wish to hold.

Stage IV

Bank		Public
Assets	Liabilities	
£100 currency	£190 deposits	£400 currency
£90 bonds		£1,910 bonds
		£190 deposits

The bank is thus in a similar position to before. It now has to deal with
day-to-day business on a larger volume of deposits, but if we continue to
assume that a 10% cash reserve figure is sufficient, the £19 will be all
that is needed in the till, and £81 (£100 less £19) will still be lying idle.
Once again, as a profit-maker, the bank buys bonds of this value.

Stage V

Bank		Public
Assets	Liabilities	
£19 currency	£190 deposits	£481 currency
£171 bonds		£1,829 bonds
		£190 deposits

And once again the public finds that it has excess cash holdings, which
it duly redeposits with the banks (£81).

Stage VI

Bank		Public
Assets	Liabilities	
£100 currency	£271 deposits	£400 currency
£171 bonds		£1,829 bonds
		£271 deposits

The bank has £100 currency again! Since only £27.1 is needed to service
deposits now totalling £271, it still has £72.9 surplus cash available for
further buying of bonds.

And so it goes on. We can omit further stages, not just because the
arithmetic is getting complicated, but because, on the assumptions made,
the final outcome becomes predictable. Although the bank continues to
buy bonds with its surplus cash and the public continues to redeposit the
cash proceeds with the bank, at each stage the bank finds it needs to
retain a larger absolute amount of cash (although the same proportion) as
a reserve against withdrawals.

The final stage will be reached when the whole of the bank's cash holding is required for servicing deposits. And since the public is insisting that £100 cash be held with the bank, the pyramid of deposits which can ultimately be supported on this cash base must be ten times £100, i.e. £1,000. The balance sheet of the bank and the public when the process has fully worked itself out will, therefore, look like this:

Final stage

Bank		Public
Assets	Liabilities	
£100 currency	£1,000 deposits	£400 currency
£900 bonds		£1,100 bonds
		£1,000 deposits

We should stress that the activities of the bank have led to no increase in the *wealth* of the community. The public still owns only £2,500 assets – which is what it started with – but it now holds it in a different form. The bank certainly has assets of £1,000 which it did not have at the outset, but it has liabilities of just the same amount. All that has happened is that the amount of *liquidity* in the economy has increased.

'Liquidity' is the degree to which an asset gives the holder immediate command over resources, goods or services. Since money can be used to buy any of these things directly, it is by definition perfectly liquid. Bonds are less liquid because, although they are easily marketable (saleable for cash), the price which they will fetch is uncertain.

In the process of credit creation, a bank makes the wealth held by the public more liquid by accepting claims against itself in exchange for less liquid bonds. However, although the bank has not added to total wealth in the process, it has most definitely created more *money* by its operations. The exchange of bank deposits for bonds is just as much the creation of money as the issue of banknotes by a central authority.

There are limits to the extent to which banks can create money in this way, corresponding to the assumptions made in the model. We first assumed that the public demand for cash balances remained constant at £400. If people felt inclined to hold more cash as their bank deposits increased and bond holdings fell, the amount redeposited with the bank and the consequent credit multiplier would be correspondingly reduced. (Conversely, if the bank is able to attract more initial cash, it increases its ability to create further deposits.) Another 'leakage' might occur if the sellers of bonds or recipients of the proceeds were not clients of the bank and did not, therefore, redeposit the currency which came into their hands. If, for example, such proceeds were used to finance payments to the government sector, this would – unless the taxes were paid out in equivalent benefits – amount to a destruction of money.

The really crucial assumption underlying the process of deposit creation is, however, the fact that the bank is able to operate safely on a fractional reserve basis. If there was doubt or suspicion in customers' minds about the security of their deposits and the bank's ability to encash those deposits on demand, then the possibility of the public testing the bank's soundness by frequent 'runs' would entail the bank having to maintain a high reserve–deposit ratio to prove itself. The fact that there is a high degree of public confidence in the banks' ability to meet their obligation is what makes quite tiny cash ratios possible in practice.

The essence of banking is thus to conceal or minimize the difference between currency and bank deposits. So long as the public has sufficient trust in bank soundness, it will not bother to distinguish between cash and deposits. Banking turns out to be a highly sophisticated confidence trick.

PROBLEMS OF DEFINING MONEY

The 'quantity of money' sounds a definite enough concept, and we have so far treated it as comprising banknotes, coin and bank deposits. However, limiting the definition to just these assets is not as straightforward as it seems.

On the one hand, it could be argued that if money is money because it performs the twin functions of a medium of exchange and a store of value, then not all bank deposits should be included. A medium of exchange gives *immediate* command over resources; time deposits, requiring a period of pre-withdrawal notice, do not strictly satisfy this criterion. If, on the other hand, this is regarded as quibbling and time deposits are included, then, for the same reason, so also should be a number of other assets such as Post Office savings accounts and deposits with finance houses and building societies, which can similarly be turned into cash after a short period of notice. The case for their inclusion is strengthened by the fact that many such deposits are withdrawable on demand up to stipulated amounts.

There are thus difficulties in drawing a rigid distinction between two groups of assets: money and non-money. If we define money in terms of certain qualities which it should possess and which enable it to perform monetary functions, we have to admit that 'moneyness' or 'liquidity' is

Table 14.1. 'Narrow' money, 1985

	(£ billion)
Notes and coin in circulation with the public	12.9
Banks' till money	1.6
Bankers' balances with the Bank of England	0.2
Mo	14.5

Table 14.2. Notes and coin in circulation, 1985

	(£ million)
end January	12,006
end February	11,976 low
end March	12,036
end April	12,188
end May	12,106
end June	12,111
end July	12,346 high
end August	12,310
end September	12,097
end October	12,005 low
end November	12,041
end December	12,612 high

an attribute which may be found in a much wider variety of assets than banknotes, coin and bank deposits.

Official definitions

Confusion about just what constitutes the 'money supply' is reflected in the fact that the Bank of England publishes different series of statistics based on alternative definitions.

'M' is the symbol generally used to denote the money supply, and the narrowest measure of money is that which equates it with cash – notes and coin. This is not so simple-minded a definition as might be thought at first, because if we add the cash in the banks' tills, and their balances with the Bank of England, we get a 'base' which serves as one of the important limits to the banking system's ability to expand its lending, in the way we described earlier. This definition of money is known as Mo, sometimes referred to as 'narrow' money – see Table 14.1.

Table 14.3. Money supply M1, 1985

	(£ billion)
Notes and coin in circulation with the public	12.9
Private sector non-interest-bearing sight deposits	22.4
Private sector interest-bearing sight deposits	25.2
M1	60.6

Table 14.4. Money supply £M3, 1985

	(£ billion)
Money as defined in M1	60.6
Private sector time bank deposits, original maturity up to two years	59.8
Private sector holding of certificates of deposit	3.1
Private sector time bank deposits, original maturity over two years	1.9
£M3	125.4

The amount of notes and coin in circulation varies from month to month, because the Bank of England responds to demand, increasing the quantity to cope with the seasonal demand at Christmas and in the holiday season, and reducing it once the January sales are over – see Table 14.2.

Over the years the quantity of notes and coin in circulation has grown from £9,122 million in 1978 to the present level of £12,612 million: a rise of 38% in seven years, not matching the fall in purchasing power. This is yet another reflection of the fact that notes and coin are just 'small change' and that most payments are made in other ways.

The commonest of these other ways is by using a cheque drawn on a current account or 'sight' account at a bank. This standard definition of money, which we have been using so far, is therefore 'notes and coin plus current or sight accounts at banks'. (The latter are known as 'demand deposits' in the United States.) Officially, this is the M1 definition, as set out in Table 14.3.

As we have just pointed out, the dividing line between sight deposits and time deposits is not clear cut, because at the worst it takes a few days to convert one into the other, and usually much less. If therefore the definition of money is broadened to include time deposits, the 'quantity of money' increases considerably – see Table 14.4.

Table 14.5. Private sector liquidity, 1981–5 (£ million)

		1981	1982	1983	1984	1985
'Money'		83,248	90,667	100,736	110,814	125,592
of which:	Notes and coin	10,767	11,221	11,866	12,147	12,714
	Sight deposits	25,766	29,436	33,324	40,017	48,892
	Time deposits	44,987	48,221	53,550	56,697	61,495
	CDs	1,728	1,789	1,996	1,953	2,491
Other money market instruments (net)		3,942	2,840	3,167	3,418	3,016
Shares and deposits with building societies		47,078	51,054	60,063	74,574	88,864
National Savings Bank[a]		4,562	5,444	6,156	6,693	7,218
National Savings		1,811	1,765	1,774	1,796	1,813
(less savings institutions holdings)		(3,949)	(4,860)	(5,418)	(6,013)	(8,841)
Certificates of tax deposit (net)		997	2,066	2,030	2,337	2,767
PSL2 (seasonally adjusted)		137,385	149,237	168,467	193,685	220,472

Note: [a] TSB deposits in 1981, included from 1981 in 'time deposits'.

All the figures above are in sterling, so that strictly speaking this is 'sterling M3', usually written £M3. If we add private sector bank accounts in foreign currencies, which in December 1985 totalled the equivalent of £19.8 billion, we get plain M3. Since it is now quite easy to switch into and out of foreign currencies, it is as well to keep an eye on both measures.

What has happened to M2? It is not much used, but was originally devised as a measure of the potential purchasing power of consumers. It includes what are known as 'retail' interest-bearing deposits: savings accounts in banks, building societies, National Savings Bank and so on. M2 consists of banknotes and coin, non-interest-bearing sight deposits and these 'retail' deposits – exactly the kind of financial resources which a typical consumer might possess. As we have seen, building society deposits are very large, so M2 was £146.1 billion in December 1985.

The idea of a spectrum of assets of decreasing degrees of liquidity is well illustrated by another concept, that of 'private sector liquidity' or PSL2. Table 14.5 shows how holdings of various financial assets have changed over the past few years.

In percentage terms 'money', defined as £M3, has fallen from some 61% to 57%, while building society deposits have increased from just over 34% to about 40%. Within the category of money, as defined in

this table, notes and coin have declined in importance from 13% of
'money' to 10%, while sight deposits have increased from 31% to 39%.
The behaviour of the interest-earning assets is interesting. Time deposits
(part of £M3) plus building society deposits (not part of £M3) together
totalled 67% of PSL2 in 1981 and 68% in 1985, with very little variation
in between. But the share of building society deposits rose from just over
half of this (51.2%) to 59.1%. This shift into an asset which earned high
interest but was becoming steadily more liquid as building societies
became more like banks would have slowed down the growth in the
money supply over this period, as measured by £M3, even though
'liquidity' was growing rapidly. It illustrates the perils of relying on any
one definition of 'money'.

There are thus a variety of definitions of the 'money supply' or 'money
stock' or 'quantity of money' (all of which terms mean the same thing).
There is no *right* definition, because there is no clear dividing line
between money and other assets. Choosing between the alternatives measured by the authorities might therefore seem a peculiarly arbitrary or
academic question. But when governments elevate 'control over the
money supply' to the status of the key regulator of economy, as they did
in the early 1980s, then the matter is far from academic. In such circumstances, the question of *which* money supply is to be controlled and by
what means assumes considerable importance, as we shall see in Chapter
18.

BRITISH BANKING

Like much of British industry, British banking now has an oligopolistic
structure as a result of integration during the last hundred years. Competition is between the few. Ordinary 'high street' business is almost entirely
in the hands of the 'big four' banks: Barclays, the Midland, Lloyds and
National Westminster in England and Wales. The Bank of Scotland,
Clydesdale and the Royal Bank of Scotland predominate north of the
border.

These are all examples of what are now called 'retail banks' with a
wide network of branches and dealing with individual and business
customers often with relatively small accounts. They are distinguished
from 'wholesale' banks whose business is confined to very large deposits
in excess of £1 million (although the retail banks also deal at this end of
the market too).

Table 14.6. Assets and liabilities of UK retail banks (£ billion, rounded, June 1986)

Assets		Liabilities	
Sterling:		1	Notes issued by Scottish and Irish banks
Notes and coin	2		
Balances with Bank of England	0.5		*Sterling deposits by:*
	—	12	UK monetary sector
Subtotal 2.7, 2.2% of £ deposits	2.7	4	UK public sector
Market loans:		89	UK private sector
With discount market	4	11	Overseas depositors
Other UK monetary sector	19	8	Certificates of deposit, etc.
UK monetary sector CDs	4	—	
UK local authorities	2	123	Sterling deposits, of which sight deposits 55
Overseas loans	2		
	—		
Subtotal 30, 24% of £ assets	30		*Deposits in other currencies by:*
Bills	4	7	UK monetary sector
Advances to:		5	Other UK depositors
UK public sector	—	30	Overseas depositors
UK private sector	79	6	Certificates of deposit, etc.
Overseas	4	—	
	—	47	Other currency deposits
Subtotal 84, 66% of £ assets	84	31	Items in transit, etc.
Investments in:			
British government securities	6	202	Total liabilities
Other	3		
	—		('Eligible liabilities' totalled
Subtotal 9, 7% of £ assets	9		£93.6 billion)
Sterling assets £130 billion			
Other currencies:			
UK monetary sector	12		
UK private sector	4		
Overseas	33		
Investments	5		
Subtotal assets in other currencies £56 billion	56		
Miscellaneous assets, sterling and other currencies, etc.	20		
Total assets	202		

The banks have a dual responsibility. As private, commercial concerns, with their capital subscribed by stockholders and shareholders, they are expected to make profits. On the other hand, they have a responsibility to their customers to safeguard their deposits. In the long run these responsibilities can hardly conflict, but it is perhaps worth stressing that the commercial banks are part of the private sector. Any concern with the national interest is therefore incidental. 'We are bankers, not statesmen,' said the chairman of one of the banks before a government committee set up to examine how the monetary system worked, with the clear implication that the banks would consider it fair game to find and exploit any loopholes in government restrictions which might conflict with their profit-making activities.

The retail banks broadly function along the lines described in our model by creating deposits hugely in excess of the currency which they hold. Bankers have sometimes been at pains to dispute this, claiming that they do not create money but simply lend what has been deposited with them. The first part of the statement is clearly untrue as the figures show. But that they re-lend only what has been deposited with them does appear to be the case from the point of view of a single banker.

If, for example, Lloyds received an additional cash inflow of £10 million, it would certainly not immediately create £100 million of fresh deposits (continuing to assume a 10% cash ratio). It would, however, feel able to lend some £9 million, and that, as far as it was concerned, would be that. But when the loans were used to make payments, the recipients would probably also be depositors at some bank or other, and the £9 million would mostly flow back into the banking system. To the extent that some returned to Lloyds, it would be indistinguishable from any other deposit of cash and would be used for yet further creation of deposits. Thus any fresh deposit of cash with a bank would be shunted round time after time until deposits had increased to the point where all was needed by the banks as part of their reserves. The banking system as a whole would have created money; any *one* bank would merely have re-lent what was originally deposited with it.

The process of deposit creation and the consequent balance sheet of a retail bank is enormously more complicated than that illustrated in the model, as can be seen from the principal assets and liabilities of the retail banks in 1986 shown in Table 14.6. Both sides of the balance sheet are far more complex than they once were because of the extent to which the banks now involve themselves in international business.

The deposit liabilities take a number of forms. First there are current accounts which customers hold for settling their normal transactions. Because they are immediately withdrawable (and therefore called 'sight deposits' in Table 14.6), they earn no return (although sometimes interest is offered on accounts kept above a certain level). Generally, interest is payable only when customers are prepared to lodge funds with the banks for minimum periods, the interest being higher the longer the time that the depositor is prepared to forgo liquidity. Thus there are deposit accounts withdrawable at short notice, savings deposits earning rather more and 'negotiable certificates of deposit'. CDs, as the last have become known, consist of large sums mostly deposited by companies for fixed periods between three months and two years. As such, they earn much higher rates than the other types of deposit. These days, about a third of deposits are held in current accounts.

The item 'eligible liabilities' is important. It is not an *additional* form of liability, but that part of the total (in sterling) designated as such by the Bank of England for the purpose of determining what amounts each retail bank must hold as 'bankers' deposits' with the Bank itself. These, together with notes and coin held in the banks' own tills, constitute the first of its assets – equivalent to the 'cash ratio' referred to in our model. Before the war the banks in fact did observe a cash ratio of 10%. In the post-war period it has sharply fallen, and today it will be seen that cash comprises only a tiny proportion of the total assets.

Beyond that, what light does the assets side of the balance sheet throw on the 'backing' there is for deposit liabilities? To begin with there are 'market loans' and 'bills', broadly what used to be termed 'money at call and short notice'.

The loans are very short-term, repayable on demand or in a matter of days, and can therefore be used to meet any cash shortage which the banks might face. Mainly they are to the discount houses or to other elements of the banking system itself.

'Bills' need a little more explanation. A commercial bill of exchange is an instrument of short-term credit, generally for three months. If the seller is agreeable, the financing of a transaction can be postponed by the creditor 'drawing' a bill of exchange on the debtor, who 'accepts' the bill by signing it (the amount of the debt including an interest payment for the loan). If the creditor wants cash now rather than in three months' time, it can be taken to a specialist institution known as a 'discount house', which discounts the bill by paying its cash value less an interest charge for holding the bill to maturity (when it will receive payment from the original debtor whose name was on the bill).

The commercial bill of exchange was originally popular in financing international trade transactions around the turn of the century and then declined in importance with the development of bank overdrafts. This was accompanied, however, by an increasing volume of business in Treasury bills issued by the British government to raise short-term funds. Subsequently, the trend has been reversed, with 'bank bills' assuming more importance and the Treasury bill issue being reduced in size.

Many of the people who own bills will wish to turn them into cash, while other people who have a temporary surplus of cash will wish to invest in an interest-earning asset which can quickly be turned back into cash when the need arises. The sellers of bills will also include those who wish to borrow money on a short-term basis, and the most important of such borrowers is the government, which always has the problem of matching the outflow of payments and the inflow of taxes.

Buyers and sellers meet in the discount market in the City, where a market is made by the discount houses. These specialist companies carry a portfolio of bills which they are ready to sell, and will always buy bills if the price is attractive. They thus ensure that there is always an active and sensitive market in operation.

An excess of money, i.e. an excess of would-be buyers of bills, will tend to drive up their price, and this has the effect of lowering the rate of interest which holders of bills would earn. Conversely a shortage of money, i.e. a shortage of would-be buyers of bills, will tend to lower the price of bills and raise the corresponding rate of interest which they yield.

The Bank of England, as a major issuer of Treasury bills and a supplier of cash whenever necessary, can through its own actions affect the discount market and regulate the level of interest rates. Indirectly, through the banking system, it can regulate the availability of credit and its cost. The mechanism is subtle and complicated further by the esoteric way in which the financial institutions of the City have developed. We can, however, think of the discount market as a device through which the Bank of England, as the monetary authority, pumps money into the system or drains it out – so regulating its price, the rate of interest.

Of the remaining assets, 'investments' comprise holdings of government stocks, and 'advances' provide the main source of the banks' income. The financing of trade, industry and professional and personal expenditure is the most lucrative part of retail banks' business and requires the greatest acumen and judgement.

British banks have a long-standing preference for financing working capital rather than fixed capital expenditure. Their ideal remains the self-liquidating 'seed-time to harvest' type of lending: for the payment of running costs or purchases of raw materials rather than for investment in machinery and plant. Although they have become more interested in the provision of long-term credit, the picture is very different from the traditional industrial banking of, for example, the USA and West Germany, where the banks have always been deeply involved in the affairs of the particular firms to which they have lent.

The distribution of bank assets among the various alternatives is the result of conflicting pulls. From their customers' point of view, banks must aim at maximum *liquidity*: keeping assets in a form which enables them to meet all possible withdrawals by depositors. But *profitability* considerations imply a concentration on less liquid assets. Generally, the more liquid an asset, the less profitable it is for the banks. Thus, cash is perfectly liquid, short-term loans almost so, and bills discounted will be due to mature very shortly; none of them usually yields a high rate of return. The 'earning assets', on the other hand, are both more profitable and relatively illiquid. Investments are perfectly marketable – the Stock Exchange ensures that they can always be sold – but perhaps only at prices which involve a capital loss. For advances, on the other hand, marketability exists only if the bank has insisted on collateral security which can be disposed of if necessary. However, since many advances are unsecured, they will be self-liquidating only if the banker has correctly judged the credit-worthiness of the borrower. Distribution of bank resources is therefore a compromise between the competing ends of profitability and liquidity.

Other banks and financial intermediaries

We have so far been concentrating on the 'retail banks'. But throughout the post-war period there has been spectacular growth in the variety and range of banking institutions in the UK and a great internationalization of the banking business.

Much of this other banking is of a 'wholesale' nature; that is, it deals with deposits and loans of large sums, generally for fixed terms and frequently in foreign currencies. Key members of the system are foreign banks with London offices. Also engaged in this business are the British merchant banks or 'acceptance houses' (so-called because their original business was to establish the credit-worthiness of international traders and, by being prepared to put their name on a commercial bill of exchange, to reduce the rate at which it could be discounted), British overseas banks and subsidiaries of British deposit banks.

As well as banks, there exist a large number of other financial intermediaries like pension funds, insurance companies, investment and unit trusts – mainly collecting small savings and re-lending them in large sums to business and government. We shall return to them when discussing the capital market in Chapter 15.

Building societies

Building societies may be briefly dealt with here since by and large they both borrow and lend in relatively small amounts, at least compared with these other financial institutions. And there is an increasing overlap between the business done by them and the retail banks.

For the individual family, the purchase of a home is the largest it is ever likely to make. The cost of a house is so large in relation to most people's annual income that if they had to save the purchase price they would have reached the end of their working life before they had saved enough. So, as with most large purchases, they borrow the purchase price and repay the debt over a period of time. In the case of home purchase, the loan is secured by the house or flat itself and is called a mortgage. Building societies, as their name implies, originally helped their members to build their own houses, but are now financial institutions which accept deposits and lend the resulting funds to home buyers. Because home ownership has been seen as socially desirable, various tax advantages are available for borrowers and lenders, so that deposits with building societies offer an attractive yield, and in recent years a growing range of other financial services as well.

Mergers and take-overs have been frequent in this sector of finance as in others, and now a few very large societies dominate the scene. At the moment their legal status distinguishes them from other 'deposit takers', particularly the banks, but it seems likely that here, as elsewhere, the distinction will disappear, and lending for home purchase will become just one of the range of services offered by a high-street financial equivalent of a supermarket. The big four banks, for example, are very active in this field. At the same time, building societies are constantly extending the range of their operations to compete with banks in areas like money transmission (through payment of depositor's bills, the issuing of cheque-books and the provision of cash points).

The great bulk of the assets of building societies consist of mortgages, although they must hold liquid assets as well to cover depositors' with-

Table 14.7. Building societies, 1981–5 (£ million)

	Inflow of funds (total)	Liabilities (shares, deposits, etc.)	Assets	
			Mortgages	Other
1981	7,924	62,147	49,039	11,833
1982	11,097	74,483	57,186	15,894
1983	12,797	87,190	68,114	17,595
1984	16,283	103,311	82,868	18,973
1985	17,648	121,239	97,397	23,842

drawals. The size of the building societies can be judged from Table 14.7. It is worth keeping in mind that the corresponding figure for the total liabilities/assets of the UK banking system was about £750,000 million at the end of 1985, of which £243,200 million was in sterling. Total sterling deposits were £208,700 million.

The Bank of England

In its youth, the Bank of England was just a particularly large and rather privileged commercial bank competing vigorously for deposits. It now stands aloof at the apex of the banking system and confines itself, apart from an insignificant residue of private business, to handling the accounts of a few highly important customers.

First, it is the government's banker. It looks after the Exchequer accounts, and has the further responsibility of seeing that its client is always in a position to meet its commitments. If government spending exceeds income from taxation, the shortfall must be made good by borrowing. Direct loans from the Bank itself are traditionally limited to overnight Ways and Means advances to cover temporary miscalculations; but it is the job of the Bank of England to organize the government's major borrowing operations, through the issue of bills or bonds.

The retail banks, as we have already seen, each keep part of their cash reserves in the form of a deposit with the Bank of England, such accounts being convenient for settling payments between themselves or between the private and public sectors of the economy. However, the Bank does not act as a bankers' banker to the extent of giving them overdrafts; generally, as a result of a historical reluctance to seem dependent on a fellow banker, British banks have dealt with cash shortages through the agency of the discount market.

Thus, if the banks face a cash shortage, they simply withdraw some of the short-term loans that they make to the 'money market', leaving the discount houses in some embarrassment. But they can always in such an event go to the Bank of England and know that they will be accommodated – at a price.

The Bank of England's underpinning of the banking system, which is what this amounts to, evolved only very gradually during the nineteenth century. After a series of painful and disruptive 'confidence crises' in the then fragmented banking system, the Bank came to see that it could not just stand by and watch the structure collapse. Its obligation instead to 'lend without stint in times of crisis', articulated by Walter Bagehot in the 1870s, was a crucial element in the evolution of low cash ratios. In acting as 'lender in the last resort', the Bank of England underwrites the liquidity of the whole system and eliminates the possibility of cumulative runs on the banks arising from loss of confidence by depositors.

The basic function of a central bank is, however, to implement the monetary policy of the government, a responsibility assumed by the Bank of England long before its position was formalized by nationalization in 1946. The enabling Act gives the Bank and Treasury combined almost complete coercive authority over the banking system. In practice the Bank has preferred to rely on more traditional technical and persuasive pressures.

The post-war history of monetary policy is tortuously complex and best left to specialist students of the subject. Suffice it to say that both the objectives and the mechanics of monetary policy have been subject to a multiplicity of changes over these years. What they have in common are the technical complexities that have always been encountered, and a relative lack of success in achieving the desired results.

Very broadly indeed, three types of monetary policy may be distinguished:

(1) Attempts at direct control over the quantity and/or quality of bank advances and other types of credit in order to encourage certain types of spending (like investment) and discourage others.

(2) Indirect control over the total and ingredients of spending by manipulation of interest rates.

(3) More recently, regulation of the money supply in the belief that this was the key technique for reducing the rate of inflation in the economy.

The first two of these may be termed 'Keynesian' in their approach. The third is associated with 'monetarism'. We shall return to some of the major issues involved in the debate between the two schools of economic thinking and their policy implications in Part III.

15

LLLLLLLLLLLLLLLLLL

The Capital Market

From the account we gave in Part I, it can be seen that of the £282.5 billion United Kingdom disposable income, £240 billion went to the personal sector, which spent £213 billion on consumption and saved £27 billion.

Money is not only the unit in which these flows can be measured; it is the prerequisite for them to take place at all. Money is the 'medium of exchange', and there has to be enough of it available to both buyers and sellers if the economy is going to continue to function. Unfortunately, as we all know from experience, the flows of money into and out of our purses and wallets do not coincide, either in their timing or their quantity. We need ways of keeping any temporary surplus safely and profitably, of supplementing our supplies when they are temporarily inadequate and of making long-run accumulations of funds.

As we have seen, it is the banks which primarily meet the first of these needs. Building societies too compete for short-term deposits of funds and are, of course, the main source of finance for home purchase, a major capital asset in the case of many families.

THE CITY

Apart from the need to keep balances of cash and to undertake home purchase, many households try to provide for the future. Thus most of us recognize that the period during which we are able to earn an income is limited; we shall need an income when we retire. We may also wish to ensure security for our families in case we die or become incapacitated. We may wish to purchase assets other than homes which are so large in relation to our income that 'saving up' would seem to be impossible. Financial institutions have evolved which allow us, even encourage us, to do all these things.

These institutions – like pension funds, insurance companies and unit trusts – enable the accumulation of small savings to be channelled towards those who require long-term funds, principally government and enterprises. The meeting-place of those providing such funds and those demanding them is the so-called 'capital market' situated in the City.

The square mile of London around St Paul's Cathedral formed the original city, resting on its Roman and Norman foundations and rebuilt after the Great Fire of 1666 under the influence of Wren. During the Victorian and Edwardian period of British supremacy it became the trading and financial centre of the world. Such was the dominance of Britain in world trade, both as a market, as a source of manufactures and as a carrier, that even trade between third countries was routed through London-based markets, financed and insured by London institutions and priced and paid for in sterling.

In these very exceptional circumstances the City developed a very wide range of financial and business skills, and an equally wide range of specialized financial professions and institutions. It was very much a close-knit brotherhood, guarding its exclusiveness but admitting money and talent from outside as long as it played the game under the same rules. Many of the most famous City names reflect such infusions from Europe (Rothschild, Warburg, Kleinwort), from the United States (Morgan, Merrill Lynch) and from the Nonconformist, often Quaker, banking families of the English provinces and Scotland. But others can be traced back to the City merchants of Tudor or Stuart times.

At the centre of the City are the Bank of England and the Stock Exchange. We have already had something to say about the former and have seen how one of its jobs, in concert with the Treasury, is to regulate the flow of government securities – the 'IOUs' which the government issues against the money it borrows. These, together with the securities issued by private institutions, are the assets which are traded on the Stock Exchange.

THE STOCK EXCHANGE

The Stock Exchange has a dual function. First, it is where government, firms and other institutions go to raise fresh funds through new 'issues' of securities. And it is also a 'secondary' market in that it provides a buying and selling place for second-hand securities.

'Security' is a general label for the great variety of stocks and shares which are now available and whose prices are listed in the daily columns of the financial press. Shares represent a title to ownership in a firm. Stocks, on the other hand, are loans, to government or companies, which earn the lender a fixed-interest return.

Gilt-edged

The most important stocks are found in the gilt-edged market of which the issues of the British government comprise the chief element. These head any list of Stock Exchange securities under the title 'British funds'. For example, one will find there 'Treasury 14% 96' or 'Exchequer 12% 99–02'. The names themselves are virtually meaningless; what matters are the numbers attached to them.

Government stocks are issued in £100 units, and the figures 14%, 12% and so on refer to the interest payable and are based on the nominal value of the stock. Thus someone buying one £100 unit of 'Treasury 14%' will receive £14 interest per annum, and this will be so whether the price paid for the stock in the market was £50, its nominal value of £100 or a great deal more.

Some of the stocks in the British funds list have two dates attached, some one date and others none at all. These dates indicate the period of the loan and show when the stock will mature and the loan be redeemed or repaid. Most stocks are double-dated, e.g. '99–02', and this means that the government has the option of repaying the loan at any time between 1999 and 2002 but no later than that. 'Treasury 14% 96' has only one date attached, which means that it is certain the government will repay this stock in 1996. Finally there is undated stock, like '2½% consols', with no definite repayment commitment. Although such stocks are in principle repayable, it is very unlikely in practice that the government will ever redeem its undated stock.

It may seem strange that there are people foolish enough to put money into a loan which will never be repaid. But we have to remember that buyers are purchasing an entitlement to interest of the stated amount. Secondly, they can always dispose of them again in the stock market, where they have a definite value based on the stream of interest payments that they will yield.

The extreme case of undated stock is the clearest illustration of the Stock Exchange acting as a secondary market, performing an important role in making such assets more liquid. 'Liquidity' is the degree to which

an asset gives immediate command over resources. Money is therefore
perfectly liquid, and the marketability which the Stock Exchange provides greatly increases the liquidity of the assets that are traded there.
Without a stock market, irredeemable stock in particular would be a
highly illiquid and unattractive way of holding wealth. The same would
be true, to a lesser degree, of other securities, to the nature of which we
now turn.

Company securities

Private firms issue stocks similar to government bonds which are known
as 'debentures'. Someone buying a debenture stock is merely making a
loan to a company. Its possession gives no say in how the company
should be run. And the income, a fixed-interest payment, does not
automatically increase with the firm's profits. But the return on debentures is relatively certain, because the firm has to meet its fixed-interest
obligations before any other claims.

Next call on a company's profits comes from preference shareholders.
'Preference shares' carry only limited rights of participation in the running of the firm (voting rights when dividends are in arrears, for example)
and they yield only a fixed or limited dividend; but cumulative preference
shares imply that if the company is unable to meet its obligations in any
year, the arrears of dividend become payable in the following year.

After debenture stockholders and preference shareholders have been
satisfied, some part of the remaining profits may be ploughed back into
the business. The left-overs, if there are any, are distributed as dividends
to the 'ordinary' (or 'equity') shareholders. But although the ordinary
shareholders are thus last in the queue, they are the owners of the
company and, in theory at least, elect a board of directors to carry out
their policy in running the firm. In practice, the passivity of shareholders
means that many boards are no more than self-perpetuating oligarchies;
the practice has developed, indeed, increasingly to issue *non-voting*
shares.

Since dividends depend on prior claims being met, and also on the
board's decision about the proportion of profits which should be ploughed back, ordinary shares are much riskier investments than other types of
security. Equity-holders may get no return at all on their capital. On the
other hand, since dividends are related to profits, they also stand to gain
a good deal in prosperous years.

Once again, the role of the Stock Exchange as a secondary as well as a primary market makes shareholding a much more attractive proposition than it would otherwise be. Purchasing shares in ICI does not commit the buyer to the fortunes of that firm for ever; nor do the shares represent a title of ownership to some specific part of ICI's capital, a particular machine or part of a machine which would have to be sold if the shareholder wished to withdraw. If participation in an enterprise implied this degree of involvement, relatively few people would be interested in the venture. The great advantage of securities is that they are transferable, and the Stock Exchange exists as a highly organized market in which such transactions may take place. Those buying ICI shares do so in the knowledge that they can always dispose of them without difficulty – although not necessarily at a satisfactory price.

THE SUPPLY OF FUNDS

The flow of funds into and out of the stock market involves very large sums indeed. In 1985, for example, the turnover on the Stock Exchange amounted to some £390 billion. However, as the word 'turnover' suggests, this does not represent the amount of 'fresh' funds entering and being deployed through the capital market for the first time. Since the Stock Exchange is, as we have said, chiefly a secondary market, the bulk of these transactions took the form of buying and selling existing securities, and were frequently either a reshuffling of past savings into different stocks and shares or the channelling of new savings into second-hand securities. In fact, *new* issues of government bonds in 1985 totalled £15,136 million (with £5,581 million old stock being redeemed); the amount of company stocks and shares freshly issued in the same year was £4,266 million.

To some extent private individuals are themselves responsible for directing their savings into the stock market. Until recently this has been limited to a tiny proportion of the population and quantitatively this remains true today. However, the flotation of the British Telecom, the TSB and British Gas in 1985 and 1986 led to several million first-time share buyers, although how many will continue to hold shares in the long run remains to be seen.

The great bulk of personal savings that reach the Stock Exchange do so, however, through the 'institutional investors'. These institutions have developed as intermediaries assembling quantities of relatively small

Table 15.1. Pension funds, 1982–4 (£ billion)

| | Net acquisitions during year | British govt securities | Ordinary shares | | Land and property | Total assets |
			UK	Overseas		
				Assets at end of year		
1982	7.4	18.2	36.0	9.5	10.5	84.2
1983	7.8	21.7	46.6	14.7	11.1	107.2
1984	8.0	23.9	61.6	16.3	12.3	130.3

savings and then accepting responsibility for their direction into profitable outlets. We have already seen how the banks perform this role and themselves engage in stock market activity by holding part of their assets in the form of government securities. We now briefly glance at some other major institutions: pension funds, insurance companies and investment and unit trusts.

Old age and poverty have always gone hand in hand, and regrettably they still do. Most of our old people are relatively poor, and most poor people are old. This is because the universal state pension system is based on the accumulation of small weekly payments into a 'fund', where they earn interest. In the future, the interest should yield enough to pay for a pension in retirement. Although contributions grow through the accumulation of compound interest, small contributions still imply a small pension, especially when the number of pensioners, and the number of years they survive to draw their pensions, has steadily increased. In relation to average earnings before retirement, British state pensions are much less generous than their European counterparts; but then the contributions are smaller too. State pensions are seen as a safety net, and many employees in business, and in central and local government, contribute to other pension schemes as well. What happens to the flood of payments in respect of these 'occupational pensions'? They go into a fund, and the managers are required by law to invest the money in such a way as to combine security with income. The flows into such funds are extremely substantial, and fund managers therefore find themselves in command of very large sums looking for a profitable and secure home. In recent years they have spread their investments as shown in Table 15.1.

A pension normally ceases when the pensioner dies, so that to safeguard the income of remaining dependants some other form of insurance is

Table 15.2. Insurance companies, 1982–5 (£ billion)

	Net acquisitions during year	Short-term British govt securities	Long-term Ordinary shares		Land and property	Total assets
			UK	Overseas		
1982	6.4	16.3	22.8	22.2	4.8	16.0	79.8
1983	6.8	18.8	25.8	28.0	7.3	17.2	95.8
1984	7.9	20.0	27.7	35.9	9.3	18.7	112.9

Table 15.3. Investment and unit trusts, 1981–4 (£ billion)

	Investment trusts	Unit trusts
1981	8.9	5.9
1982	10.1	7.8
1983	13.4	11.7
1984	15.3	15.1

needed. The possibilities are numerous, and make *life insurance* an almost universal way of saving. But there are other hazards as well – of accident, of damage to property, of ill-health – against which insurance is needed. The inflow of premiums to the insurance companies makes them one of the biggest concentrators of small savings into large-scale investment funds, as Table 15.2 shows.

Pension funds and insurance companies are therefore the major purchasers of government securities and company shares. For the sake of completeness we should add investment trusts and unit trusts. These are financial institutions which buy and hold securities on behalf of other people. Investment trusts do this by using the proceeds from the sale of their own shares. Unit trusts deploy their funds similarly but, as their name implies, do so by selling 'units' to the general public (which they are always prepared to buy back). Both provide a spread of risks and opportunities and expert management of funds which individuals could not secure themselves. Again they serve to concentrate small savings into sizeable funds for investment in a wide range of financial securities. Their total investments in recent years are shown in Table 15.3.

Table 15.4. Industrial and commercial companies: sources of funds, 1981–5 (£ billion)

	Total	From internal sources	From external sources		
			Banks	UK share issues	Total
1981	32.3	20.1	5.8	2.4	10.1
1982	27.3	16.3	6.6	1.3	10.0
1983	32.4	24.6	1.6	2.5	6.6
1984	38.5	31.0	7.1	1.4	7.2
1985	45.6	31.9	7.7	4.3	12.9

Table 15.5. Capital flows, 1975–85 (£ billion at current prices)

	1975	1977	1979	1980	1981	1982	1983	1984	1985
British investment overseas									
Direct	1.3	2.4	5.9	4.9	6.1	4.3	5.3	6.0	7.3
Portfolio	—	—	0.9	3.2	4.3	6.7	6.5	9.6	18.2
Total	1.3	2.4	6.8	8.2	10.4	11.0	11.8	15.5	25.5
Foreign investment in Britain									
Direct	1.5	2.5	3.0	4.4	2.9	3.0	3.4	0.4	3.4
Portfolio	0.2	1.9	1.5	1.5	0.3	0.2	1.9	1.4	7.1
Total	1.7	4.5	4.6	5.9	3.3	3.2	5.3	1.8	10.4
Balance (inflow +)	+0.4	+2.1	−2.2	−2.3	−7.1	−7.8	−6.5	−13.7	−15.1
Balance on portfolio	+0.2	+1.9	+0.6	−1.7	−4.0	−6.5	−4.6	−8.2	−11.1

THE DEMAND FOR FUNDS

Turning now to those seeking to *raise* funds through the Stock Exchange, we have seen that government was responsible for almost double the amount of new issues of stocks and shares made by private companies. We have also already noted that the amount of net private capital formation over these years was itself at a low ebb; but even within that total, firms have been far more reliant for fresh funds on 'internal financing', the ploughing back of undistributed profits. Also, in recent years, they have become more dependent on bank borrowing. Both points are illustrated in Table 15.4, which shows the sources of funds for industrial and commercial (as opposed to financial) companies.

This has led to criticism of a failure in the capital market to accommodate the needs of British industry, a criticism reinforced by the huge outflow of funds that has taken place overseas since the abolition of exchange controls in 1979. (Until that time official permission had to be sought to obtain the foreign currency needed to purchase overseas assets.)

Table 15.5 shows the dramatic increase in overseas investment as compared with the inward flows of capital from abroad which were taking place at the same time. 'Direct' investment is that by companies in setting up subsidiaries. 'Portfolio' investment consists of buying stocks and shares.

The combination of a huge outflow into overseas investment and low level of investment in British industry seems at first sight clear evidence that home industry has been 'starved' of funds by a capital market set on maximizing returns regardless of the national interest.

However, this is a somewhat simplistic argument, resting as it does on two assumptions. The first is that funds, if they had not been channelled overseas, would have been put into net domestic industrial investment. But this would not necessarily have occurred. It would have been open for fund managers, for example, to have preferred alternative outlets – non-financial assets like land and property, or existing stocks and shares – if they thought that to do so would provide a more profitable rate of return. This leads to the second questionable assumption: that a shortage of finance has been a major contributor to the problems of British industry. It can be argued that other factors – the impact of high exchange rates, the deflationary policies pursued by government and the high rate of interest – have been more important constraints on British industry. In other words, it is the weakness of the *inducement* to invest that has limited the extent of new capital formation and hence the opportunities for profitable use of funds.

However, particularly in view of the spate of merger and take-over activity which has dominated public attention in recent years, the Stock Exchange is increasingly charged with 'short-termism'. By this is meant that those providing the inflow of funds on to the market, including the major institutional investors, are essentially concerned with the value of shares in the fairly immediate future, maximizing short-term capital gains. Companies investing heavily in research and development or new plant which may yield substantial long-term benefits may therefore be relatively neglected. This is reflected in their share prices and makes them susceptible to take-over by predators more interested in 'asset stripping', selling off their instantly profitable elements, than in encouraging their long-run development.

Market prices will reflect the most efficient use of savings only if they are the result of investors rationally estimating future prospects of different companies – what Keynes called 'enterprise'. If instead they reflect speculative assessments of market psychology and how it will determine prices over the coming months, then they will be poor guides to how scarce resources can best be used. What Keynes had to say in 1936 remains an apposite warning for today: 'Speculators may do no harm as bubbles on a steady stream of enterprise. But the position is serious when enterprise becomes the bubble on a whirlpool of speculation. When the capital development of a country becomes a by-product of the activity of a casino, the job is likely to be ill-done.'

There also seems some substance in the argument that the capital market has not been geared to provide sufficient 'venture' capital of the kind required by new, small and growing businesses. Investment in such businesses at this stage of their lives is risky; there are the chances of failure, and success might not bring rewards commensurate with that risk. The ordinary banks provide working capital, usually through an overdraft, but long-term industrial investment is rarely if ever undertaken. The larger 'merchant banks', which do provide or arrange long-term finance, are interested in much bigger things.

Attempts have been made to fill the gap. The big banks now have investment subsidiaries; government finance is available in many areas; organizations like British Steel and the National Coal Board help new industries to become established in areas where they have run down their own operations. The hope is that the new firms will become established and be able to finance their continued growth through the 'normal' channels, because the investing institutions should ideally be moving their assistance to the next generation of firms.

To do this, their investment has to be marketable; they have to be able to sell their shares. This means the conversion of the private company into a public company – 'going public' by means of an offer of shares. This is neither simple nor cheap. A Stock Exchange listing is given only to companies that meet quite stringent requirements of size (amount of issued share capital) and information about their trading activities. The assistance of a large financial institution, like a merchant bank, is usually necessary. Once this step is taken, however, the new company will be able to raise capital much more easily and cheaply through the issue of shares. Firms which meet these requirements are known as public limited companies or p.l.c.s.

The advantages of a Stock Exchange listing, and hence a quoted value for the company's shares, are the opportunities it presents for raising additional capital. It means, in effect, that the shares are tradeable, and hence that they are the kind of asset which the large financial institutions will willingly hold.

This has meant that there is, as it were, a queue of firms which have (in their view) grown large enough to justify a quotation, and whose owners wish to obtain a wider market for the shares they own. To meet this need, a subsidiary market has grown up – the Unlisted Securities Market, a kind of second-rank exchange which nevertheless provides an active market in the shares of smaller firms, and the 'over-the-counter' market where shares can be traded, but where the matching of buyers and sellers is not automatic and instantaneous.

Despite these new developments it is still often pointed out that in other countries the transition from hopeful youth to profitable maturity is made easier by the greater willingness of financial institutions to invest in, and to support, new ventures, and that the British capital market is too cautiously conservative in its approach.

'BIG BANG'

Membership of the Stock Exchange has always been exclusive and strictly controlled. Its practices have been in some ways traditionally rigid and in other ways (since everyone tended to know everyone else) extremely informal.

Until recently, members fell into two distinct groups; they were either brokers or jobbers. Brokers bought and sold stocks and shares on behalf of their clients and charged a fixed commission on each transaction.

Brokers never handled shares themselves, because this was the function of the jobbers. Each jobber (in practice a member of a firm or partnership) dealt in a limited range of stocks and shares and would always quote a price at which they would sell and a lower price at which they would buy. In effect, they 'made a market' and also made a profit on the 'turn', the difference between their buying and selling prices. Neither group was affected by rises and falls in prices; the broker's commission was the same whether buying or selling, and the gap between buying and selling prices which yielded the jobbers' incomes was always there. Membership, as many people have commented, was a licence to print money.

Such a system fell foul of the fair trading legislation, which was extended to services in 1976. In the early 1980s the Stock Exchange was faced with the choice of reforming itself or having its practices challenged in court. It chose the first option. The resulting changes, fully introduced by October 1986, were so sweeping and dramatic as to earn the title 'Big Bang'. The break with time-hallowed practice and techniques was, for an institution so tradition-ridden as the Stock Exchange, quite revolutionary.

To those not involved, the changes seem less momentous. In the first place, membership is now open to foreigners and outsiders. Second, the age-old distinction between brokers and jobbers has been abolished. Thirdly, and most radically for those concerned, the brokers' system of fixed commissions is to be discontinued, and they will henceforth have to compete on price as well as service.

The large financial institutions such as pension funds, insurance companies and investment trusts, whose orders to buy or sell are measured in millions of pounds, will be able to drive down commissions to such low levels that some observers question whether all the present firms will survive, despite the very extensive amalgamations which preceded 'Big Bang'.

This opening up of the British securities market to competition is by no means the whole story, however. These days, far more business is done in London in non-British securities in the so-called 'Euromarkets' – now more sensibly retitled the International Capital Market. This market began to take shape in the 1960s at a time when non-Americans were beginning to accumulate large quantities of dollars, the result of a massive flow of capital out of the USA. The banking system was able to find governments and firms to borrow these dollars against interest-earning securities attractive to the holders of dollars. So were created the 'Eurobond' (the security) and the 'Eurodollar market' on which these bonds were floated and traded. Not long afterwards the Eurodollar was joined by Euro-sterling and the Euro-yen, and the market is now so large that it dwarfs the turnover of the Stock Exchange itself – a change paralleling what we saw in Chapter 14 has taken place in banking.

The leaders in this business are the very large US banks and their associates; though for reasons of banking law, tax rules and the position of London midway in time between Tokyo and New York, it was their London branches which handled it.

So much money is now flowing round the world that the smallest movement in interest rates or exchange rates, the merest whisper of political instability or industrial unrest, or even totally unfounded rumours, will send billions of dollars this way or that. Thanks to technology, the news travels in less than a second, and the money must respond as quickly if its owner is not to sustain a loss or forgo a chance of gain. Hence the growth of large financial conglomerates, equipped with all the electronic gadgets, a full range of specialized services and the financial resources to handle the largest deals.

Organizations such as these, headed usually by a British, US or European bank, have replaced the traditional jobbers and brokers on the Stock Exchange. By March 1987 the trading was no longer taking place on the floor of the Exchange but within and between the linked dealing rooms of the big institutions.

One advantage of the old system, with its divisions of functions between broker, jobber and merchant banker, was that conflicts of interest were rare. A merchant bank advising a client about a share issue or a take-over bid was not itself advising other clients to buy or sell, nor was it setting prices in the market as a jobber. Once these separate functions take place within one institution, then the opportunities to exploit inside information are suddenly magnified. The regulation of behaviour under the new regime is still unfinished business.

The new inhabitants of the Stock Exchange are so-called 'market-makers', instead of jobbers, and they will quote the prices at which they are willing to buy or sell stocks and shares and the quantity, through the electronic system SEAQ – the Stock Exchange Automated Quotations System. Interested buyers or sellers can receive this information in detail on their screens and deal with their chosen market-maker directly or through a broker. Alternatively they can contact a broker to obtain this information and place their deal through him; and since each will be dealing in a wider range of securities, quoted prices should be more competitive, and the spread between buying and selling prices should be smaller. On the broking side, competition for business, and especially for large orders, will lower commissions. Whether the new institutions will be as anxious to serve small customers with occasional orders is open to doubt.

Here, though, the general decay of barriers between financial institutions may help. A high-street branch of a bank or building society could generate enough business to warrant the attention of a broking firm, even though the individual orders were small and few.

The end point, not yet reached in London, is for all the sales and purchases to be routed though the system, rather than just to be recorded and reported by it.

So far we have talked generally about 'stocks and shares', using the phrase to cover every variety of tradeable security. From the point of view of economic theory and policy, however, the market for government securities is of special importance, since through its sales and purchases in this market the government tries to regulate the supply of money and the rate of interest.

The new market-makers in this market (there are expected to be over twenty of them initially) will act as both jobbers and brokers, and the Bank of England will issue new stock through them. Six 'inter-dealer brokers' will help to keep the market fluid and reactive but will not be able to sell outside the market. 'Money brokers' will provide facilities for borrowing or lending stock, and finally a number of other dealers will act mainly as brokers dealing with outside clients. Although the system is new and different, much of the mystique of the old gilt-edged market seems to have survived.

Concentrations and growth in industry lead to parallel growth in the size of institutions in the financial sector. We are currently seeing the growth of financial conglomerates to service big, multinational business – and the disappearance, through merger and take-over, of the previous separate, specialist units. As a result, the rules are having to be rewritten. The City has traditionally been a rather exclusive club, or collection of overlapping clubs, which vetted new applicants for entry. Everyone knew everyone else, and a surprisingly large volume of business was done verbally, on a basis of trust. One did not need rules and regulations, because gentlemen could be trusted to behave like gentlemen!

The new game, now being played on an international scale, is investment banking. This brings together the hitherto separate functions of making loans and issuing securities. The large sources of funds – the pensions funds, insurance companies and investment trusts – need to be 'matched' with the borrowers through the issue of the right mixture of securities, and this has to be done on a world-wide basis. So a very large organization, containing within itself all the necessary skills and able to carry out all the functions which have hitherto been the special tasks of independent firms, will be needed. By international standards (that is, by US standards) the embryonic British investment banks are small, and it may be that while the City remains a major financial centre, its largest firms will be US or Japanese multinationals.

16

LLLLLLLLLLLLLLLLLLLL

Public Finance

Government is heavily involved in finance. It intervenes in a variety of ways to regulate the finance of the private sector: in attempting to manipulate the money supply, in influencing interest rates and in generally regulating the financial markets of the economy.

In this chapter, however, we shall be concentrating on the state of the government's own finances. Government is, after all, by far the biggest spender in the economy. Where do its funds come from? What does it spend them on? And what are the effects of its financial activities on the rest of the economy?

GOVERNMENT INCOME AND EXPENDITURE

Bearing in mind that government comprises both central and local authorities, the sources of its income are as shown in Table 16.1.

The upper half of the table deals with central government income. It can be seen that the three main sources of revenue are taxes on income (35.5% of the total in 1984), taxes on expenditure (31.3%) and National Insurance contributions (17.3%). The 'other' elements mainly refer to petroleum revenue tax.

Taxes on personal and corporation incomes are levied directly on the individuals and enterprises. Since National Insurance contributions are similarly deducted at source, it is customary to group the two together as 'direct taxation'. (National Insurance contributions definitely *are* taxation, despite the fact that governments occasionally trumpet 'tax cuts' – reductions in income taxes – while at the same time offsetting the fall in revenue by a rise in National Insurance contributions.)

Direct taxes still account for over half of central government income. However, although the proportion has remained fairly constant over the

Table 16.1. Sources of government income (% and £ billion)

Source of income	1971	1981	1984	1985
Central government income (%)				
Taxes on income paid by persons	32	26	25	24
Taxes on income paid by corporations	7	8	11	11
(Total taxes on income)	(39)	(34)	(35)	(36)
Taxes on expenditure (total)	(32)	(30)	(30)	(30)
Customs and excise (including VAT)	26	24	26	27
Other indirect taxes	6	6	4	3
National Insurance and National Health contributions paid by employees	7	7	8	8
National Insurance and National Health contributions paid by employers	7	8	9	8
(Total National Insurance)	(14)	(15)	(17)	(16)
Other current income	8	9	9	9
Taxes on capital	3	1	1	2
Borrowing requirement	3	10	8	8
Total central government (= 100%), £ billion	20	105	133	146
Local authorities' income (%)				
Rate support grants/other non-specific	33	39	33	32
Specific grants	4	9	16	17
Total current grants from central government	37	48	49	49
Capital grants from central government	2	1	1	1
Rates	27	33	31	32
Rent	9	10	7	7
Other current income	7	8	6	7
Borrowing	18	1	6	4
Total local government (= 100%), £ billion	8	32	41	42
Total general government, £ billion, net of intra-sector transactions	24	120	148	160

years there has been a tendency for the National Insurance element to rise more than taxes on income. Also, within the totals, the proportionate fall in recent years in personal income taxes has been accompanied by a higher employee–employer ratio in terms of National Insurance contributions.

The other main component of central government revenue is that from indirect taxation, mainly levied on expenditure of one kind or another. It can be seen that this has increased relative to personal income tax since 1981.

Personal income tax is progressive. That is, the higher income groups pay not only an absolutely higher amount but also an increasing proportion of their greater incomes in taxation. National Insurance contributions and indirect taxes, on the other hand, are basically proportionate taxes; we pay out similar percentages of our incomes or expenditure regardless of whether our incomes are high or low. It can therefore be argued that the changes which have taken place have resulted in a greater degree of post-tax inequality than before.

Turning now to the lower half of Table 16.1 which deals with local government sources of funds, it is interesting to see the relatively small part of its income which local government raises itself. Mainly this comes from rates and rents and in recent years it has barely exceeded half of the total. The traditional method of finance has been for central government then to supplement local sources of revenue through 'rate support' and other grants based on complex formulas.

This dependence on central government grants can be used, as it notably has been in recent years, to force local authorities to follow central guidance in respect of their spending programmes, whether they wished to do so or not. Some large Labour-controlled authorities attempted to defy the Conservative government and were subsequently, if not consequently, abolished.

Local authorities have a number of legal obligations to provide services, of which education is the major item. They are therefore squeezed between the demand for these services and the amount of money which (in the view of the central government) is sufficient to provide them – with their own taxes (the rates) acting as the balancing item. They have in consequence had two equally unwelcome courses of action: to reduce services, or at least the cost of supplying them, if that was possible; or to raise rates. It is not surprising that the relationship between the two levels of government has been poor in recent years.

The extent to which the government has been successful in holding down local authority spending may be judged by reference back to Table 12.1. The services with which local authorities are mainly concerned are education and housing. It will be seen that, in constant 1983–84 prices, expenditure on education fell from £16.5 billion in 1979–80 to £15.8 billion in 1985–6. The fall in housing expenditure over the same period was much sharper: from £8.2 billion to £3.1 billion. In this case, the statistics mix current spending and capital investment, and the spending total is made to look smaller by netting out sales of assets. The steep decline in expenditure on housing primarily reflects the extensive sales of local authority houses and flats to their occupiers, with local authorities not being allowed to spend this windfall income.

Governments also require individuals and firms to perform certain services and to incur expenditure. The costs of smoke abatement, sound insulation, safety precautions and so on are borne by individuals and do not appear under 'environmental services' as government expenditure, even though the expenditure is carried out on government instructions.

Much more important is what are called 'tax expenditures'. These are private expenditures which can be offset in whole or in part against tax liabilities. Some desirable goods or services are provided and paid for, and government's *income* is reduced, instead of its expenditure being increased, as might otherwise have happened. Think of the case just mentioned, the sale of council homes. These are being bought by the tenants on mortgage, and the interest on the mortgage can be offset in part against income tax. Local authority spending on repairs and maintenance falls, but since central government's income is also reduced, it is not easy to calculate whether total public involvement in the provision of housing has been increased or decreased as a result. Tax relief and rebates are exactly equivalent to expenditures but much less obvious. Tax relief for owner-occupiers is the largest of these items, estimated at £3,710 million in 1979–80. Pension contributions and insurance premiums were subsidized to the tune of £1,650 million.

The government's use of economic resources can be measured by general government expenditure on goods and services and its contribution to fixed capital formation. In 1985 this was about £81 billion or 23% of gross domestic product. This is a measure of the resources used by the government – resources which are therefore not available to provide goods and services for private consumption, or for firms to use in capital formation.

The rest of government spending, about £78 billion – see Table 16.2 – represents *transfers* of income from one group of people to another. The recipients simply treat this extra money as part of their income and spend or save it; the payers find their incomes correspondingly reduced and so consume and save less. A part of government spending is met through borrowing, rather than from current income from taxes, and this represents a transfer to the recipients (whoever they may be) in the present generation from those who will be taxed to repay the borrowed money and the interest, i.e. some members of a future generation.

Table 16.2. Total general government expenditure, 1985

	£ million	%
Current expenditure on goods and services		
Wages	43,800	27.5
Other	30,200	19.0
Gross domestic capital formation	7,100	4.5
'Resource use'	81,100	50.9
Current grants to personal sector	46,100	28.9
Current grants abroad	3,400	2.1
Subsidies	7,700	4.8
Capital grants to personal sector and public		
corporations	3,500	2.2
Debt interest	17,500	11.0
'Transfer of claims'	78,200	49.1
Total	159,300	

Just as we are all being taxed, and all receiving income of some kind, so we are all paying off our parents' borrowing and saddling our children with debt. 'Transfers' are exactly that; they simply redistribute claims on resources. This part of public expenditure absorbs no resources except for those involved in administering the system, and in this sense it is costless. Keeping this distinction – between 'resource use' and 'transfers of claims' – clear in one's mind will help in understanding the arguments about the proper role of government.

GOVERNMENT BORROWING

In addition to its revenue from taxation, government has a further source of funds available. To the extent that its tax haul and other income falls short of its level of spending, it can turn to borrowing. The amount of such borrowing – the Public Sector Borrowing Requirement (PSBR) – has become a matter of almost obsessive concern to recent British governments. Its reduction has been a prime aim of policy. In order to understand the arguments that surround this issue we must first explain the nature of government borrowing activity.

Why borrow?

The first reason why governments borrow is simply that the inflow of tax payments is not spread evenly over the year. For example, certain personal and corporation taxes are paid in two half-yearly instalments; revenue from expenditure taxes is also likely to be bunched at times of high spending like Christmas. These inflows may not match the outflow on government expenditure programmes. Borrowing (and repayments) therefore take place to compensate for these ups and downs of inflow and outflow.

On top of this, governments may deliberately budget to finance a higher level of spending than can be funded from taxation. Such 'deficit financing' may be a conscious application of Keynesian demand management policies, with government spending more than it receives from taxation in order to inject a higher level of demand into the economy and thus stimulate employment. Or, like private companies, it may decide to finance investment programmes partly through borrowing in the knowledge that they will subsequently yield a return which will make the projects self-financing. It is also possible (as critics would emphasize) that government borrowing can be used as a substitute for unpopular taxation, enabling spending programmes to be maintained without bringing home to the electorate the true costs involved.

The mechanics of borrowing

The first point to note is that government borrowing has nearly always been *internal*. It very seldom has taken the form of 'going cap in hand' to other governments or international institutions like the IMF. Generally, it is government raising funds from *us*, and it has a variety of instruments enabling it to do so.

Thus, for example, it can borrow from the small saver through the medium of National Savings certificates, investment accounts with the Post Office Savings Bank, Premium Bonds or save-as-you-earn schemes.

Of much more specialized appeal are Treasury bills: short-term assets (generally three months) which are offered for tender each week and mostly bought by financial institutions which make their profit from the difference between the price they pay for them and their full face value, which they receive when they mature.

Finally, there is the issue of gilt-edged securities on the Stock Exchange. These are government bonds, 'IOUs' on which the government promises to pay the holder a fixed interest payment annually. They are issued for various periods, at the end of which the government will repay

Table 16.3. Government borrowing (£ million, rounded)

	1975–80 average		1980–85 average		% change
Central government borrowing requirement (CGBR) on own account	22,500		37,500		+ 66.9
Local authorities borrowing requirement (LABR)	10,100		5,600		− 44.7
Public corporations borrowing requirement (PCBR)	10,600		7,000		− 34.4
PSBR	43,200		50,100		+ 15.9[a]
CGBR on own account	22,500	(52.1%)	37,500	(74.9%)	
for on-lending to LAs	4,000	(9.3%)	9,600	(19.3%)	
for on-lending to PCs	8,800	(20.3%)	8,300	(16.6%)	
	35,300	(81.7%)	55,500	(110.8%)	
LAs net borrowing from markets	6,100	(14.0%)	−4,100	(−8.1%)	
PCs net borrowing from markets	1,900	(4.3%)	−1,300	(−2.7%)	
PSBR	43,200	(100.0%)	50,100	(100.0%)	
as % of GDP at market prices					
CGBR (own account)		2.9%		2.7%	
CGBR, total		4.6%		4.0%	
PSBR		5.6%		3.6%	

Note: [a] Remember that these are not constant prices; five years' inflation has to be considered.

the existing holder in full. It is the guarantee of interest payment and principal repayment, backed by a government's ability to raise any required amount of taxation to do so, which gives them their 'gilt-edged' label.

Government securities (or stock) of this kind are a popular asset for individual and institutional savers to hold because there is a thriving market on the Stock Exchange in second-hand securities. However, although they are therefore always marketable, there is no certainty as to the price at which they can be sold. To illustrate this, take a typical British government stock, issued in units of £100 and carrying a rate of interest of 10%. Each unit of stock will therefore give its owner £10 a year, and we know that it will be redeemed at its face value of £100 in 1995. How much would a buyer be willing to pay for it? Obviously this would depend on two things: how much could be earned from alternative financial assets, and how near the date of redemption is. If other securities

are yielding 15%, and if 1995 is too far ahead to enter into the calculations, then the price offered would be not be more than £66.66 – the
amount on which £10 represents a 15% return.

There is therefore generally an inverse relationship between the price
of a security and the ruling rate of interest. If, in our example, the going
rate of return fell to 12%, the price of the unit of stock would rise to
£83.33. The annual £10 payment is 12% of this sum. It will be seen that
quite large gains or losses in the market value of securities could take
place if interest rates changed.

How much is borrowed?

Such has been the attention drawn by recent governments to the question
of government borrowing that it is easy to confuse the PSBR with government spending itself. But in fact the amount of government spending
that is financed through borrowing is only a small proportion of the total
– less than 7%. Table 16.3 shows the make-up of the PSBR between the
various arms of government and also indicates that as a proportion of
GDP the PSBR is even tinier.

Part of the decline in the PSBR in recent years has been due to the
government's somewhat bizarre accounting procedure of crediting the
proceeds from privatization sales to current revenue. Part of the government's borrowing, on the other hand, could be offset against fixed capital
formation (some £7,156 million in 1985), so that it would seem logical to
put the creation of public assets on the other side of the ledger.

Why worry about the PSBR?

If the PSBR can easily be confused, at least in the public's mind, with
government spending as a whole, there is a similar confusion about the
relationship between the PSBR and the money supply which appears to
be perpetrated by policy-makers themselves. Thus it is frequently suggested that government spending in excess of that funded from taxation
is financed by the printing of new money – a 'resorting to the printing
presses'.

But, as we have already indicated, the instruments of public borrowing
generally draw savings from the public, individuals, financial institutions
or firms, and to that extent they certainly do not involve any creation of
new money. Table 16.4 confirms this.

Table 16.4. Counterparts to changes in £M3 (£ billions)

Item	1979	1980	1981	1982	1983	1984	1985
Public sector borrowing	12.6	12.3	10.7	5.0	11.6	10.2	7.6
(of which central govt)			(10.4)	(7.9)	(14.5)	(10.2)	(11.8)
less Govt borrowing from non-bank priv. sector	10.9	9.5	11.3	10.6	10.8	11.1	9.1
equals Borrowing from elsewhere	1.7	2.6	−0.7	−5.7	0.8	−0.9	−1.4
Sterling lending to UK private sector	8.6	10.0	11.4	17.6	12.9	16.5	20.9
Domestic counterpart to changes in money stock[a]	10.3	12.9	10.7	11.9	13.7	15.6	19.5
(corrections are made here for foreign, external and other items)							
Changes (increases) in money stock £M3	6.6	10.9	9.3	7.5	9.5	9.8	15.1

Note: [a] This magnitude is called 'domestic credit expansion' and was given great attention in the late 1970s.

Provided that the government borrows from the public there is no increase in the money supply, since all that happens is a transfer of spending power from one to the other. When government borrows from the banks, the money supply does increase, since the banks pay for government securities by, in effect, giving the government bank deposits in exchange. But it is clear from Table 16.4 that government has borrowed almost entirely by selling securities to the public. Only in 1979, 1980 and 1983 did it borrow from the banking system; in other years it 'over-borrowed'. This should have had the effect of *reducing* the money supply, because government securities do not count as money, whereas the sums paid to the government in exchange for these securities would have been part of the money stock.

A further objection to government borrowing is that it has had the effect of 'crowding out' the private sector. The mechanism through which this is alleged to operate is via interest rates. Government borrowing competes for a limited amount of available finance and in the process pushes up interest rates to levels at which private borrowing is deterred. Once again, this does not seem particularly plausible.

Interest rates in recent years *have* reached unprecedently high levels. (Note that it is the *real* rate of interest which is significant, i.e. after allowing for inflation. At many times in the past, this has been negative, with money interest rates being below the level of price rises. Recently,

Table 16.5. Public and private borrowing, 1981–5 (£ billion)

	Central government	Companies	Personal
1981	10.4	10.1	6.2
1982	7.9	10.0	9.8
1983	14.5	6.6	8.7
1984	10.2	7.2	6.4
1985	11.8	12.9	10.1

Table 16.6. Destination of sterling lending to UK private sector

Destination	1981 £b.	1981 %	1982 £b.	1982 %	1983 £b.	1983 %	1984 £b.	1984 %	1985 £b.	1985 %
Personal	6.2	55	9.9	56	8.7	64	6.4	38	10.1	48
Industry and commerce	0.7	6	1.0	6	1.8	13	4.0	24	4.5	21
Financial institutions	1.9	17	2.0	11	3.2	23	3.1	19	5.2	25
Other (balance)	2.6	22	4.7	27	—	—	3.1	19	1.1	5

with inflation much lower and money rates of interest staying high, the real rate of interest has risen sharply.)

Certainly, government's need to refinance old debt as well as to fund its current deficit means that it must sell a large quantity of securities every year; if it can do so only by lowering the price, it will raise interest rates. But such a situation is made more likely by the policies followed by recent governments in trying to limit the money supply along the lines we shall be discussing in Part III.

Another factor making for high interest rates has been the frequent need to attract funds into sterling in order to maintain a required exchange rate. Moreover, to the extent that the finance available for various uses is limited, it is interesting to see the relative significance of government, corporate and personal borrowing within that total – see Table 16.5.

It is as reasonable to conclude from such statistics that it is personal borrowing, at least as much as that of government, which has been 'crowding out' private sector industry. And since this lending by the banking system accounts for most if not all of the increase in £M3 over

Table 16.7. National Debt, 1913–85

	£ ooom.	Approx. % of GDP
1913	0.6	25
1919	7.4	155
1939	7.1	150
1945	21.4	270
1972	35.8	55
1985	190.8	56

the past few years, it is interesting to see from Table 16.6 that the major destination is the *personal* sector; i.e. these are loans for home purchase or other consumption.

THE NATIONAL DEBT

The National Debt is the sum total of government borrowing which remains outstanding, and it has risen hugely over the past three-quarters of a century – see Table 16.7.

These figures show that the major jumps in the level of government borrowing have taken place during the two world war periods; at those times, for obvious reasons, it became necessary, if sufficient resources were to be released for war production, to effect a greater transfer of purchasing power from private into government hands.

The table also reveals, however, the difference between the periods 1919–39 and from 1945 to the present day. Whereas in the inter-war years the National Debt was cut by some £300 million as state activities dwindled again to their peacetime scope, the debt has vastly increased since 1945. The government has for the first time become a net borrower in time of peace, largely reflecting its much greater involvement in the economy. It is important, however, to bear in mind the effect of inflation on amounts involved. Although the total debt increased by 60% in money terms between 1945 and 1972, it fell sharply as a proportion of gross domestic product. It would have taken nearly three years' national income to pay off the 1945 debt, whereas the 1972 debt could have been cleared in seven months.

However, no government even aims at repaying the debt. This suggests that we are spending beyond our means, and that government borrowing

Table 16.8. Public sector debt, 1985

	£ billion
Market holdings of securities	146.7 (42% of 1985 GDP)
Notes and coin in circulation	13.8
Other liabilities	7.5
Total	168.0
less Holdings by local authorities and public corporations	−0.9
Net total, central government	167.0
Local authority debt	41.0
less Holding by CG and public corporations	−25.3
Net local authority	16.1
Debt of public corporations	33.1
less Held by CG and local authorities	−25.3
Net public corporation debt	7.8
Public sector consolidated total	190.8 (55.8% of GDP)

Table 16.9. Government liquid reserves, 1985

	£ billion
Gold and foreign exchange reserves	11.0
Commercial bills	7.1
Other liquid assets	8.4
Total	26.6
Local authorities	1.4
Public corporations	1.0
Consolidated liquid assets	28.0 (8.5% of GDP)
Net public sector debt	161.8 (47.3% of GDP)

Source: *Bank of England Quarterly*, March 1986.

stores up trouble for the future. Government may manage to obtain a larger share of the national cake now, but does it do so only by imposing a burden of indebtedness on future generations?

As we have already stressed, most of the borrowing undertaken by the British government is internal; the government issues securities which are bought by its own citizens, using domestic currency. Even if they are bought by foreigners, it is understood that the interest and the principal will be paid in domestic pounds.

Against this, one should set the liquid reserves held by government, i.e. those immediately or quickly available for meeting any call from holders of government debt – see Table 16.9.

It is only rarely that the debt takes an external form, with government borrowing foreign exchange. Such external borrowing requires interest and repayment in a foreign currency, so that the servicing of such loans is a charge on the external balance of payments. Many developing countries which have borrowed large sums in the past now find that their earnings from exports of goods and services are swallowed up in debt repayments. But that is certainly not the case with the UK, which is a net creditor overseas.

We have also discussed the reasons for internal or domestic borrowing: when revenue will not cover expenditure (for instance, during a recession); when large sums are needed for long-term capital expenditure; or to cover the huge increases in spending during wars and similar emergencies. The first of these should be reversed during a subsequent boom, when tax revenues rise. Debt incurred for the second purpose can be serviced and then redeemed from the fruits of the investment. War-generated debt, on the other hand, does not in itself make any productive contribution which will ease its repayment. From this point of view it creates an additional 'servicing' requirement which post-war generations have to meet.

The 'burden' of the National Debt is genuine only to the extent that that it contains a foreign element whose repayment depends on lower consumption and increased exports. So long as it is domestic, then the *real* effect will have taken place in the past with the initial reallocation of resources from the private to the public sector. All that remains for future generations is a mere transfer payment from one section of the community to another. The servicing of the debt involves only an internal redistribution of income to the holders of the debt from the taxpayers.

Since to a very large degree these are the same people, even the redistribution is minimal.

So the 'burden' of the debt is a myth, as long as it is internal. It can be termed a 'burden' only in as far as higher taxation may be required to service the debt or repay the principal. But interest payments are only 10% of total government spending, and capital repayment is effected as a rule through the issue of new securities to replace the old ones.

Indeed, gilt-edged stock is such a useful way of holding wealth that if government debt did not exist some substitute would have to be invented. Unless for some reason (and it is hard to think of one) the government decided to raise taxes to such a level in 1990 that it could pay off the debt coming due in that year without issuing any new securities, there is no question of the 1990 generation having to repay debt incurred in 1960 or 1965 by its parents. The 'burden' of the National Debt is an example of the dangers of thinking about a national economy as if it were a household economy.

17

International Institutions

International factors now heavily constrain the ability of any British government to regulate the economy. Before going on in Part III to discuss the major policy issues of recent years, we therefore need to sketch the international framework within which the United Kingdom economy, and its government, now has to operate. The economic relationships between nations are governed by a number of treaties and agreements and are monitored by institutions which are world-wide in scope – the International Monetary Fund and the General Agreement on Tariffs and Trade, for example. Since 1973 the United Kingdom has been part of the European Economic Community (now called the European Community), and must conform with its rules and practices.

THE INTERNATIONAL MONETARY SYSTEM

Although the global bodies have been in place for a longer time, their influence on the UK is perhaps less now than it was, being overshadowed by the European Community. But it is worth beginning with these broader, world-wide institutions. There is room for confusion right at the start, because the functions and activities of these institutions do not match their names very closely.

The International Monetary Fund (IMF), for example, has a similar relationship with individual states to that of the central bank within a state with other financial institutions. In particular, it is a 'lender in the last resort' and a regulator of their financial behaviour.

What is called the World Bank, on the other hand, is a purely lending institution, whose proper name is the International Bank for Reconstruction and Development (IBRD). It has another lending agency called the

International Development Agency, and the main concern of both is now the economic development of the Third World.

The International Monetary Fund

The IMF used to be the regulator of exchange rates. It was established after the Second World War in an attempt to prevent the pre-war chaos of unstable exchange rates and also their use as weapons of economic warfare. The US dollar was given a fixed value in relation to gold, and then all other currencies were given an agreed exchange rate against the dollar and therefore also against each other. The signatories committed themselves to keep their currencies within narrow limits around this central value, by selling their currency if its price threatened to rise and by buying it if the price threatened to fall. The former creates no serious difficulty, because countries can create as much of their own currency as they wish. The latter gave rise to the problem which bedevilled British economic policy from 1945 until the early 1970s, because the only means with which a country can *buy* its own currency is by exchanging it for the limited amounts of gold and foreign exchange which it holds. The IMF's function was essentially to stand ready to lend foreign exchange to any country which needed to extend its reserves in order to maintain the value of its currency. It was also the body which would approve a change in the dollar value of a currency if and when it became clear that the old rate was not defensible or reasonable.

Countries could borrow foreign exchange from the IMF quite freely up to a limit determined by their original gold contribution, but any further borrowing was on progressively more stringent conditions. The IMF became involved in the management of the borrowing country's economy and had to approve its proposals for rectifying the problems which had forced it to borrow – a humiliating situation for a sovereign state.

The UK experienced this process when in the mid-1970s the reserves, under pressure to pay for oil imports at the new higher prices, were on the point of running out. Strongly influenced by monetarist thinking, the IMF prescribed drastic cuts in government spending and penal rates of interest in a package of deflationary measures to be applied by the British authorities. Since other countries were reacting in a similar way to the deficits induced by oil price rises, and to the rate of inflation, 1975 saw a world-wide recession.

It was North Sea oil which came to Britain's rescue. The balance of payments moved into surplus, the pound floated upwards, and the IMF loans were repaid.

Just as the central bank of a country can increase the supply of money or credit, so the IMF could, if it wished, increase the supply of international money. It has in fact done so, partly by selling off some of its gold at a handsome profit, and partly by increasing and adjusting the 'drawing rights' of its members. It has not gone far enough for some – notably the debtor countries of the Third World – but too far for others, which are worried about the inflationary effects of an increase in international liquidity.

However, the IMF has in the process created a useful new unit – the SDR or Special Drawing Right, which is a 'basket' of sixteen major currencies containing 0.40 dollars and appropriate fractions of the others. It was originally defined as the value of 0.888671 grammes of gold, which in 1971 was $1.00; hence its name, 'paper gold'. Like its European equivalent, the ECU or European Currency Unit, it is a valuable unit for statistical purposes and has been adopted by international airlines for accounting purposes and by central banks for international transactions.

The efforts of the UK to maintain the exchange rate of the pound finally came to an end in 1967, when the pound was devalued. This gave sterling a breathing space, but the position of the US dollar was now critical to the survival of the system of fixed exchange rates. By this time there was a vast amount of mobile money in the world, derived from the earnings of the oil-producing countries, the cash balances of the growing number of multinational corporations and the very large capital outflows which had been taking place from the United States. This money – known as 'hot' money because of its extreme volatility – moved from one currency to another under the influence of the interest rates being paid, but much more in response to expectations about devaluation or revaluation. This made it extremely difficult to defend a currency against a speculative run, and the expansion of IMF drawing rights mentioned above was inadequate to the task.

Floating exchange rates

The US dollar was and is by far the most important reserve currency, as well as the leading trading currency (all transactions in oil, for example, are in dollars). The world therefore needs enough dollars to facilitate the flow of international payments, and the problem of the 1950s was a dollar shortage. But if, on the other hand, too many dollars are thought to be available, then 'confidence in the dollar', which equates with nations' readiness to hold dollars in their reserves, will tend to decline.

From the mid-1960s the US balance of payments went into deficit, and there was a considerable outflow of dollars. This was not because of imports exceeding exports; US trade was in surplus. The deficit was the result of capital outflows. This was due in part to overseas investment by US multinationals, in part to military assistance for Europe and Asia and especially to the cost of the Vietnam war. Certain countries, led by France, began to convert some of their surplus dollars into gold, and the US gold reserve shrank from £18 billion in 1960 to £11 billion in 1970.

Since the US dollar was the key currency to which all others were linked, any loss of confidence in its reliability was a serious threat to the whole system. Another international conference held at the Smithsonian Institution in Washington produced a general realignment of currencies – in effect a devaluation of the dollar and an upward revaluation of the Japanese yen and the West German mark – and a looser system of fixed exchange rates. But the 'Smithsonian agreement', as it was called, did not provide a permanent solution to the international payments problem. The US deficit was not cured, and dollars continued to accumulate abroad, especially in West Germany and Japan. Britain 'floated' the pound in 1971, followed first by the currencies of Canada and Switzerland, and then by those of Italy and Japan. In March 1973 attempts to create a new system of fixed rates were finally abandoned, and the world entered a new regime of freely floating exchange rates. In retrospect, it is clear that no new set of rates, even had one been agreed, would have survived the massive shock of 1974 when oil prices quadrupled.

Although there is now no need for countries to use reserves of gold and foreign exchange to defend the fixed value of their currencies, governments and central banks do still intervene in the foreign exchange markets, in part to even out very short-term fluctuations, and in part to try to avoid the rate from going to levels which they regard as too high or too low.

Too low a value, while it might stimulate exports, would also raise the domestic price of imports and thus add a further stimulus to inflation. For Britain in the mid-1970s this was a serious threat. Too high a value, and a country's exports will become too expensive in foreign countries, while cheap imports threaten the domestic sales of its own industries.

Britain experienced this situation in the early 1980s, when the pound, sustained by oil exports at very high prices, rose to levels which were strongly criticized by the business community.

The focus of attention of the IMF has more recently turned towards the problems of those developing countries that had to go deeply into debt in order to pay for their oil imports (Brazil and Argentina) or that embarked on rapid development using borrowed money which they expected their oil exports would enable them to repay. The subsequent fall in oil prices helped the first group but created serious difficulties for the second group. The problem of servicing their debts is common to both, and the IMF, as their 'lender in the last resort', is much involved in trying to find solutions and imposing 'financial discipline' which can create severe hardship and represent a major setback to the process of development.

Apart from this, however, the tendency in recent years has been for the major powers to deal with economic problems outside the formal IMF machinery. The 'Group of Five' (the USA, the UK, West Germany, Japan and France, with Italy protesting at exclusion) is the core of a wider grouping of industrial countries in the Organization for Economic Co-operation and Development (OECD). This body originated from the Organization for European Economic Co-operation (OEEC), which advised on the restoration of the war-shattered Western European economies through US aid – the Marshall Plan. It has a secretariat in Paris and is a fertile source of economic statistics and analysis.

TRADE AND TARIFFS

The intention of the mainly Anglo-Saxon designers of the post-war world was that there should be an international organization with authority to regulate world trade, just as the IMF was to regulate the world's money. There was a certain amount of lip-service paid to the ideal of free trade, though the USA wished to retain its protective tariffs and was not averse to protection as such. What it did oppose were discriminatory tariffs, like the Commonwealth preferences operated by Britain before the war, which gave British manufactures an advantage in the Canadian and Australian markets, and Canadian and Australian wheat a similar benefit in the British market. So the International Trade Organization (ITO) would prevent discrimination and other unfair trading practices and would foster 'freer' – if not free – trade, just as the IMF would ensure stable exchange rates and freely convertible currencies. But its start was delayed. Anglo-American co-operation broke down, and the Havana Conference in 1947–8 was complicated by Third World demands for preferential treatment. A charter was eventually signed, but the US Senate failed to ratify it, and the ITO was stillborn.

The General Agreement on Tariffs and Trade (GATT) had been agreed as an interim measure, and it now took over. It is a very loosely knit organization of over ninety countries, which meet periodically to discuss the working of the agreement and ways of improving it. The original agreement was amplified and enlarged in the 1950s and 1960s. The organization, if one can call it that, has a small secretariat in Geneva and, since 1960, a permanent council.

In the periodic conferences, which have often in the past been associated with an incumbent US President in the form of the 'Kennedy round' or the 'Nixon round', each country negotiates a set of tariff concessions (reductions) with its major trading partners. 'Reciprocity' – that is, finding mutually advantageous reductions – is the basis for this horse-trading, in which the European Community, having a common external tariff, negotiates as a unit. The GATT rules then require that these concessions must be applied to *all* countries. The treatment given to the 'most favoured nation' must be unconditionally extended to all other nations.

GATT does not prohibit the formation of customs unions (groupings in which members remove tariffs against each other while retaining a common external tariff against non-members) and 'free trade areas', and it has sometimes proved difficult to distinguish between preferential or discriminatory arrangements ('bad') and regional trade groupings ('good' or at least 'allowed').

Direct restrictions on trade through quotas, quantity limits and all the other 'non-tariff' restraints are also GATT's business and have now become almost as important as tariffs in restricting trade flows. GATT does not deal with monetary restrictions, which are the business of the IMF.

The existence of these international agreements and organizations means that any British government has its freedom of action curtailed. Certain actions are against the rules or against the spirit of the agreements and would, if taken, invite not only censure but also retaliation. And although the USA might have been large and powerful enough to ignore the IMF, the UK, now low in the second tier of economic power, is not.

THE EUROPEAN COMMUNITY

The international institution which is now dominant in Britain's economic affairs is the European Community (formerly called the European Economic Community or EEC). Although British statesmen were prominent among those who argued for European reconciliation and unification in the post-war period, the UK did not sign the Treaty of Rome which established the EEC in March 1957. Instead it fostered, and joined, the looser European Free Trade Association (EFTA) along with Norway, Sweden, Denmark, Portugal, Switzerland and Austria. A 'free trade area' is a group of countries which agree not to impose quotas or tariffs on trade with each other but leave each country free to make its own decisions about its trade with third parties. EFTA aimed to reduce and ultimately abolish tariffs on industrial goods, but its prime purpose as far as the UK was concerned was to act as a bargaining counter with the EEC. By the time the UK applied for membership of the EEC in 1961, the process of dismantling tariffs on industrial goods had begun within, and between, the two trading groups.

General de Gaulle effectively vetoed British entry in 1963, and it was not until 1970 that a second application was made, which eventually succeeded. The UK, along with Ireland, Denmark and Norway (which later withdrew), joined the EEC in January 1972. The original EEC of the 'Six' – Belgium, Luxembourg and the Netherlands, forming the Benelux group, with France, West Germany and Italy – was then fifteen years old and not only had completed the dismantling of all internal tariffs (1966) but had established a common agricultural policy, free movement of labour and the basic institutions of the Community: the Council, the Commission and the Parliament. They had begun discussions on a common fisheries policy and transport policy and the restructuring of agriculture, and were looking forward to full monetary and economic union. Britain had to accede to policies and institutions which had been designed by, and for, the original members.

The Common Agricultural Policy

In particular the UK had to accept the Common Agricultural Policy (CAP), which meant a considerable shift in its trading patterns and a sharp increase in food prices. The UK had traditionally imported large quantities of food, bought cheaply on the world market. Under Commonwealth preference, Australia, Canada and above all New Zealand supplied considerable quantities of food; but Ireland, Denmark and Holland also depended to a considerable extent on the British market. In the 1930s British farmers could not compete with these cheap and high-quality products, and British agriculture was moribund.

In contrast, the war placed a premium on agricultural output, and the 1947 Agriculture Act set a framework within which it was intended that farm output and income should never again relapse to their pre-war levels. Agriculture was to be supported in a variety of ways, but especially through the mechanism of 'deficiency payments'. Under this system British farmers sold their output on the open market, in competition with low-cost overseas producers, and initially received what were, in effect, 'world market prices'. They were then paid the extra sums needed to bring these up to previously agreed guaranteed prices for various products – high enough to ensure the required amount of domestic output and adequate farm incomes.

Within the EEC, on the other hand, food prices were set to begin with at a level which would yield reasonable agricultural living standards. Any imports of food still necessary would then pay a levy, which was the difference between the external world price and the internal EEC price.

Both were systems intended to support domestic farmers and secure a higher level of output than would otherwise have been achieved. However, under the British method, farmers were subsidized by the taxpayers. Consumers could buy at lower world prices. Under the CAP, farmers were directly subsidized by the consumers. When the UK entered the CAP, it involved a choice between paying a levy on all non-EEC food imports or shifting purchases to EEC sources. (During negotiations for entry, an attempt was made by Britain, with very limited success, to safeguard the position of New Zealand and ex-colonial suppliers of sugar.)

In economic analysis, 'trade diversion' from low-cost producers outside to higher-cost members within the grouping is regarded one of the detrimental effects of a customs union. France in particular was anxious to obtain as big a share as possible of the UK market for its farmers.

Diversion of trade in manufactured goods was less likely because GATT negotiations, EFTA and the EEC had between them reduced tariffs on industrial goods to quite low levels by 1973. Here the UK expected to gain from the favourable 'trade-creation' impact of a custom union, together with the 'dynamic' benefits of associating with a group of countries that had been achieving much faster economic growth. By gaining access to a potential market of over 250 million people – a market comparable in size with the USA – Britain hoped that its industries would be able to reap economies of scale. There was also the fear that not joining would lead to industrial stagnation or decline.

As we have seen, the industries which have grown and in which Britain competes effectively are the service industries, especially financial services. Unfortunately, this is an area where 'harmonization' (the removal of idiosyncratic national differences in legislation which hamper European-scale operations) still has a long way to go.

Another obstacle to the creation of a single European market is the continued existence of national currencies, between which the exchange rates may vary. The problems that this can cause are illustrated by the difficulties that have bedevilled the CAP as a result.

A common European currency?

A common European price is fixed for, let us say, butter. This is then translated into pounds, punts, francs, marks, lire, etc. What happens if the exchange rate now changes so that, for example, more francs are obtained for each West German mark? French farmers still get the agreed price in francs. But it is now worth the while of West German housewives literally to cross the Rhine to buy their butter, since it will cost them less in marks than it did previously, or less than West German butter would cost them now. French farmers will find it lucrative to sell their butter across the river because by doing so, and then changing their marks into francs, they will get more for it. It has therefore proved necessary to devise an enormously elaborate system of 'monetary compensation amounts' and 'green' currencies keep the CAP working more or less as it was designed to do.

Partly because of this the creation of a common currency has always been seen as a desirable objective – indeed as an essential element in a genuine European market. In 1972 when the global fixed exchange rate system began to break down, the 'Six' accordingly introduced the 'snake', a system under which their six currencies moved up or down together within narrow limits. This has now developed into the European Monetary System (EMS). The UK, characteristically, did not join but does tacitly co-operate with the other governments.

As with any system of fixed exchange rates, the EMS means that no country can pursue an economic policy which would cause its currency to depreciate in relation to those of fellow members. Temporary ups and downs can be met by a central fund, but a fundamental divergence means a realignment of currencies. So there are considerable pressures to align general economic policies as well as currencies. Since the dominant currency is the Deutschmark, it is likely to be the rather conservative monetary stance of West Germany which wins out over expansionary (some would say inflationary) policies such as those adopted during the early phase of the Mitterrand government in France.

The British government has said, up to now, that the time is not ripe for joining the EMS, fearing perhaps that the exchange rate at which we entered, boosted by North Sea oil, could not be maintained.

Britain as a region of Europe

Once a country has joined a common market in which capital and labour can move freely, then any regional problems which already existed within its borders will tend to be magnified. Capital will move to areas where profits are greatest: to locations with the best communications, nearest to materials or markets. In Europe this tends to mean the 'golden triangle' of South-East England, Holland, Belgium and the Rhineland, with Paris and Northern Italy on its fringes. Cities like Liverpool and Glasgow, once the gateways to the Atlantic trade, now face the wrong way and are part of a depressed 'outer belt'. It is salutary to talk to someone from Vienna, who sees Europe from its centre and to whom Scotland is as far away and as 'foreign' as Egypt or Morocco.

There is a clear danger that the existence of a European-scale market will lead to the draining of wealth and employment from weaker areas and a concentration in the already stronger. Looked at 'from Strasbourg', i.e. from a European point of view, the free movement of goods and factors of production is economically advantageous since it means a larger total Community output and income. But does Britain benefit if, for example, ICI's new petrochemical plant is located in Rotterdam, or Vauxhall Motors' new assembly line is in Barcelona? (It is as little consolation for the UK to know that the Community as a whole has gained as it is for Merseyside to be aware that the *British* economy as a whole is more prosperous as a result of IBM, for example, setting up a computer plant in Southampton.)

Free trade and resource movement may well lead to greater overall wealth, but the key question is how it is shared out. If it is unevenly distributed initially, will it spread or 'trickle down'? Will the Dutch eventually go to buy their bulbs from the Liverpool Garden Centre, or the Spaniards spend their holidays in Scotland?

Experience of regional disparities within the UK itself suggests that the disequalizing process is a cumulative one, and that economic activity gravitates towards the already more prosperous centres through a kind of positive feedback. That is precisely why Britain and other countries have for many years applied policies deliberately designed to counteract these forces, however ineffective they may have been.

Recognition of such problems, and attempting to deal with them, is one of the features which distinguishes an economic community from a mere customs union. Provision was accordingly made in the Treaty of Rome for action at least to ameliorate if not to eliminate the geographical inequalities that would be the likely consequence of economic integration. Such policies are mainly the responsibility of two institutions. The European Investment Bank devotes over 80% of its funds to regional developments, and the European Social Fund spends about three-quarters of its budget on aid to poor regions. However, the resources set aside for this purpose are inadequate.

The recession which began in 1978–9 has been associated with exceptionally rapid technological change and with the growth of competing industries in those Third World countries known as the NICs, the newly industrializing countries like Brazil and South Korea. Assistance with retraining, with the establishment of new high-technology industries and with other sources of employment is now needed on a vast scale in almost every Western European country, not just in the depressed old industrial regions. (At present, the poor South of Italy itself absorbs about a half of the funds available).

The trouble is – and this affects the UK in particular – that while the European Community has a well-established and effective mechanism for transferring larger sums of money from consumers to farmers, the funds available for these other purposes are minute by comparison. Thus nearly three-quarters of Community funds go on the CAP, with regional policy receiving only about a sixth of that amount. Either the Community has to be given greater resources than it now gets from agricultural levies and its small share of VAT, or the agricultural programmes have to be drastically curtailed and the money redirected. Neither would be easy to achieve.

In 1981 Greece became the tenth member of the Community. Being much poorer and much less industrialized than the other members, it needed a long transitional entry period. Now Spain and Portugal have joined and together they pose some difficult problems. All three countries will represent a further call on regional funds. Also, with Southern Italy, they can produce large amounts of Mediterranean products. Shall we add orange and lemon mountains to the lakes of wine and olive oil that already exist?

PART III

POLICY AND PERFORMANCE – PAST, PRESENT AND FUTURE

18

Shifts in Macro-Economic Policy

What has been happening in the British economy in recent years must have been particularly difficult for the casual observer or non-economist to understand and interpret. Indeed (although this is unlikely to elicit much public sympathy), it has often been bewildering for economists themselves.

In the first place a sea change took place, particularly from 1979 onwards, in the attitude of government policy-makers towards what could and should be done in influencing the broad direction that the economy was taking. For the previous quarter of a century there had been a general consensus on such 'macro-economic' matters, with similar objectives being pursued by governments of different political hues, using similar policies in attempting to achieve them. In the latter part of the 1970s that consensus had begun to crack. By the early 1980s it was shattered. The new lines of division were mainly between those who persisted in thinking that the economy was amenable to rational ordering through government action and those who had reverted to an earlier *laissez-faire* belief that a great deal of macro-economic intervention was both futile and even damaging.

Secondly, the subject of economics itself suffered a deep rift. It is a commonplace that economists are never able to agree. But the extent to which they became split during these years had not been seen since the nineteenth century. Recent economic controversy has been about not minor considerations but the very nature of what makes the economy function.

The two types of dispute are interlinked. The theoretical arguments between opposed schools of economists provided a rationale for the policies that have been implemented. And those in turn have created grist for the economists' mill in suggesting evidence in support of one view or another.

Meanwhile, and to a large extent as a result, the economic landscape has itself been transformed to a degree which would render it almost unrecognizable to a time-warped observer from the early 1970s. Mass unemployment, widening inequality, the decline of manufacturing industry and the continued attempt to weaken the public sector – all would be inconceivable let alone incomprehensible to an observer from that point in time.

In this chapter we outline some of the bases of recent macro-economic controversy, followed in Chapter 19 by an account of the parallel arguments and changes that have been taking place on the micro-economic front.

THE KEYNESIAN CONSENSUS

For much of the post-war period, governments were in agreement about the four main objectives of economic policy:

(1) Full employment.
(2) Price stability.
(3) Economic growth.
(4) Balance of payments equilibrium.

As we have seen, 'full employment' is not a precise concept because a good deal of social convention enters into its definition. Firms and their employees work a traditionally defined day, week and year. If necessary, the working day can be extended through overtime, and the week by Saturday working. More output can be obtained from the capital equipment by working a second or even a third shift. The amount of arable land can be increased by ploughing up pasture or even, as happened in the Second World War, by cultivating golf courses and playing-fields. So we have to understand full employment in this sense: not the absolute maximum, but the full use in a normal way of the economy's resources. It is because we cannot define full employment precisely that there is room for argument about when it is reached.

However, most people in the United Kingdom would agree, even today, with the proposition that it is better to have more goods and services to enjoy than less, though they may and do argue about what are 'goods' and what are 'bads'. Put another way, most would prefer that resources should not lie idle when they could be usefully employed.

The second objective of post-war consensual economic policy was the achievement of price stability or at least an acceptable rate of inflation. One problem here is that the borderline between sufficient demand to ensure full employment and an excessive level of demand which will start to drive prices upwards is very narrow; the two levels of demand are not far apart and may even overlap. Inflation, once it starts, tends to feed on itself or accelerate, and its consequences in terms of income distribution, social conflict and external trade may, as we have discussed, be undesirable.

Thirdly, it would seem to follow naturally that if the flow of goods and services produced by a fully employed economy is a good thing, then an increase in that flow is also desirable. 'Economic growth' was therefore a further goal of economic policy. Whether economic growth is always worth striving for depends, of course, on the composition of output, the distribution of the benefits and the costs involved. But although economic growth is not synonymous with higher living standards, it remains a generally necessary if not sufficient condition for their achievement.

The last of the commonly accepted policy objectives was to achieve soundness or 'equilibrium' in the balance of payments. In practice it was found that one of the consequences of a high level of demand and prices in the UK was that goods and services which might have been exported were diverted to meet internal demand, while increased imports were being sucked in. In the 1940s, 1950s and 1960s this meant trouble, because the need to maintain a fixed value for sterling used up the limited reserves of gold and foreign exchange. Since the 1970s, in a regime of floating exchange rates, the consequence is a fall in the value of the currency. This too is not painless. Import prices rise and add to inflationary pressures. The 'terms of trade' move adversely, and the standard of living will fall if this continues.

Demand management

It is worth briefly recalling the mechanism of how the economy works through our basic model of the flow of income and product in the economy; illustrated in Figure 10 (page 70).

We defined the gross domestic product as the quantity of new goods and current services which the economy produced in a year, and we measured this flow by looking at the amount which was spent on these goods and services. This gave us 'gross domestic product at market prices', and we could adjust this figure to allow for the fact that the prices would include an element of tax or be reduced by a subsidy. Making this adjustment would give us GDP at 'factor cost', and the advantage of doing this was that we then got a figure which matched the payments made in the form of wages, rent and profits, i.e. the income side of the flow diagram.

The goods and services are produced by firms, which in an economy like ours means predominantly by privately owned enterprises; but we must not forget that some of these goods, and some very important services, are produced by central and local government.

The basic Keynesian proposition was that the volume of goods and services produced will reflect the demand for them. This in turn would determine the levels of income and employment. If, in particular, full employment was to be attained, then it was necessary for governments to intervene and deliberately *manipulate* total demand and its components. Such 'demand management', as it was termed, could be implemented by using the instruments of government spending and taxation (known as fiscal policy) and to a lesser extent the availability of credit and its price, the rate of interest (Keynesian monetary policy).

Demand is conventionally split into four: demand from overseas buyers, or 'exports'; demand from government for its current use; demand from firms and government for capital goods for use in production, called 'investment'; and demand from ordinary consumers or households for goods and services, called simply 'consumption'.

Each of these elements of aggregate demand comes from a different group of people and institutions and will be influenced by different factors. Demand for British exports, for example, will be determined to a very large extent by the level of economic activity in the economies of our major customers. Another major influence will be the relative price of British goods. There is not a great deal that a British government can do directly about some of these factors, but it can exercise indirect influence through its policies on domestic costs and inflation, and through manipulation of the exchange rate.

By contrast it might be thought altogether straightforward for government to raise or lower its *own* expenditure. However, experience suggests that there is a certain asymmetry in its scope for action. In practice, it is a great deal easier to increase spending than it is to reduce it. There is never any shortage of suggestions about ways of spending more, but candidates for cutting are not so forthcoming.

The third form of demand is spending on investment, of which there are three components: spending on plant, equipment, machinery, buildings and roads, i.e. on 'capital goods'; spending (by individuals, firms or government) on dwellings, included here because they are such a long-lived asset; and net increases in the physical stocks of finished goods, work in progress and raw materials held by firms. By their very nature, decisions about spending money on things like these are forward-looking and depend on guesses about future demand. Firms will not expand or even renew their capital equipment unless they foresee a future demand for the goods and services it will produce. They will reduce the level of stocks if they expect future demand to fall, and since they can do this quite quickly this is the most volatile aspect of investment.

The government can raise or lower its own contribution to capital formation and can influence the spending of firms in two ways. It can subsidize the purchase of capital goods by firms, and it can alter the terms on which firms can borrow money to spend on capital goods through its control of credit and interest rates. Less specifically it can change the expectations of firms about the future of the economy by pursuing a generally expansionary, growth-oriented policy, or a restrictive, deflationary policy.

Last but not least we come to personal and household consumption, the largest spending flow of all. Its level depends above all on the incomes of households. If these are large and expected to continue or increase, so spending will be high. If incomes fall, or if the future looks uncertain, then spending will decline. A cushion of wealth helps to sustain spending, of course, but very few are in this fortunate position. Most households, however, have access to credit, and their spending is thereby made less dependent on current income.

Again we ask what the government can do to influence this element of demand. It is evident that by changing the levels of taxation, and the levels of the transfer payments it makes, it can increase or decrease the disposable incomes of households and thus influence consumption (as we explained in Chapter 8). That part of consumption which depends on credit, like investment spending, is to some extent responsive to the availability and cost of credit.

We can now sum up these macro-economic objectives and the Keynesian 'instruments' which a government can employ in an attempt to achieve them.

It will be seen that the methods of achieving objectives (3) and (4) may conflict with measures aimed at securing objectives (1) and (2), and

Objective	Instruments
(1) Full employment	Increase aggregate demand by: Reduction in taxation = increase in disposable income Increase in own spending on goods and services Easing of credit/expansion of money supply Lowering of interest rates
(2) Economic growth	Develop expectations of future high demand Stimulate investment in new capital via low interest rates and tax incentives Carry out or subsidize research and development
(3) Stable prices (or low inflation rates)	Keep aggregate demand somewhat below maximum capacity levels Introduce prices and incomes policies
(4) Balance of payments equilibrium (surplus or tolerable deficit)	Stimulate exports within limit of GATT rules Keep interest rates high enough to deter capital outflows Keep aggregate demand low enough to prevent higher imports Devalue currency

that the devaluation remedy in (4) will make the attainment of (3) more difficult. For this reason there has been a search for additional instruments, especially some means of making a direct rather than an indirect attack on objectives (3) and (4). Import controls have been suggested; prices and incomes policies have been tried since the late 1940s.

Despite all the difficulties, the UK succeeded in attaining full employment right through the 1950s and 1960s. Fears of a post-war slump proved groundless, and measured unemployment fell to astonishingly low levels. There was even a considerable immigration of workers from the Commonwealth to supplement the inadequate domestic work-force. Around 1960 over 50,000 a year came in, mainly from the West Indies; later in the 1960s the flow of 25,000 to 30,000 annually came mainly from Asia.

In retrospect this level of employment has been seen by some commentators as 'over-full', and the corresponding level of aggregate demand as too high in relation to the capacity of the economy. Expectations of a higher material standard of living for consumers and of an ever-improving standard of public services grew more rapidly than the capacity of the economy to meet them. In consequence, whenever the economy was stimulated, the result was a balance of payments deficit as goods were diverted from foreign to domestic markets, and imports boomed. The upshot was pressure on the exchange rate which forced successive governments to rein back the expansion, raising taxes, cutting spending and raising interest rates to attract an inflow or deter an outflow of capital.

This alternation between expansion and retrenchment became known in the 1960s as 'stop-go', and many remedies were suggested. Attention was focused on alleged causes, and prominent among these was excessive foreign expenditure by the government, continuing to act as if Britain were still a world power with world-wide interests. This was linked with the determination to maintain sterling as an international trading currency, which effectively ruled out devaluation as a solution to a balance of payments deficit. An international or 'reserve' currency is one which is used by traders in preference to their own national currencies, partly because of its superior exchangeability and partly because of the banking, insurance, shipping and other trading facilities which it offers. Thus trade in trucks and cocoa between West Germany and Ghana might well be conducted in sterling, with the payments routed through London. Traders would either use the pounds earned for other transactions, or leave them on deposit, or convert them into their own currencies; the facilities of the City of London were at their disposal. This also meant that countries would maintain working balances in sterling to even out trade fluctuations. None of this would continue if uncertainties about the stability of the pound became serious, and the City would lose some of its lucrative business. Hence the 'strong pound' lobby which persists even to this day. It is ironic that, if anything, it was Labour governments which held this view most strongly.

A second aspect of stop-go is worth noting. On the whole the 'stop', with its cuts in government spending and its high levels of interest and credit squeezes, was a stop on capital investment. Firms were deterred not only by the cost of borrowing but also by the feeling that by the time any new capital investment came on stream another stop phase would have arrived; they began to lose faith in steady growth. Government, as always, found capital spending much easier to cut than current spending, which would mean sacking people. There is a widely held view that the consequent lack of sustained long-term investment bears much of the blame for Britain's continuing economic ills. Not only was the overall level of investment (as a proportion of GDP) lower than in West Germany, France or Japan, but such investment as did take place was spasmodic and haphazard. It contrasts sharply with the French persistence in carrying through their programme of modernization.

However, in the end devaluation had to come, and in 1967 the exchange rate was lowered from $2.80 to $2.40. The retreat of sterling left the dollar alone as the world's reserve and trading currency, and as we saw it proved unable to meet all the pressure which was placed on it. The breakdown of the fixed exchange rate system which followed at the beginning of the 1970s removed one of the constraints which had hitherto kept the expansion of aggregate demand within limits. When the 'dash for growth' associated with the Conservative Chancellor Anthony Barber took place in 1970–1, it quickly turned a comfortable balance of payments surplus into a deficit. But now it was no longer necessary to cut back; the pound could be allowed to float, and it did so downwards, gently losing a further 10% of its value.

So began a series of events, many of them external to the UK economy and beyond the control of its government, which led to a new phenomenon: a very high rate of inflation coupled with a decline in the level of output. The 'Barber boom' was fuelled by a rapid expansion of credit facilitated by the relaxation of controls on banking. Large sums of money went into the property market, but much less into industrial investment.

However, GDP rose quickly, the growth rate averaging 4% between 1970 and 1973. Indeed the boom was world-wide in these years, resulting in high levels of demand for raw materials, with prices of most of the major commodities rising accordingly. Coupled with the falling value of the pound, this meant a sharp rise in the cost of imports, but the real shock came at the end of 1973 and the beginning of 1974 when the price of oil quadrupled in three months. Since oil in some form or other enters into every other cost, this was an added inflationary factor. The annual rate of increase in the Retail Price Index climbed above 10%, reached 15% in 1974 and rose to over 25% late in 1975.

Looked at from the point of view of the balance of payments, these two events drove the UK and all the other major oil-importing industrial economies into deficit. Large sums flowed into the OPEC countries, but only a few of them, such as Venezuela and Iran, could increase their imports of manufactures very much. The major Arab oil producers had very small populations and virtually no industry, and the money simply piled up in their bank accounts.

The equivalent in a domestic economy would be a sudden increase in saving not offset by an increase in investment spending by firms or in government expenditure. Aggregate demand would therefore fall, output would decline in sympathy, and the economy would move into recession.

Essentially this is what happened on a world scale in 1974–5, made worse by the simultaneous response of most of the major economies to their balance of payments deficits and their accelerating inflation rates. All began to raise interest rates, cut back on government spending and raise taxes, with the intention of reducing their demand for imports.

The world, it seemed, had to learn again that one country's imports are another country's exports. There was a sharp fall in 1975 in Britain's exports, but the immediate effect was on stocks, which fell dramatically, and on investment.

This combination of recession and inflation became known as 'stagflation', and it posed serious problems for economic policy. The accepted remedy for stagnation or recession was to increase aggregate demand; the accepted remedy for inflation was to reduce aggregate demand. New ideas were obviously needed.

One of the responses of the Labour government was to persist in its attempts to make a prices and incomes policy effective. Whether because of this, or because of the other deflationary measures which accompanied the incomes policies, to which we shall return, the rate of inflation fell steadily from its 1975 peak to between 7% and 8% in mid-1978. Growth resumed and averaged 2.5%, but unemployment remained at a post-war peak of 5%.

The difficulties of enforcing an incomes policy became glaringly obvious in 1978–9, the 'winter of discontent'. Antagonism was particularly intense among the relatively low-paid workers in the public sector, and the resentment their industrial actions caused among the electorate contributed to the defeat of the Labour government in the 1979 election. The new Conservative government, strongly averse to government interference with markets, even the labour market, promptly dismantled the whole mechanism. The resulting explosion of wages sent the RPI back up towards 20% in early 1980.

Coming back to the oil price rise, it must be recognized that it brought about a deterioration in Britain's terms of trade and entailed either exporting more goods and services in order to *maintain* the same level of imports, or accepting a lower level of imports, or some combination of the two. This implied, in the absence of growth of GDP, that some other elements of demand would have to go unsatisfied. Government spending could be drastically cut, but not easily. Investment could drop, and it did. But only a fall in consumption would provide an amount of 'slack' commensurate with the turn-round, which was estimated at 2% to 3% of GDP.

At this time Britain imported all its oil – the North Sea fields began to produce in quantity only from 1977 onwards – and oil is priced and paid for in dollars. So the fall in the exchange rate from £2.42 in 1973 to £1.71 in 1977 was, in effect, a further increase of 30% in the oil price.

One can appreciate the difficulties which the economy faced in adjusting to this oil shock, as it was appropriately called, and the importance of incomes policies in preventing the spiralling of wages and prices, as expectations of continued inflation began to be built into all discussions.

Keynesianism under fire

By this time the successes of the post-war period of demand management were largely forgotten as Keynesianism itself came under increasing fire. Broadly these criticisms fell into three groups.

(1) Three decades of Keynesian policies suggested that the monetary and fiscal techniques which it used were decidedly clumsy instruments. Thus for successful stabilization, an inflationary or recessionary condition had to be diagnosed early enough for preventive action to be taken, and the measures then used to redirect the economy had to be rapid but controllable. On each of these counts, demand management techniques had proved to be blunt, hit-or-miss tools of regulation. Assessing the current situation, let alone forecasting the future, is a difficult exercise. And even when the need for action was finally appreciated, monetary and fiscal policies were slow – both to implement in the first place and in their impact on the economy. Moreover, they showed themselves to be even slower to reverse when that was called for. Even when it could safely be predicted that a measure would work in a particular direction, questions of by how much and when could not be answered with the same confidence.

(2) It became clear that demand management could not be relied upon exclusively to achieve the objectives set for the economy. It could deal with the problem which exercised Keynes himself in the first place: unemployment caused by demand deficiency. And it could be applied in the opposite situation where it was excessive demand which was causing inflation. (Although even here the problems of 'fine tuning' the level of demand to just the right amount might make it very difficult to strike the appropriate balance.)

But unemployment had other causes too. Regional and technological unemployment, for example, was not so susceptible to manipulation of national spending. Inflation, when caused by cost-push pressures, similarly called for a different type of solution. And a high or even stable level of demand might be necessary but was not a sufficient method for obtaining faster economic growth. What was needed, so it was increasingly argued, was a greater emphasis on the 'supply side' factors in the economy: measures aimed more directly at raising productivity or restraining income/price rises through changes in institutions, attitudes and practices. Such criticisms came, it should be noted, both from the left and from the right of the political spectrum, leading to very different conclusions about the scope and nature of state intervention that was required.

(3) Thirdly, there was rising scepticism about whether the four objectives of policy were inherently compatible. In particular, doubt was expressed that full employment could be maintained without generating inflationary pressures. Might there have to be a trade-off between the two, with rather higher unemployment being accepted as the necessary condition for bringing inflation under control?

By the mid-1970s, as we have seen, inflation had mounted to what were regarded as very worrying levels. Increasingly public attention became focused on rising prices as the main problem to be faced. Gradually to begin with, and then quite sharply in 1979, the old order of economic priorities changed. With the advent of the Thatcher administration, squeezing inflation out of the system became the paramount economic objective. Full employment as a goal lost its pre-eminent position and has not, so far, regained it.

This change in *political* priorities was accompanied, as we shall now see, by a dramatic switch of economic policy. Keynesianism was not to be reformed or supplemented as many of its earlier critics had intended. Instead it was abandoned, to be derided and blamed for what was now interpreted as thirty years of economic mismanagement and failure.

MONETARISM

What might be called 'pre-Keynesian' ideas had never completely faded away, and the accelerating rate of inflation in the 1970s caused a renewal of interest in the role of money in the economy and a shift in the priorities of the policy-makers away from growth and employment and towards the stability of domestic prices and the external price of the currency, the exchange rate.

Intellectually this shift is associated with the USA and specifically with the University of Chicago and Professor Milton Friedman, but the ideas spread in the context of world-wide inflation to the International Monetary Fund. So the adoption of targets for the growth of the money supply in 1976 and the use of cash limits rather than volume measures in the control of government spending are sometimes associated with the advice of the IMF when Britain had to borrow to cope with its foreign exchange problems in 1975. But the truth is that the Labour government of the time went further than the IMF had in fact called for in imposing monetary targets.

'Monetarism' is the modern name given to what is really a very old theory – simply that inflation is a consequence of excessive growth in the quantity of money in the economy, and of nothing else. 'Only money matters.' Inflation, a fall in the value of money, is caused by too great a supply. Control that supply, and price rises will be checked accordingly.

It is a short step to putting the blame for inflation on government, since it is only government, not trade unions or firms, that has the ability to print money. This, so it was contended, was what it had been all too ready to do during the 'Keynesian' years, effectively financing its operations by debasing the currency in much the same way as medieval kings had done.

The prime economic responsibility of government, as the newly elected Conservative administration in 1979 saw it, was therefore to halt this process and to re-establish the principles of 'sound finance'. The key regulator of the economy was to be the money supply. If that were brought under control, then other forms of government intervention would be unnecessary or positively harmful. These wider aspects of the new approach will be dealt with subsequently. For the time being, we shall focus attention on the view that 'inflation has always and everywhere been accompanied by an increase in the supply of money', and the belief that too much money is therefore what causes inflation.

The theoretical basis for the relationship between the money supply and the level of prices can be summed up by a celebrated equation known as the 'equation of exchange'. It is not really an equation but an identity, since it is true by definition, but it is usually written as

$$MV = PT$$

'M' is the supply of money (whichever definition we choose); 'V' is the velocity of circulation, i.e. the number of times that the money stock turns over during the course of a year. So M times V is the total flow of money, its effective 'supply', during that period.

On the other side of the 'equation', 'T' is a measure of the number of transactions involving money which take place in the economy during the year. It therefore has a very close relationship with 'Y', the gross national or domestic product, but T will be much bigger since it includes all the intermediate transactions which are netted out of the GDP calculations, as well as transactions in second-hand goods and paper claims such as stocks and shares. 'P' is the average amount of money involved in each transaction, i.e. the average level of prices. T, the number of transactions, times P, the average amount of money involved in each, therefore represents the amount of money which is needed in the economy: the demand for money.

At this stage, $MV = PT$ is simply a truism, since the two sides are really different ways of thinking about the same quantity, the total amount of spending in the economy. The monetarist theory goes much further, in asserting that it is the supply of money which *causes* inflation. It is M that determines P; causation runs from left to right.

Clearly this will hold good only if the remaining elements are more or less constant. Monetarists do believe that the velocity of circulation is reasonably stable, being determined by social habits which change slowly. They also believe that the economy will tend towards a 'natural rate' of unemployment – a given level of economic activity which government cannot influence. This implies that T also will change only slowly as, or if, the economy grows.

Given T, and assuming a stable V, then any expansion of the money supply will show up, after a longer or shorter delay (about the length of which there is some dispute), in an increase in P, the general level of prices. Conversely the remedy for inflation is a reduction, or at least a slowing-down, in the growth of the money supply. It is worth noting Friedman's own prescription, which is a steady, slow expansion of the money supply in line with expected economic growth, and he would shift responsibility for this out of the untrustworthy hands of the government into those of an independent central bank.

In assessing the theory and practice of monetarism, we need to look first at how control of the growth of the money supply is supposed to achieve price stability. There are also serious practical problems to consider in defining what is meant by 'money' (which we saw in Chapter 14 cannot be done unambiguously) and then in controlling its growth in a sophisticated financial system such as ours.

How, it might be asked, can monetarists put the whole blame for inflation on excessive growth in the money supply and ignore more obvious upward pressures on prices exerted, for example, by wage increases above those warranted by higher productivity? The answer is that, for them, such pay rises are a *symptom* of 'too much money' rather than themselves the cause of inflation.

Granted, for the moment, the assumption that both V and T (at full employment, however defined) are stable then the increase in the quantity of money which a higher P requires can came about only through an increase in M, i.e. a growth in the money supply, matching and in a sense 'validating' the rate of inflation. If therefore the government keeps a tight control over the money supply, there will simply be none available with which to meet the higher wage demands. Workers will either have to accept less than they had hoped for or face the consequences in terms of higher unemployment. Thus some firms, unable to pay higher wages to all their employees, will instead dismiss part of their work-force.

Once it becomes plain to all concerned that the government is not going to react to rising unemployment by reflating the economy – by expanding the money supply again – then expectations will be revised. Workers will modify their wage claims, and when they are prepared to accept a lower real wage they will be re-employed. If they are not prepared to accept a lower real wage, then their unemployment is 'voluntary' and no one's concern but their own.

In the process of eliminating inflation, wage increases will therefore be lower than price increases; real wages and thus standards of living have to go down if inflation is to be checked and reversed. But once inflation has been shaken out of the system, the economy will return to its 'natural' employment level. Confidence in the stability of the currency will be restored, saving and investment will revive, and real incomes can begin to rise again in line with any improvement in productivity.

Even if this works at all, there remain unanswered questions about how long it will take and how much will it cost in lost output. Much depends on how quickly markets respond, particularly the labour market. If there is a good deal of monopoly power, then firms may be able to raise prices and pay higher wages. If key workers can use their position to resist wage cuts or redundancies, then the cost will be borne by other, weaker groups. Since the government itself is a major employer, it may be able to enforce wage cuts directly or through strict cash limits on spending.

So monetarists see workers as having to face a choice: between a temporary reduction in living standards or (assuming some modest growth of the economy) a pause in their rise or, on the other hand, the maintenance or improvement of some people's real incomes at the cost of unemployment and a drastic decline in income for others. The monetarists's view is that a properly functioning market would provide the solution, and that once inflation is under control, workers will move out of the declining industries or areas into the new opportunities which will emerge as the economy returns to full employment.

Monetarism in practice

The official basis for monetarism in practice was the government's Medium-Term Financial Strategy in which a vital component was the setting of targets for the growth of the money supply, concentrating initially on £M3. Curiously, however, the government to begin with (in the spirit of its pro-market philosophy) removed the very restraints on the banking system's freedom to expand credit which its predecessors had used. The so-called 'corset', introduced in December 1973, was abolished, with a corresponding increase in the banks' freedom to lend and thereby to increase the money supply.

In fact, instead of relying wholly on regulating the *supply* of money directly, the government chose to operate to a large extent on the *demand* for money. It argued that, once that had been constrained, then supply would be adjusted accordingly.

Since the demand for money could come from either the public or the private sector, policy to contain it was two-edged. Private sector demand, from firms or households, was to be held back by manipulating the price of money, the rate of interest. Demand from the public sector, on the other hand, was to be achieved through reducing the government's own level of borrowing, which in turn meant holding back or cutting total public spending. This emphasis on the demand side was criticized by some, including Friedman himself, as not in fact being 'pure' monetarism.

In fact during the early years of the policy the paradoxical effect was to increase rather than reduce private demand for money. This was largely because of the deflationary implications of the government's economic stance, which reduced demand for firms' output and put them into financial difficulties which forced them to borrow more than they otherwise would have found necessary. This in turn was compounded by additional borrowing needed to service the higher interest charges that they were now having to meet.

Increasingly government became obsessed with the other arm of its policy – reducing the Public Sector Borrowing Requirement in the belief that it was closely linked to the supply of money. The nature of the PSBR is a matter that we have already examined in Chapter 16, where we also explained the error of thinking that it is synonymous with monetary growth. It is true that if the government borrows from the banking system the money supply will increase because the banks gain assets which form a base for further lending. But if the government sells securities to the public – whether to individuals, pension funds or insurance companies – the money supply is actually decreased, because the 'non-bank public' exchanges money for assets which are not money as conventionally defined. Reference back to Table 16.4 shows that only in 1982 was there any significant government borrowing from the banking system. Yet the size of the PSBR became a central point in government policy, and its reduction a major aim. There was some confusion about whether the concern about the PSBR stemmed from concern about the growth of £M3, with which as we saw it is not closely connected, if at all; or whether the concern was that excessive borrowing meant high interest rates, which cause, to use the government's own words in its Medium-Term Financial Strategy of March 1980 'greater financing problems for the private sector'. In any case, the PSBR proved difficult to reduce. Total government outlay on defence, law and order and agriculture has increased; spending on housing has decreased, and the increases in education and health have slowed down markedly. Some public corporations have reduced their losses, and others have not. But ironically the recession led to a massive increase in transfer payments to the unemployed. Without the fortuitous tax flow from North Sea oil, government would have been caught in the dilemma of raising taxes or *increasing* its borrowing requirement.

Part of the reason for failure to meet the targets of £M3 set in the Medium-Term Financial Strategy was undoubtedly that when the pressure became severe the Bank of England limited the otherwise large rise in interest rates by adding to the banks' liquidity. Strict monetarism, which would say 'control the quantity and let the market dictate the price', was not actually implemented. (And it is doubtful whether, in a complex financial system such as that of the UK, it is possible for government directly to control the money supply or to prevent stability in M being offset by variations in V, the efficiency with which any given quantity of money is made to work.)

However, high interest rates as part of *attempted* monetarism became an important contributory factor in the soaring sterling exchange rate of the early 1980s. The coincidental appearance of net oil exports made sterling a particularly desirable currency to hold. At one point it got back to its old £2.40 level, and British exporters complained bitterly that they were being priced out of all their markets. On the other hand, import prices were falling and so assisting in the reduction of inflation which was the government's main objective.

But the combined squeeze of high interest rates and a high exchange rate imposed intolerable pressures on British industry, leaving it in a very uncompetitive position abroad, facing a depressed home market of which imports were taking a greater proportion, and deterring fresh investment. The answer, reiterated time and again by government, lay in reducing home costs, particularly by a fall in real wages.

An alternative view

There is, however, another interpretation of government policy and its effects over these years, along broadly Keynesian lines of analysis. One way of reducing excessive aggregate demand, and so reducing inflationary pressures, is to restrict credit and increase its price, namely the rate of interest. The economy will react to this, on a conventional Keynesian analysis, by reducing investment expenditures and some elements of personal consumption – consumer durables. The first impact will be on stocks, which are very costly to maintain if interest rates are high; and Figure 13 (page 121) shows just how big an impact the advent of the new government had. The second element most affected will be capital formation, and again the marked fall from 1979 onwards is plain.

Add to this the government's declared intention and strenuous efforts to reduce the PSBR via a reduction in government spending, and there are all the ingredients of a typical deflationary package. The difference, perhaps, between these measures and similar previous episodes lay in the perceived shift in objectives. It was clear to most observers and, in case it was not, the government missed no opportunity of making it plain that it would squeeze inflation out of the economy no matter what the cost in unemployment or business failures. There would be no U-turn. 'TINA' ('there is no alternative') became almost a slogan. So, few people expected the recession to be short or mild. There would be no point in keeping a factory ticking over, or hanging on to key workers. The number of plant closures and redundancies increased from month to month.

The surprising thing about the 1979–81 recession is that, although disposable income fell, consumer expenditure did not. Consumers maintained or increased their spending (in real terms) partly by reducing the proportion of their incomes which they saved and partly through increased use of credit. Had it not been for this, the recession might have been much worse. The other offsetting factor was the drop in imports as a result of the fall in oil imports.

So the 'Thatcher recession' can be explained in straightforward Keynesian terms without invoking monetarist theories and without trying to define 'money' or to find out how the money supply actually behaved. (In fact, the various monetary aggregates – Mo, M1, M3 and PSL2 – which we discussed in Chapter 14 behaved in contradictory ways, adding to the difficulties of the government and the scepticism of the non-monetarists.) In brief, the attempt to reduce the PSBR by controlling government spending, and the high cost and shortage of credit, in the context of a world-wide depression so that exports were declining or stagnant, led to a typical recession. Inventories were drastically reduced, profits fell, firms closed down or reduced their operations, and unemployment rose steadily to levels not experienced since the 1930s.

Even in the short run the impact which these unpropitious factors had on wage increases was only limited: partly because there was a rebound from the severe income policies of the outgoing government; partly because of large increases in public sector pay following from the Clegg comparability study; and partly because of the government's own actions in switching taxation from the top range of income tax to indirect taxes via a large increase in VAT. The resulting sharp rise in retail prices led to compensatory wage claims. And by the mid-1980s real earnings in the private sector were rising rapidly despite the continuation of mass unemployment.

As we have noted, one repercussion of the increase in this unemployment was much greater government spending on unemployment and supplementary benefits, which made the control of the PSBR far more difficult. Increasingly capital expenditure was cut, until the country's infrastructure – its roads, water supply, drainage and public buildings – was visibly decaying. Desired and desirable growth in spending on health and education was deferred, and the pursuit of efficiency and the use of cash limits and severe restrictions on local authority spending led to redundancies in the public sector as well.

On the credit side, it can be pointed out that inflation was finally reduced from its high point of over 20% in 1980 to 5% in 1983–4, and that productivity increased sharply. It should not be forgotten, however, that although the government in 1979 inherited a lot of inflationary pressures, the rate of inflation when it took office was only 10%. Scepticism has also been expressed about the nature of the productivity increase that has taken place. Largely this was the result of wholesale closures in the manufacturing sector. In other words, the rise in productivity is chiefly due to eliminating weaker enterprises rather than improving their efficiency. British manufacturing may be 'fitter' but has it as a consequence become so much 'leaner' that it can no longer produce the contribution required from it, in particular to the balance of payments?

The lack of 'downward flexibility' in wages led to a renewed attack on trade union privilege and power, which we shall discuss in Chapter 19. Here let us continue the story of macro-economic policy a little further. Figure 13 (page 121) shows how the various macro-economic categories of expenditure changed from 1981 to 1984. GDP (and national income, which is plotted in the figure) began to increase again in real terms from 1981 onwards; average growth from 1981 to 1984 was just over 2%. Domestic capital formation rose again, though inventories did not increase and capital formation had barely returned to 1979 levels in 1984. Personal consumption, which had held up during the recession, continued to rise, as did exports with the flow of North Sea oil reaching its peak levels. On the negative side, unemployment did not fall; industrial output and non-oil exports of manufactures were stagnant or declining. Such new jobs as appeared were predominantly in services, especially financial and technical services, and in distribution, hotels, catering and the like: jobs, in other words, for professionally qualified men or part-time women workers, neither of which categories was much help to unemployed manual workers dismissed from steel, coal, shipbuilding or the assembly lines of the Midlands. There was little sign of the spontaneous recovery which was going to follow the elimination of inflation. Even the recent sharp fall in oil prices to levels which were as low as in 1972 (if not lower in real terms), which reduced inflation in West Germany to negative figures, failed to stimulate a sustained upturn in the world economy.

By the mid-1980s the general verdict was that monetarism was dead, if not buried. The money supply was rising rapidly; government borrowing was also increasing, albeit in a concealed form through the proceeds of privatization; there was a consumer boom financed through credit expansion. What, indeed, was taking place was a Keynesian pre-election boom. It was however, a reflation of the least desirable kind – with higher demand channelled into consumption, property and financial take-overs rather than industrial investment – and inevitably spilling over into a flood of imports as home industry lacked the capacity to respond to increased spending.

Debate will continue about whether or not a 'true' monetarist experiment was really conducted. But certainly the costs of attempted monetarism have been enormous. Although it would be unfair to blame the worrying state of the British economy in the mid-1980s entirely on government policies, they must be held responsible for exacerbating underlying problems. It is ironic that the UK, where monetarism was pursued with more resolute enthusiasm than in any other major industrial state, should have suffered worse unemployment, a much greater degree of manufacturing weakness and yet still a higher rate of inflation than those averaged in other Western European nations, the United States and Japan, despite the British advantage during these years in having the bonus of North Sea oil.

The future is bound to see some reversion to elements of Keynesianism, not as a sufficient but as a necessary condition for improvement of the economic prospect. How far that will be supplemented by more direct intervention (for which those on the left would argue), or whether there will be continued reliance on a freer market system to achieve the required outcome, remains to be seen.

19

Government and the Market

Conservative governments in the years following 1979 have been inspired by much more than a simple adherence to a particular theory of inflation. Beyond purely technical monetarism lay a whole philosophy: a belief that markets should be allowed to operate freely without any intervention from government, whose function should largely be limited to maintaining the framework of law and order and national security which makes this possible. 'Law' includes the preservation of property rights, and since money and monetary assets are a major form of property, the maintenance of the value of the currency is a paramount duty. This was held to mean prudent finance – a balanced budget, with spending and hence taxation kept to low levels. These principles were extended to an international scale: the free operation of trade and finance, and so a stable currency. 'A strong pound', maintaining its purchasing power internally and externally, was the primary or perhaps the only economic objective.

The level of employment, the distribution of income, the rate of economic growth and so on – these were not considered the responsibility or the concern of governments, beyond ensuring that the market forces which determine them should be allowed to operate with maximum freedom. Incomes policies in particular are anathema to anyone holding these beliefs. If trade unions wish to claim excessively high wages and so create unemployment, that is nothing to do with the government. Once workers see that the money with which to pay these high wages will not be provided, they will modify their behaviour. If firms choose not to invest in new technology, on a judgement that the returns will be inadequate, then since they will bear the consequences of being wrong there is no call for government to persuade them or bribe them to do otherwise. If new investment flows overseas because movement of capital is free, again the commercial judgements which give rise to these decisions must be respected.

It is a minimalist, almost a 'do-nothing' approach to economic policy which responds to the inevitable question 'Why doesn't the government do something?' with the twofold answer that it is not the proper function of government to do these things, and that intervention by government will probably make things worse rather than better. It has a positive aspect which should not be ignored, namely a belief that individual freedoms are best preserved by such a 'hands-off' role for governments. The bigger the government, the smaller the range of decisions which people can make for themselves. Government should restrict its activities to those which it alone can carry out; hence the suggestions that it should get out of health or education, or at least let the market in to these fields. The only thing a government can do in the sphere of economics is regulate the supply of money.

GOVERNMENT'S SHARE IN THE ECONOMY

Following from this philosophy recent years have seen a determined intention to 'roll back the public sector', to reduce the share of the nation's resources taken by government and thereby to widen the scope for private enterprise and choice.

Since in the subsequent debate figures have frequently been used which give an erroneous impression about the extent of the government's share in the economy, it is worth carefully examining the basis of the statistics.

Measures of government spending

If we look back to our basic picture of the United Kingdom economy in Figures 9 and 10 (pages 68 and 70), we see that from the overall stream of income and expenditure the government (i.e. general government) extracted £87 billion from incomes through various forms of *direct* taxation and took a net £49 billion from taxes on expenditure or *indirect* taxation. On the other hand, the government paid out very large sums: £70 billion in pensions and other supplements to incomes, and £81 billion in respect of goods and services. In relation to total final expenditure, which in 1985 was £450 billion, general government was involved in one way or another with about 30% of measured economic activity.

Table 19.1. The government's share of national product

Category of spending	Percentage of GDP					
	early 1970s	1975	1979	1980	1982	1985
General govt expenditure on goods and services (G)	17–18	22	20	22	22	21
G as above plus general govt share of gross domestic capital formation	22	27	23	24	24	23
General govt total current spending	32–33	39	38	40	43	42
General govt total current and capital spending	38	45	42	45	46	45

Note: Both figures may change. Government spending, however defined, may rise or fall, but so also may GDP. The increased percentages in 1975 and 1980 are partly due to a fall in GDP in those years.

Around this fact there revolve the most acrimonious arguments about the size of the government's share in the economy, the nature of its interventions and the way in which things should be changed. It therefore becomes very important to be clear about our definitions. The first distinction which we must make is between general government's contribution to total expenditure on national product, and total government expenditure.

It will be remembered that when we were trying to measure the size of the UK economy we 'added up' all the goods and services which it produced in the course of a year, using the prices of the goods and services as the unit of measurement. The *volume* of output was measured by the *expenditure* on it. Using this concept, the share of general government has been as shown in Table 19.1.

Now 20% of all the available goods and services does not seem an obviously disproportionate share, when all the functions which central and local governments have to carry out are remembered. Yet for the past ten years or more critics have argued that the level of government spending has been excessive; and, since 1975, although more particularly after 1979, successive governments have been trying to reduce it, or at least to restrain its growth. They have commonly referred to the government's slice of the total as being of the order of 45% rather than the more modest share that we have just indicated.

Table 19.2. Government spending and GDP (£ million, at current prices)

	1980	1981	1982	1983	1984	1985
General govt total spending	104	117	128	138	146	159
GDP	230	254	277	301	319	351
Spending as % of GDP	45.2	46.1	46.2	45.8	45.8	45.3

The nature of this confusion is a matter we have already touched upon. It arises from the fact that in the definition we have used so far we have been concentrating on government's claim on *real resources*, and the goods and services which those resources produce. 20% to 25% has been the proportion of those resources which governments at all levels have taken and used for public purposes.

If we translate this percentage into actual sums of money, we find that in 1980 and 1984 current expenditure on goods and services, and capital expenditure, amounted to £52.7 billion and £74 billion respectively. But in the same year the *total* expenditures were £104 billion and £146 billion, roughly twice as much.

The difference is made up of a series of payments for which nothing was received in exchange. In other words, these were not payments for goods and services, but simply transfer payments of money from the government to individual members of the population. These sums will eventually be spent, or saved, and the government will get some of them back again through taxation, but until they reappear as expenditure on gross domestic product under the heading of 'consumption' or 'investment', they are *not* part of gross domestic product.

As Table 16.2 (page 233) illustrated, the two big items are current grants to the personal sector and debt interest. The first of these consists of pensions, unemployment and supplementary benefits, and similar payments to individuals and families. The second, debt interest, goes to holders of government securities of various kinds. Financial institutions are dominant amongst these holders, but their earnings from interest payments are often redistributed via insurance claims, private pensions, etc. to individuals.

About half of total government spending, therefore, simply represents money taken from one part of the population (the taxpayers) and transferred to another part. In practice nearly all of us belong to both parts at once; most us receive some kind of payment and pay some kinds of tax. Money goes out of one pocket and comes into the other. This part of

Table 19.3. Comparisons of government spending and taxes (% of GDP)

	1960	1965	1970	1975	1980	Increase 1960–80
Sweden						
Spending	31.1	36.0	43.7	49.0	65.7	+34.6
Taxes	32.2	39.6	46.9	50.7	57.1	+24.9
West Germany						
Spending	32.0	36.3	37.6	47.1	46.9	+14.9
Taxes	34.8	35.3	37.5	40.8	42.8	+8.0
France						
Spending	34.6	38.4	38.9	43.5	46.2	+11.6
Taxes	34.9	38.4	39.0	40.3	45.4	+10.5
United Kingdom						
Spending	32.6	36.4	39.3	46.9	44.6	+12.0
Taxes	30.3	33.4	40.7	40.7	40.4	+10.1

government spending has also remained remarkably constant. It was 49.3% in 1980, 49.4% in 1984 and 49.1% in 1985.

Much of the 'panic' about the size of government spending has been generated by the rather peculiar habit of expressing total government spending (of which only half is spending on goods and services, i.e. part of GDP) as a percentage of gross domestic or national product. Remembering that this is therefore rather a bogus statistic, it is interesting to note that it too has been remarkably stable – see Table 19.2.

This is not a particularly high percentage by historical standards. Government spending on *goods and services* has been astonishingly constant at around 20% of GDP ever since 1946. *Total spending* fell from roughly 45% in 1946 to around 35% in the mid- and late 1950s, rising as we have seen to 46% in the 1980s. What caused increasing alarm (apart from the questionable use of statistical evidence) was a marked jump in 1975–7, which resulted from the continued growth in government spending at a time when GDP fell.

Is government spending in the UK very different from spending in other countries? Is it comparatively high? This is not what the comparative figures in Table 19.3 suggest.

What is 'too high' or 'too low' with respect to both expenditure and the taxation needed to cover it depends on a social and political consensus that the objectives of the various spending programmes are acceptable, and that the level of spending on them is reasonable, or the reverse. France, West Germany and the UK are very similar, while Sweden accepts a higher proportion of both taxes and spending. Much depends too on the impact of the taxes; high rates of income tax show up as a deduction from pay packets, whereas high social security contributions by employers are hidden from the majority. One big difference between France and West Germany, on the one hand, and the UK lies in the way that social security spending is financed.

Taxes on income and wealth represent nearly 40% of total taxation in the UK, contrasting with 30% in West Germany and 21% in France. Social security contributions, on the other hand, represent 43% of total French taxes, 39% of West German taxes, but only 18% in the UK.

'Crowding out' the private sector

The case for reducing the share of government in the economy is often put in terms of 'releasing resources for the private sector'. It is argued that the latter is in some sense 'crowded out' by the public sector. However, it is difficult to see just what this could mean.

If the economy were operating at full employment, then it might be true that public and private sectors were competing for limited real resources. More of one would mean less of the other, except to the extent that both could be accommodated through economic growth. (Even in this situation, however, it is important to remember the degree to which public and private forms of economic activity are complementary and interdependent.) But when, as today, the economy is running well *below* full employment, there is no inherent reason why both public and private sectors should not be able to command greater resources.

A more sophisticated view is that the crowding-out effect is financial. Government's attempts to increase its spending generally involve higher borrowing. This, it is claimed, pushes up interest rates to levels which inhibit private sector borrowing. However, such a view rests on the assumption that there is a fixed pool of finance available; there is no reason why this should be so unless government policy itself is financially restrictive – which, of course, it has been while monetarist policies have been followed. In any case, there are other calls on finance than government. Why should the high interest rates be the results of excessive government borrowing rather than, for example, the demands for finance arising from consumer spending or investment overseas?

To conclude, it is untrue to say that the slice of resources taken by government in the UK has been much different from that in other comparable countries, or that it has markedly increased. Nor do the arguments for reducing that share seem particularly cogent or persuasive. And in the event, as we have seen, attempts to reduce the proportion of government spending have not been very successful. The total has remained remarkably stable although the composition has changed. To some extent this has reflected intended policy: for example, higher spending on defence, less on housing. But it has also arisen as a side-effect of broader economic policy, with attempted cuts in various areas offset by rising expenditure on unemployment benefits and other social 'transfers' stemming from recession and widening inequalities.

LUBRICATING THE LABOUR MARKET

Trade union power

The view that government had become too dominant and ponderous, inefficient and destructive of initiative and enterprise stemmed from the Conservative belief in the virtues of markets and market solutions to economic problems. The Conservatives accordingly aimed at both a slimming of the public sector and the achievement of greater efficiency through the introduction of more business-like methods. As we shall see in the following section, there was also the intention through a massive privatization programme of returning nationalized industries to private ownership and management, while making those which remained more responsive to commercial pressures, and expanding individual choice in matters like health and education. For now, however, we look at attempts, not only to withdraw from many areas where previous governments had intervened, but also to make the market system work more effectively through eliminating various 'imperfections' which marred its operations.

There was, in particular, a determination to make the labour market more 'flexible'. We have seen how trade unions, once blamed for inflation, now come to be regarded by those of monetarist persuasion as responsible instead for unemployment – by maintaining a wage level too high for the labour market to 'clear' itself.

Policy was directed in the first place therefore at weakening the power of the trade unions and their leaders, partly for the economic reasons just mentioned, and partly because of the political memory that the Heath government had been brought down by the miners' strike in 1973–4. The previous Labour government had also attempted to restrict union

2

84   *Policy and Performance – Past, Present and Future*

power; by the mid-1970s there was a measure of consensus in the political 'centre' that reforms were needed.

The main legislation introduced to curb union power was in the 1980 and 1982 Employment Acts and the 1984 Trades Union Act. These laid down new rules for picketing which in effect eliminated the scope for 'sympathy' strikes. They limited the possibility of closed shops and required ballots before strike action. Together they have undoubtedly weakened the power of the unions to resist plant closures and job losses. But as important in contributing to a lessening of union influence must have been the general economic climate of these years.

There was still confrontation between the government and the unions, mainly over redundancies in the nationalized industries. Unions strenuously attempted to resist the run-down of manufacturing industry and especially of their traditional base in steel and coal, with the latter providing the main battlefield.

Coal since nationalization has steadily lost its position as the UK's primary source of energy, but for many years the process of run-down was amicable because the pace was slow. Young miners whose pits were worked out could be re-employed nearby, and older workers were glad to accept the relatively generous retirement terms. Between 1960 and 1970 employment fell by over 50% as production was concentrated into fewer but more productive collieries. (The number of working collieries fell by nearly 60% in the same period.) Coal was now vulnerable because of its dependence on the Central Electricity Board as its only major customer, and pressures to 'break even' or to operate profitably led to a further programme of closures of 'uneconomic' pits, to which the miners' union responded by strike action. It eventually lost a very bitterly fought battle.

Generous redundancy payments have subsequently proved tempting, with a job loss of a further 50,000 in coal-mining since the end of the strike. More generally, well over 2 million jobs have been lost in manufacturing since 1973, and the decline continues. So do pockets of union resistance, as in the printing industry.

Work and welfare

In addition to these broad legislative reforms, there has been a great deal of discussion about the possible role of welfare payments in creating a disincentive to work and too high a floor for the wage levels which would be necessary to clear the labour market.

A common line of argument from the political 'new right' is that the 'cushion' of unemployment and supplementary benefits discourages the unemployed from seeking work, and those in low-paid work from seeking advancement, since the increased earnings result in lower benefits.

Certainly it is possible for the taxation and the welfare system to combine in creating some undesirable situations. Let us consider first the often-repeated allegation that unemployment benefits act as a disincentive to accepting low-paid work. On the supply side of the labour market workers are thought of as evaluating each job on offer and deciding whether or not to apply, and then, if a job is offered, deciding whether or not to accept it. They are thought to have in mind a 'reservation wage', a wage rate below which they would not consider working. A very important element in such calculations must be the level of income when *not* working. If the alternative to work were starvation, or the Victorian workhouse, a very low wage would be accepted, and the reservation wage would be virtually zero. If unemployment or supplementary benefit is available, the reservation wage is correspondingly higher. How much higher?

Factors making for a high reservation wage might include:

(a) generous benefits;
(b) high costs of working (travel, clothing, meals out, etc.);
(c) unpleasantness of work/attractiveness of leisure;
(d) undeclared income (underground economy, home-grown vegetables, etc.).

Factors working in the opposite direction might be:

(a) miserly benefits;
(b) social/family disapproval of unemployment;
(c) guilt about idleness;
(d) pleasures of work/boredom of idleness.

This is a very difficult field to research since it is not one where honest answers can always be expected to questions, and any large-scale links between benefit level and unemployment can be swamped by other economic factors such as boom or slump. There is some evidence to suggest that generous benefits might *lengthen* periods of unemployment by reducing the pressure to accept the first available job. There is little to suggest that many unemployed people prefer – or are even content – to live on their benefits. In the words of Professor A. B. Atkinson, one of the principal researchers in this field, 'there is at present no strong evidence that there are a large proportion of volunteers among the unemployed watching the monetarist experiments of the early 1980s. It does appear to be a conscript army.'

This does not mean that the tax and benefit system has no effect, still less that it could not be reformed to increase the benefit from working. Because of the interactions between the benefit system and the tax systems, increased income can increase tax liability while *at the same time* rendering a person ineligible for means-tested benefits. The relatively simple calculation of gains and losses envisaged above has to be complicated by considering 'wage less tax and NI contribution' and the additional expenses resulting from loss of benefits such as rent rebates and free school meals.

Two examples of the workings of what has become known as the 'poverty trap' will illustrate the problem. (The system is constantly changing and currently undergoing review, so the cases are based on the situation in the early 1980s.)

Case 1. How much would a married man with two children of school age have to earn at work if he is to *increase* spendable income by £10 a week? The calculation (using 1982 levels) would have been as follows: *

Income from supplementary benefit		Income from work	
	£		£
Supplementary benefit	43.05	Gross wages	???
Child benefit	10.50	plus Child benefit	10.50
Rent rebate	14.60	less Tax	25.49
Rate rebate	6.40	less NI contribution	11.55
Other benefits, say	10.71	less Rent and rates	21.00
	———	less Work-related expenses	10.00
	85.26		———
less Rent and rates	21.00	Target spending power	74.26
Net spending power	64.26		

The gross wage required – the sum to replace the ??? and to make the right-hand column add up – is £132: in other words an average manual wage. There would be little incentive to accept a low-paid job, unless the very strong social pressures are remembered. This explains why so many people have argued for a reduction in the levels of benefit, especially for

* Data from Hermione Parker, *The Moral Hazards of Social Benefits*, IEA Research Monograph No. 37, 1982.

young people who could never expect to earn average wages when starting work.

Case 2. This example illustrates how the system may perversely discourage young people from taking up training:

2nd-year trainee hairdresser		Unemployed on supplementary benefit	
Wage	31.00	Supplementary benefit	18.60
less Tax	0.26	Housing addition	2.55
less N I contribution	2.76	Disregarded earnings	4.00
less Fares to work and			
college, lunch	7.00		
Net income	19.68		25.15

The system got into this kind of muddle for a number of reasons. In part it was because of legitimate and laudable concern about poverty, especially in families with children, which led to an expansion of benefits. In part it was a legacy of inflation which brought more and more low-paid (relatively speaking) into the income tax net, so that the level at which income tax starts being paid is below the poverty level at which entitlement to various benefits begins. In part it is because National Insurance is still thought of as 'insurance', with the flat-rate contribution entitling everyone to a flat rate of benefit. Hence a benefit big enough to be useful as the sole source of income requires a contribution which takes a lot (proportionately) out of a small wage.

However, the existence of such anomalies provides little in the way of support for the contention that many of the unemployed are simply 'scroungers'. The fact is that the jobs are not there. So long as the number out of work continues to exceed registered vacancies by over two and a half million, the question of how many are deterred from work by over-generous welfare payments remains an academic one.

Improving the quality of the work-force

The fact that the major industrial disputes of the past few years have been about plant closures, job losses and the introduction of new technologies is sometimes taken to indicate the reluctance of workers to change – in contrast to the mobility, both geographical and occupational, ascribed for example to the United States work-force. Certainly a way must be found of shifting people from declining industries to growing ones and from unneeded occupations to new ones, although, once again, the priority must be in creating the job opportunities themselves.

Other countries have put a great deal more government effort into initial education and training, into retraining as technology changes and generally into cushioning the impact of industrial change without slowing it down. Attention has been drawn to the much greater involvement of West German and Japanese workers in the technicalities of the processes in which they are involved; a reflection of their superior technical education. Sweden's programme of retraining has attracted praise, and Japan's lifetime security in its large industrial firms is associated with the recognition that the 'job' will change, probably more than once, during a working lifetime.

Attention has already been drawn to the 'bulge' of new entrants to the work-force in the early and middle 1980s. The number of babies born each year in the 1960s was about 950,000, and in the mid-1980s about 110,000 of them are gaining a first degree, 11% to 12% of each cohort. That figure compares very unfavourably with most other developed economies, but it is at the next level – the crucially important technicians and executives – that Britain's failures are exposed. Less than 4% of the age group gained a technical or business certificate or diploma at a higher level, so that a bare 15% to 16% in total are 'qualified'. Very few of the remaining 85% will obtain skills via the traditional route of apprenticeship and technical college, and a high proportion move straight from school to unemployment. In some inner-city areas this proportion has in fact been 80%.

In Britain as elsewhere the focus of attention has rightly been on young people, the group which has experienced very high levels of unemployment. Failure to gain a first job after leaving school is a shattering experience, tantamount to rejection by adult society. So 'job experience', the opportunity to gain some taste of work, linked to a greater or lesser amount of training, has been one strand of the various and changing schemes introduced since 1975. The original Work Experience programme was replaced by a Youth Opportunities Programme, which in turn has grown into a much broader Youth Training Scheme, under which, it is intended, every young person will get some training for work. This was at least a move, however late in the day, towards developing an education and training system comparable to what had been operating for years in West Germany and France.

The second facet of these employment programmes is 'job creation':

the deliberate creation of work opportunities in the community in which the young unemployed could undertake useful tasks of construction, clean-up, social service, and so on. There was little or no element of training, though it was hoped that the mere fact of having been employed would help participants when their period of employment on the scheme was over. The original Job Creation Programme ended in 1978, but was replaced by a Special Temporary Employment Programme, designed for the 19–25 age group and for the long-term unemployed of any age. The emphasis is still on projects which will improve the environment or help the community, but the range and scope of the programme are greater.

When these programmes were started, unemployment on a large scale was a new event, and it was hoped and believed a temporary consequence of the oil shock. The programmes themselves are 'cheap', because the alternative is to pay out unemployment or supplementary benefit. In the early years too, quite a high proportion of the participants succeeded in obtaining permanent employment when they left the programme. But as unemployment became more severe and apparently more permanent, fewer did so; less than a third of the Youth Opportunities Programme participants got a job when they left.

So 'temporary' programmes are developing into a permanent change in the general education and training provision, and increasing thought is belatedly being given to the 'future of work'. Has there been a fundamental change in the relationship between the level of output and the volume of employment which it generates?

For the moment, questions of redefining full employment (through job sharing, shorter working periods, educational sabbaticals and the like) remain as points for future discussion. Increasing the mobility of the labour force will be useful only if there are jobs to move to, whether the move be from a depressed area to the more prosperous South, or from unskilled to skilled occupations. There is little point in training young people to use specific as opposed to general skills unless there are vacancies in that field. It can hardly be repeated too often that at the top of the immediate economic agenda must be the provision of a much larger volume of work to make serious inroads into the present backlog of unemployment.

PRIVATIZATION

The third main strand of government policy aimed at enhancing the role of the market has been the thrust towards privatization. Generally, this term is associated with the transfer back into private ownership of nationalized industries. But it has also taken the form of 'hiving off' elements of social service provision and a general encouragement to the private sector to expand its operations in areas such as education and health.

We examined the origin, nature and problems of nationalized industries in Chapter 12 and outlined the long, generally unsatisfactory debate that has taken place over the years about how nationalized industries should be managed. No unequivocal substitute for 'making the biggest profit' was ever introduced, and all the industries suffered from frequent changes in direction and emphasis. For example, the steel industry had five different ministers in six years and, whether by accident or design, five different directives on pricing. Attempts to separate out the 'public service' functions from the commercial operations and to account for them differently were made, for example, British Rail was overtly subsidized for maintaining uneconomic branch lines. Otherwise the latest criteria have centred on trying to ensure a reasonable return on past investment and on stricter scrutiny of new investment proposals.

Early attempts to control the finances of the nationalized industries were stepped up in the difficult days of 1978. 'Cash' or 'external financing' limits were introduced, so-called because what was limited was the industries' call on government to cover losses and to finance investment. This reflected the general drive to limit government spending and the Public Sector Borrowing Requirement, of which the demands of public corporations are part. Financial considerations dominated over longer-term objectives.

Given the variety of industries, it is not surprising that their record was patchy. Financial returns are very difficult to interpret, because of the heavy burden of fixed debt which most of these industries carry, but growth and productivity are less prone to distortion. Growth was, in fact, below the average for all industry, which itself was a not very spectacular 2.7%; but it has to be recognized that coal and rail transport were declining industries, even if air transport and telecommunications were not. Productivity actually fell during the early 1970s in many industries, and despite the generally good record of gas, electricity and telecommunications, there remained the feeling that, by the standards of private industry, performance was poor.

Given its generally pro-market orientation and its desire to reduce the scale of government, it is not surprising therefore that the incoming Conservative government in 1979 saw privatization as a major element of

Nationalized industry	Year nationalized or reorganized	Current or planned action
Bank of England	1946	Always subject to govt control; change of status minimal. Change unlikely.
British Gas	1949	Sold 1986.
National Coal Board (British Coal)	1946	Privatization, e.g. of open-cast coal, discussed, but no current plans; pit closures continue.
Central Electricity Generating Board, etc.	1948	Profitable industry; privatization being considered.
(reorganized)	1958	
British Rail	1948	Non-rail assets – hotels, land, workshops – being sold off;
National Bus/National Freight	1947	Management and work-force bought Nat. Freight; competition open since 1980 for
(reorganized)	1969	buses.
British Airways (as BOAC and BEA)	1946	Groomed for privatization in 1987; work-force reduced, now profitable.
British Airports Authority	1966	Due for privatization.
Post Office and Telecom	Govt dept until 1969; split in 1980	British Telecom sold; PO more commercial in attitude.
Steel denationalized	1951	Drastically pruned; some parts reorganized and privatized.
renationalized	1954	
British Shipbuilders	1977	Broken up, and parts sold.
British Aerospace	1977	51% sold in 1981.
British Petroleum (BP)		Parts of govt's shareholding sold since 1967.
British National Oil Corporation	1976	Britoil, owning oilfields and engaging in exploration, separated.
Royal Ordnance factories	1974	Being sold off.
Rolls-Royce	1973	Sold off 1987.
British Leyland	1975	Being broken up and sold off when possible.

its programme. By the mid-1980s it had made very substantial progress in achieving its desired transfer from public to private ownership, and of subjecting the remaining nationalized industries to commercial constraints.

Other enterprises, such as Cable & Wireless and Amersham International (an offshoot of nuclear research, supplying radioactive materials to industry and medicine), have also been sold in whole or in part, and there have been minor prunings and adjustments elsewhere, e.g. hovercraft and ferries. The total effect of these changes will be to reduce the nationalized industries mainly to coal, rail, steel and electricity generation and distribution – still a substantial sector of the economy.

Arguments for privatization

To some extent, nationalization was seen by some of its earlier advocates almost as an end in itself. The same is true of privatization, which has often been pursued with a similar ideological fervour.

Economically, the case that has been put forward for restoring nationalized industries to private ownership has been threefold. Privatization, it is claimed, will increase efficiency. Second, it reduces the Public Sector Borrowing Requirement. And thirdly, it results in wider share ownership.

With regard to efficiency, it must be agreed that for management to be given *any* stable set of objectives to pursue can only help in concentrating its energies and make for more purposeful operation and planning of the enterprise. Maximization of profit might provide at least a clearer aim, so long as government does not continue to intervene with attempts to qualify it, which is far from certain.

More substantively, the argument that privatization will lead to greater efficiency must rest on the assumption that privatized concerns will be working within a more *competitive* framework, in which they will be forced to the wall if they are unsuccessful. Two points need to be made. First, *if* competition exists (particularly from foreign enterprises), then how will government react to privatized companies failing to hold their own? It was, after all, just such a situation which led to Conservative administrations taking firms like British Leyland and Rolls-Royce into public ownership in the first place. Secondly, and more worrying, is the fact that some of the industries which have been, or are likely to be, privatized – e.g. British Telecom – are monopolies faced with no significant competition whatever. High profits in such instances, facilitating privatization and doubtless to be used as evidence of their success in the future, in fact largely take the form of 'monopoly rents' rather than a reward for efficiency. Ironically, once such monopolies are transferred into the 'free' market there is an immediately recognized need to set up bodies (like OFTEL) to *regulate* them.

Moreover, the notion of 'efficiency' which privatization is claimed to promote is itself suspect. In Chapter 12 we discussed the distinction between 'commercial' and 'economic' criteria, pointing out that the former were based only on those private costs and benefits which appeared in the balance sheet of an individual enterprise. But, we argued, there are important 'externalities', costs and benefits arising outside the enterprise which must be taken into account in assessing *economic* efficiency. Nationalization in practice may well be criticized for the confusion which prevailed in dealing with both these and wider social considerations. But privatization involves either their total neglect or, once again, regulatory intervention to ensure that attention is paid to them.

Thus many of the newly privatized industries will be widely expected to continue their past social practices; for example, it will still be necessary for telephone services to be provided to isolated communities in the Highlands and Islands of Scotland, or to the scattered farms in Central Wales, even though such services can never be commercial. There are fears that many villages might lose their bus services, just as they have lost their branch railway, because they can never generate enough traffic to provide a profit to a private operator. Will county councils still provide a subsidy? More important, perhaps, is the pricing policy of such private monopolies. To what extent will they be allowed to exploit their mono-poly through discrimination or through charging what the traffic will bear?

Apart from greater efficiency, a second argument for privatization is the contribution that it can make in helping to 'reduce the burden on the Exchequer'. There is a dual basis for this assertion: the proceeds from the initial sale of public assets which goes into the government coffers and thereby reduces its borrowing requirement, and the fact that in future years privatized industries will when necessary undertake their own financing through the capital market rather than depend on govern-ment to do it for them.

Both points are dubious. The sale of *capital* assets is a once-and-for-all operation rather than a regular source of finance. The propriety, anyway, of including the sale of capital assets as a negative item in *current* ac-counting is, as we have already suggested, highly questionable – as, for that matter, is the prime attention that has been given to the level of the PSBR itself. As to the future, the 'burden on the Exchequer' in terms of the need to tax or borrow will actually *increase* to the extent that privatized industries are those which were profit-making; the profits will stay in private hands rather than accruing to government. And the calls they make on the capital market will be much the same whether they are privately or publicly owned.

The third gain from privatization, according to its advocates, is the resulting spread in share ownership. Certainly considerable success can be claimed in this respect, with the flotations of British Telecom, British

Gas and the TSB in particular attracting many millions of new savers into equity ownership. How many retain their shares rather than simply take a quick profit remains to be seen. But certainly the uninformative nature of the advertising campaigns preceding such privatizations must give cause for disquiet in suggesting (some would say accurately) that the Stock Exchange is a means of satisfying speculative greed rather than a market in which considered estimates of future prospects are made. *Politically*, wider share ownership may make it more difficult for future governments to renationalize. *Economically*, it probably is of little significance. There already exist, as we have seen, a wide variety of financial institutions concentrating small savings into investible amounts. And except where a very large proportion of the shares of an enterprise are held by its own workers, little contribution can be expected in breaking down the 'them'-and-'us' syndrome.

As well as privatization of nationalized industries, there has been a sustained emphasis on the virtues of private rather than public provision in areas of social concern such as health and education. The wholesale attack on the Welfare State proposed by theorists of the political 'new right' has not so far materialized. Indeed ministers are able to point to higher levels of public spending in such sectors than have ever been attained before.

However, such financing is below what is required by the increased demand on such services – in the case of the NHS, for example, because of an ageing population and expectations of improved and more available treatment. It is in this sense that 'cuts' have been made, coupled with encouragement to private sector providers of such services.

The economic case for such a switch rests partly on efficiency considerations but primarily on the increased *consumer* choice which it is claimed would be achieved. Reduce taxation, so it is argued, let the money stay in consumers' pockets and leave them 'free to choose' between the range of alternatives that market provision would offer.

We have indicated some of the dangers implicit in such an approach. Lack of technical expertise may make it difficult for consumers to make choices rationally between different models of sophisticated consumer durables like video recorders or cars. The same applies to a far more acute degree in areas like health care, where the average patient is both profoundly ignorant and generally in no fit state to exercise choice, and where the problem is greatly compounded by the potentially far more serious consequences of error. Moreover, on such basic matters, maximum freedom of choice for the individual can have detrimental effects on others. It is hardly a totalitarian position surely to deny individuals the right to spend as *little* as they choose on health or education, when it is their children or other members of society who may suffer as a result.

However, the principal objection to private rather than public provision stems from the unequal distribution of income and wealth on which consumer choice is based. It is an objection which applies not only to the extreme proposals for dismantling the Welfare State but also to encouraging a coexistent private sector alongside state services. The latter might seem an obvious extension of consumer sovereignty in offering a real choice between alternatives. But two questions must be put.

First, freedom of choice for whom? If private medicine or education is on offer, then who is free to take advantage of them? Since the market responds to the demands only of those with the ability to pay, it is inevitably the higher income groups which will mainly benefit, even though the greater *need* may exist amongst the poorer members of the community.

Secondly, is there none the less a net gain in consumer sovereignty in that *some* at least have greater freedom of choice, or is the exercise of that freedom perhaps at the expense of *reduced* choice for others? There are reasons for thinking that the latter may well be the case. Thus tax benefits and staffing inducements may have the effect of draining resources from the public to the private sector. And the provision of what is thought to be 'superior' private education or health care (which may not, in fact, always be so) attracts precisely that clientele which would be most persistent and effective in bringing about improvement within the public sector if they had no alternative but to rely upon it.

Here, as is commonly the case, increased reliance on market forces will be disequalizing in its effects when the starting position is one of initial inequality. The market is undoubtedly a very useful mechanism for allocating much of the nation's resources. But its working in the real world is very far detached from that of the economic textbook. This was recognized by economists long ago, and it was to deal with key areas of 'market failure' in practice that interventionist policies were introduced. The neglect of these long understood defects of the system makes the recent unqualified espousal of the market by certain 'new right' economists so disturbing; the retreat which they propose from intervention has little economic, let along social, justification.

INDUSTRIAL POLICY

Our major industrial rivals have not been imbued with the same ideological trust in the workings of the market system. Far from standing off, they have generally been active in supporting their industries (particularly the manufacturing base) by a variety of measures. Their policies have entailed an economic involvement which contrasts markedly with the *laissez-faire* approach of recent UK governments in ensuring that industry is kept up to date by an adequate level of new investment. In achieving this, they have not hesitated to apply selective state pressure and assistance to ensure that financial and other potential obstacles are overcome. This has enabled them to take a much longer time perspective than the typical private investor would do, and to support the development of a new area of industry from basic research, through development and testing, to established and successful manufacture. Thus France has its system of 'indicative planning', which is essentially a programme of guided investment designed to modernize and rejuvenate French industry. Italy uses the state holding companies inherited from pre-war Fascism to expand and modernize its steel, chemical and automobile industries. The Japanese Ministry of Trade and Industry has become an exemplar in all the discussions about industrial policies and is perhaps an extreme example of the concentration of administrative and financial power behind 'Japan Inc.'

The USA is an apparent exception to the rule, and also a country with a relatively low rate of growth. But industrial productivity is much higher there than in Britain, and the massive purchasing power of the Department of Defense ensures that US technology is right up with the leaders.

Earlier British governments did make attempts at similar policies. The National Plan of 1965 owed a great deal to what was seen as the success of French planning (while perhaps misunderstanding the degree to which it was purely 'permissive' rather than relying on control over the capital market and specific intervention at the level of the individual enterprise.) The National Enterprise Board, created in 1975, showed similarities to the Italian central state holding company, the Industrial Reconstruction Institute. Although it had been a Conservative government in the early 1970s which had first dabbled with indicative planning and laid the basis for a vigorous industrial policy in the 1972 Industry Act, which provided for generous investment incentives and other assistance to the private sector, it is perhaps significant that it was the following Labour government which encountered strong resistance to its industrial initiatives – perhaps inflamed by the rhetoric with which they were surrounded and the consequent suspicion that they were a back-door form of nationalization or socialization. There was particular opposition to the concept of 'planning agreements' introduced in the 1975 Industry Act which suggested, not unreasonably, that recipients of government assistance should in return make specific commitments about matters such as location, investment and exports. What might have offered a fruitful contribution towards industrial regeneration was effectively killed off. Later, so too was the National Enterprise Board. Despite its constructive record in trying to restructure and modernize the machine-tool industry and British Leyland, and regardless of the plea from its chairman, Sir Lesley Murphy, for its work to be continued 'free from doctrinal hostility', it was run down by the incoming Conservative government in 1979, ideologically so much opposed to government interference.

What is left? First, a considerable residue of expenditure designed to support major industries: Rolls-Royce and the Rover Group most prominently, perhaps, but also considerable help to shipbuilding, steel and aerospace. The 'frontiers of technology' support is focused on information technology, microprocessors, and so on. And there is continued state involvement in research and development, albeit with a marked bias to atomic energy, nuclear physics, aerospace and similar defence-oriented activities. The scale, however, is small, and there is growing evidence that in crucial areas like information technology the world is once again passing Britain by.

Industrial policy has not completely disappeared, but the belief that industrial decisions are best left to industrialists, and that the state should withdraw wherever possible, is now dominant. The danger is that the private decision may, as in the past, be to invest elsewhere – leaving British industry in no state to meet any future rise in domestic demand.

20

The Economic Consequences

We have now outlined the philosophies and practices of economic policy that have prevailed in recent years. The macro-economic approach has been dominated by a revulsion from Keynesianism and its replacement by attempted monetarism. Paramount priority has been given to the control of inflation, to be achieved by restraining the growth of the money supply. There has been a determined effort to reduce the role of the state and to replace it by more smoothly functioning free market forces. Micro-economic policy has involved withdrawal from the economic stage by government wherever possible.

What have been the consequences and what are the future prospects for the economy? Those on the right of the political spectrum will say that it is too early for any such assessment, and the processes which have been set in train must be persisted with for a longer period before bearing fruit. Others argue that possibly irreversible damage has already been inflicted as a result of positively malign measures in some areas, and costly neglect in others.

All that we shall do here is indicate three aspects of the economy about which debate is likely to be most polarized: the alleged 'deindustrialization' of the economy; the state of the balance of payments; and the extent of inequality which is emerging in British society.

DEINDUSTRIALIZATION

'Deindustrialization' is a term which refers to a decline, in some sense or other, of *manufacturing* industry in particular. It is a subject which has attracted a great deal of attention from economists and politicians over the past decade. There has been discussion about its precise nature, its causes and whether it should be a matter for concern.

The sort of statistical data which fuels such discussion has already been introduced at various points in this book. *Employment* in manufacturing industry had declined since 1970; sharply during the recession of 1973–5, remaining stable during 1975–8, then plunging steeply to level off, in 1985, at barely two-thirds of its 1970 level. Manufacturing *output* peaked in 1973 and then dropped to a level in 1981–2 almost 20% lower than that peak. It has since risen, but only to its 1975 level. Using index numbers, we have seen that manufacturing output fell from 113 in 1974 to 101 in 1984 (1980 = 100), and employment in manufacturing industry contracted from 115 in 1975 to 81 in 1984 (1980 = 100).

The picture is made uglier still by reference to the foreign trade sector (see Figure 16, page 306), where there is a combination of deepening 'import penetration' – the proportion of domestic consumption of manufactures which is imported – and a declining UK share in world exports of manufactures.

Traditionally, Britain was an exporter of manufactures and an importer of food, raw materials and energy. In 1955–60, for example, exports of manufactures were three times the value of imported manufactures; in 1970 exports were only 25% more than imports; and by 1983 the balance was negative. It was only a surplus derived from oil exports, which must be temporary, which veiled the widening deficit.

It can be argued that the British situation is far from unique. All developed economies have seen some decline in manufacturing during these years. A *relative* reduction in the importance of manufacturing is indeed likely to characterize more affluent economies, as consumers spend a greater proportion of their increased incomes on services such as tourism or leisure pursuits; but in Britain it has been an *absolute* decline. Elsewhere too the fall has often been mostly confined to employment – once again, to be expected as manufacturing becomes more capital-intensive – and coinciding with higher employment in the service sector; in Britain, it has been accompanied by reduced *output*, and the loss of two million jobs in manufacturing has not been offset by expanding opportunities in other sectors.

Similarly, it is not surprising that established industrial producers should find that they command a declining share of world exports of manufactures as newly industrialized countries enter world markets to an increasing degree. Such competition has come from South Korea, Taiwan, Hong Kong and Singapore; from India; from Brazil, Argentina, Mexico and others in Latin America; and from Turkey. The share of the 'less developed economies' as a whole in world manufacturing and in

Table 20.1. Percentage shares of world exports of manufactures

	1963	1973	1976	
West Germany	15.5	17.0	16.0	
France	7.0	7.5	7.5	
USA	17.0	12.5	13.5	
All OECD countries	80.5	82.5	83.0	
United Kingdom	11.0	7.0	6.5	
Newly industrializing countries	2.5	6.5	7.0	10.0 (1980)

exports of manufactures has increased remarkably; they now account for over 15% of world output of manufactures and, as Table 20.1 shows, for a growing proportion of world trade.

As a result of this, more of the internal demand for manufactures in these growing economies has been satisfied by domestic production, and these countries have also competed successfully with the older manufacturing countries in third markets – even in the domestic markets of the developed world. But what is disturbing is the *extent* to which the British share of world markets in manufactures has fallen – a halving from 18% in 1959 to the present 9% – and the fact that such a marked fall is unmatched by any other major industrial nation.

The comparatively poor performance by the British economy in these respects is not a new phenomenon. Its origins can be traced back to the latter half of the nineteenth century when the USA and Germany became major industrial powers. Since 1945 they have been joined, in particular, by Japan with spectacular rates of growth in manufacturing output and exports, and nearer home by Italy and France.

Since the 1960s the progressive elimination of protective duties on manufactures culminating in Britain's accession to the EEC has exposed British industry to extreme competition in its own markets. And Britain has not, on the whole, been successful in the European and world markets now open to its exports. This 'inability to compete' has as many explanations as there are writers about it. The comparative weakness of the British economy has been blamed on dilettante management, trade unions resistant to change, a financial system not properly geared to the needs of industry, too much or too little government spending and a whole range of other economic and social factors.

There is probably an element of truth in many of these hypotheses, and there is no doubt that the problem is deep-seated and long-term.

Table 20.2. Redundancies, 1977–85 (000s)

1977	1978	1979	1980	1981	1982	1983	1984	1985
158	173	187	494	532	400	327	245	235

Table 20.3. Redundancies by industry group (rates per 000 employees)

	Manufacturing	Services	All sectors
1977	13.8	2.1	7.2
1978	16.7	2.2	7.8
1979	19.9	1.9	8.3
1980	59.6	3.9	22.1
1981	65.9	5.9	25.1
1982	48.7	5.8	19.1
1983	40.2	5.0	15.9
1984	25.4	4.2	11.8
1985	25.3	3.6	11.2

But in addition to these factors, it is difficult to avoid the conclusion that recent policies have done much to exacerbate adverse underlying trends.

A particularly critical period in the decline of manufacturing was 1979–81. These were the years in which the basis for 'monetary discipline' was laid – amounting, as we have seen in Chapter 9, to a severe deflationary pressure being exerted on the economy. With demand depressed and interest rates high, it is hardly surprising that massive redundancies resulted – see Table 20.2.

These figures are for the whole economy. The extent to which redundancies were concentrated in manufacturing is evident from the figures in Table 20.3.

It is clear that in these years the decision-makers in industry decided that the 'squeeze' would be not only severe but prolonged. There was no point in keeping marginal plants open nor in hanging on to the workforce in the hope that the recession would be temporary. Firms were forced out of business or slimmed to survive. A third possibility was to shift operations abroad, an option taken by a number of major enterprises – with the West Midlands, until recently the industrial heartland of the economy, being a particular victim of the foreign exodus.

All these responses were reinforced by the 'strength' of sterling at this time, buoyed up by very high interest rates, by a growing oil surplus and by confidence on the part of foreign investors that the control of inflation was now the prime target of British economic policy. The result of the high pound was, of course, that U K manufactures were priced out of many export markets, while imports of manufactures were relatively cheap in the British market.

Is the consequent acceleration in the decline of British manufacturing reversible? Can Britain, once its oil exports begin to decline, revive manufacturing industry, reduce imports and expand exports? The answer to these questions must depend to some extent on the state of the capital stock of industry, and here the data we presented earlier on net capital formation (in Chapter 9) show that net investment in manufacturing has been *negative* since 1980. Britain has directed its investment into distribution, banking and financial services, into the public sector and into housing – not into manufacturing.

It is important to be clear about why the decline of manufacturing matters. It is not because manufacturing is somehow 'wealth-creating' in a way which other activities are not. Service occupations are just as much part of 'production' as work in the foundry or the factory, leading to the satisfaction of consumer wants. Nor should the loss of employment involved be the major cause for concern, since potentially there are vast numbers of jobs that could be created in the service sector; the quality of many social services is almost judged by how many nurses or teachers, for example, are available in relation to patients or students.

What distinguishes manufacturing and makes it peculiarly important is its capacity to earn the nation foreign currency through exports. Services too can be exported – and are, on a very large scale. But such invisible exports have not expanded at anything like the rate required to fill the increasing gap left by the fact that manufacturing, far from being a net earner of foreign exchange, is now an additional drain.

This, then, is the key definition of deindustrialization: a reduced capacity to pay for the desired level of imports. A reversal of past trends, with a revitalization of manufacturing, would not necessarily create a large number of new jobs. But a stagnant or declining manufacturing sector does represent a constraint on employment creation in other occupations. Drawing people off the dole into productive activity which does not yield foreign exchange earnings will, by increasing their incomes, worsen any

Table 20.4. Oil sales and trade balance, 1974–84

Volume of sales	1974	1976	1978	1980	1982	1984
Gas (billion m³)	34.7	38.3	38.5	36.4	35.4	35.8
Oil (million tonnes)	0.4	11.8	53.1	79.3	101.9	125.3
Imports and exports (£b.)						
Imports	4.1	5.1	4.2	5.8	6.0	7.8
Exports	0.7	1.2	2.3	6.1	10.7	14.9
Visible balance on oil	−3.4	−3.9	−2.0	+0.3	+4.6	+7.1

balance of payments problem as they spend a substantial proportion of those higher incomes on imports.

Since Britain may well be facing years of intensifying balance of payments pressure, the degree of manufacturing decline must therefore be regarded with considerable anxiety.

WHEN THE OIL RUNS OUT

There has been frequent reference already to the major changes which took place in the UK and the world economy during the 1970s as a result of the 'oil shock' – the sudden quadrupling of OPEC prices in 1973–4. In one sense this rise came at a fortunate time for the UK because in 1975 the first oil came ashore from the new discoveries in the North Sea. This offshore oil was inherently expensive when compared with, say, Arabian or Libyan oil, because a whole new capital-intensive technology of sea-going and sea-withstanding exploration and exploitation platforms had to be developed. High prices for crude oil meant that the massive investment paid off, though the recent dramatic collapse of oil prices has raised questions about future exploration.

In 1978 the price of oil was about $13 or £7 per barrel, but it rose steadily to a peak of nearly $35 in early 1982, equivalent to £18. Although the dollar price then began to fall, staying at just under $30 in 1983–4, the decline in the dollar/sterling exchange rate which began in 1982 meant that the sterling price continued to rise. Oil prices then collapsed, going below $10 in mid-1986, and although there has been some recovery, the future remains uncertain. In real terms, allowing for general price inflation, the sterling price of oil doubled between 1978 and 1984.

As a result, the North Sea has been, for most companies, a profitable investment, and exploration has continued to discover new fields, though none as large as the Forties or Brent or Statfjord finds.

The figures for output, import and export of oil make interesting reading in the context of the economic history of the ten years between 1975 and 1985 – see Table 20.4.

However, the 1984 level of production is expected to represent a maximum, and output from the fields currently being exploited and developed will begin to decline sharply from the late 1980s. Ignoring output from new fields yet to be proved, the UK will cease to be self-sufficient by about 1990. One cannot, of course, ignore the probability of new finds, and so estimates of when the UK will again become a net importer of oil vary from 1995 to well into the twenty-first century.

Policy towards the oil industry itself has reflected the changes which have taken place in the government's approach to the economy as a whole. Labour treated North Sea oil as a national asset and had the power to regulate the rate of exploitation through the British National Oil Corporation. The Conservative government of the 1980s abolished the royalty element and restricted the powers of the BNOC. Since then it is the market, i.e. the major oil companies, which makes decisions about how much to spend on exploration and how rapidly to deplete the oil reserves that are discovered. Britain, despite its temporary position as the sixth biggest oil producer, is not a member of OPEC and does not co-operate in output restraints.

What has been the impact of North Sea oil on the British economy? First, it has made a very considerable contribution to GDP and accounts for more than 5% of the total. Its influence is such that any reduction in output, even such as the normal summer drop as demand eases and maintenance takes advantage of good weather, actually causes a fall in GDP. More importantly, perhaps, this new and expanding contributor to GDP masked the decline in manufacturing industry which we discussed above. (Similarly, the fact that the North Sea takes over 25% of the UK's total industrial investment has concealed the declining investment in other areas of the economy.)

Secondly, oil has become a major contributor to the revenue of the government. Taxes and royalties on North Sea oil reached nearly £9 billion in 1983 – a third of the yield from income tax and two-thirds of that from VAT. Without this contribution the government's deficit, and the Public Sector Borrowing Requirement, would be enormous, unless other tax rates were drastically increased. In effect oil revenues have

Table 20.5. Visible trade balances, 1974–84 (£ million)

Visible trade balances	1974	1976	1978	1980	1982	1984
Food, beverages and tobacco	−2,441	−2,963	−2,792	−2,382	−2,637	−3,527
Basic materials	−1,630	−2,215	−2,165	−1,960	−1,989	−2,852
Oil	−3,357	−3,947	−1,984	+315	+4,643	+7,137
Manufactures and semi-manufactures	+1,970	+4,917	+5,066	+5,457	+2,371	−3,785
Total visible trade	−5,351	−3,929	−1,542	+1,361	+2,331	−4,101

Table 20.6. Oil's contribution to the balance of payments, 1974–84 (£ million)

	1974	1976	1978	1980	1982	1984
Imports of goods	−125	−536	−185	−144	−451	−246
Imports of services (net)	−207	−647	−547	−478	−692	−687
Interest, profits and dividends due abroad	−10	−24	−744	−2,215	−2,623	−3,032
Overseas investment	+231	+1,142	+791	+848	+1,038	−41
Total	−111	−65	−500	−1,989	−2,728	−4,006
Oil trade (from above)	−3,357	−3,947	−1,984	+315	+4,643	+7,137
Net contribution	−3,468	−4,012	−2,484	−1,674	+1,915	+3,131

enabled the government to cope with the rapidly growing spending on unemployment benefits without drastic cuts elsewhere in its budget or tax increases.

Thirdly, oil has made a major contribution to the balance of payments. The 'visible balance' on oil has changed by £10 billion since 1974, again masking a deterioration in the visible balance of trade in other sectors. Table 20.5. illustrates this.

By also taking into account invisible earnings and payments, and investment flows, we can get a picture of the full extent to which UK international payments have been attributable to North Sea oil – see Table 20.6.

As and when the flow from the North Sea declines, so these effects will weaken. Oil revenues will fall, so that either other taxes must rise or government spending must fall, if borrowing is not to increase. GDP will fall, unless some other sector of the economy simultaneously expands.

306 *Policy and Performance – Past, Present and Future*

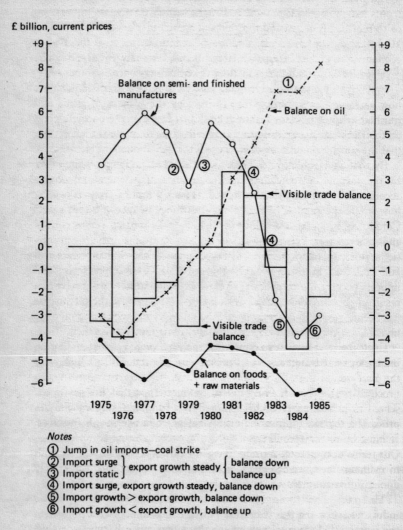

Figure 16 Visible trade balances, 1975–85

But most important of all is the degree to which the balance of payments may come under pressure. Britain will have either to import less or to replace oil exports with exports of some other goods and services. However, as we have seen, imports of manufactures into the British economy now exceed exports; and it is difficult to see how this trend can be reversed quickly to fill the gap left by the declining contribution of oil.

Figure 16 illustrates the changing pattern of trade balances and shows how as the oil contribution rose to its peak the balance of semi- and finished manufactures sank into deficit. The fact that the normal deficit on food and raw materials hardly changed seems to refute the suggestion that the surplus on oil somehow 'caused' the deficit on manufactures.

By 1986 the visible trade deficit was, it seemed, no longer being offset by the surplus on invisibles, and the balance of payments on *current* account was itself moving into the red. If such a trend were to continue, how would the gap left by declining oil earnings be met in future years? Conflicting proposals exemplify the 'hands-off' approach versus control and intervention. Thus advocates of the market mechanism are optimistic, arguing that the process will be automatic. The exchange rate will fall, and this, in turn, will bring about balance as exports rise and imports become more expensive. Manufacturing industry will revive as a result of these market forces. Also, a substantial part of the oil surplus has been invested in overseas assets, the returns from which will increase invisible earnings and so help to offset any remaining trade deficit.

Critics, on the other hand, suggest that the *capability* of manufacturing industry to respond in this way has been severely reduced. They deplore the 'lost opportunities' to regenerate British industry by investing the proceeds of the North Sea windfall, pointing out that instead it has served to maintain personal income and consumption through the depressed 1980s and to finance a massive increase in overseas investment. It must be remembered that a fall in the exchange rate is not costless. Our terms of trade will worsen; we shall have to export more if we wish to maintain the present volume of imports, or import less. Either way domestic consumption will suffer.

The only hope, these critics say, is a belated attempt at a positive industrial policy to repair the damage – unfortunately at just the time when the revenue flow from oil which might have financed it begins to decline.

There is a third alternative. If neither market forces nor interventionist measures work in bringing about a sufficient recovery in British industry (or if they are not tried), then the balance of payments situation will have

Table 20.7. Employment, output and productivity (1980 = 100)

	Whole economy			Manufacturing industries		
	Output	Employed labour force	Output per person	Output	Employed labour force	Output per person
1978	99.6	99.4	100.2	109.7	106.1	100.8
1979	102.8	100.7	102.1	109.5	105.3	104.0
1980	100.0	100.0	100.0	100.0	100.0	100.0
1981	98.5	96.6	102.0	94.0	90.9	103.5
1982	100.3	94.7	105.9	94.2	86.0	109.7
1983	103.3	93.9	110.0	96.9	82.2	117.9
1984	106.7	95.5	111.7*	100.7	81.6	123.4
1985	110.7	96.9	114.3	103.9	81.8	127.0

to be met by further deflationary pressure: reducing the level of domestic demand for imports. In other words, Britain's international books will be balanced by rising unemployment, and the reduced incomes of the newly unemployed serving to dampen down UK spending on imported goods and services. This prospect is bleak in the extreme. Indeed, it might seem out of the question that unemployment should continue to increase from its already appallingly high level. But that, after all, was what was widely said in the early 1970s about the possibility of unemployment ever again exceeding the *one* million mark.

HOW MANY BRITAINS?

In the earlier parts of this chapter we outlined some of the consequences of recent economic policy and the discussion which has revolved around present problems and future prospects. In the course of this, we have focused on broad trends, dealing with concepts like 'deindustrialization' and quantities such as the balance of payments. What remains is to reduce these somewhat remote notions to a more human scale and assess the impact of economic changes on different groups of *people* in the British economy of today.

As background, we need to look at the statistics relating to productivity. So far we have been stressing the decline in output and employment in manufacturing and the extent to which the economy as a whole has been subject to deflationary pressures. But the fact is that recent years have seen a marked rise in output per worker – see Table 20.7.

Table 20.8. Average earnings index (January 1980 = 100; all
employees)

	RPI	Whole economy	Manufacturing
1980	107.5	114.4	109.1
1981	120.3	125.8	123.6
1982	130.6	137.6	137.4
1983	136.6	149.2	149.7
1984	143.4	158.3	162.8
1985	152.1	171.7	177.6

Productivity has risen both in the economy as a whole and in the
manufacturing sector. Indeed, it is in the latter – where the fall in
employment has been greater than the fall in output – that the growth in
output per person employed, or labour productivity, has been most
marked.

We have already questioned earlier how far this 'productivity miracle'
is merely a statistical freak. To quote a commonly used analogy, if the
scores recorded by the five weakest batsmen in a cricket team are deleted,
then the average score per member of the team will consequently rise,
even though the performance of the remaining six has stayed the same.
To some extent, this is what has happened in the British economy, with
part of the productivity increase simply attributable to the elimination of
weaker elements rather than indicating a sharp improvement in underlying performance.

Whatever the cause, it is not surprising to find productivity rises
of this order reflected in higher pay. For a large part of the population lucky enough to have stayed in employment, increased earnings
have comfortably exceeded the rise in the cost of living – see Table
20.8.

Averaged out for all those who are still employed, there has thus been
a substantial rise in real incomes. We are still, however, dealing at a level
of great generality, talking of 'those who are still employed' as though
they formed a homogeneous group. But the figures we have been looking
at are, of course, averages and conceal wide variations. In breaking the
total employed down into more meaningful groups, we can start with the
data contained in the New Earnings Survey for 1985. This shows that
the average weekly earnings of professional and lower managerial employees were £238 for men and £163 for women in 1985, which repre-

sented a rise of 58% and 59% respectively since 1980. Clerical and manual groups averaged £158 for men and £106 for women, increases of 47.5% and 53%. Both occupational groups thus enjoyed a rise in real earnings, i.e. in excess of the increase in the Retail Price Index. However, the gap between them widened. The better-off gained more, relatively as well as absolutely.

These figures are for earnings, not for disposable incomes. The widening gap has been reinforced by the tax changes which have been taking place over these years. These have consisted of making direct taxation less progressive – through reductions in the rate of income tax favouring the higher earners – and a general switch towards indirect taxes. Indirect taxes such as VAT and excise duty are paid by everyone, irrespective of the level of their incomes, so that these changes too have operated to the relative benefit of those remaining in work and those in the higher income brackets.

At the other end of the scale, we have the bottom 10% of those in work who have on average received no real increase in post-tax pay, and many of whom (for example, hospital porters and refuse collectors) will have experienced actual cuts in their real earnings.

We have also already pointed out, way back in Chapter 1 (Figure 2, page 11) that national earnings figures conceal major *regional* variations in incomes. These too have become far more marked in recent years. The idea of 'two nations' – a prosperous South and an impoverished North – is clearly an oversimplification, because all regions contain areas of high unemployment, particularly in the decaying city centres. The prosperous South-East contains Brixton, Brent and Tower Hamlets as well as Hampstead and Blackheath. However, it is difficult to dispute Professor A. H. Halsey's dismal conclusion that

a pattern has emerged of a more unequal society as between a majority in secure attachment to a still prosperous country and a minority in marginal economic and social conditions – the former moving into the suburban locations of a 'green and pleasant land', the latter tending to be trapped in the old provincial industrial cities and their displaced fragments of peripheral council housing estates.*

That minority includes the sharply increased number of people in Britain – some seven and a half million families – now living within 20% of the official 'poverty line'.

The greatest divide of all, however, is that between the employed and

* Central Statistical Office, *Social Trends* 17, HMSO, 1987.

Table 20.9. Unemployment rates by age and ethnic origin, spring 1985

Age group	White	Ethnic minorities		All minorities
		West Indian	Pakistani/ Bangladeshi	
16–24	16%	34%	48%	33%
All people of working age	10%	21%	31%	20%

the unemployed. Those who are out of work, or who depend upon pensions or other types of benefit, have at best found that their payments are linked to the rate of price inflation. The fact that adjustments have tended to take place in arrears, and the reduction or greater stringency with regard to particular welfare payments like housing benefit, means that while for some of this group real incomes have remained static, for many they have actually fallen.

In either case, relative to those in work they have become poorer. The *gap* between the two has greatly widened. As we have seen earlier, unemployment has not struck evenly throughout the country or between the generations. Like disparities in income it has a deep regional dimension. And in terms of age, too, the suffering has been unequally shared. It is the young, looking for first jobs, and the old, who are nearing retirement, who have experienced much higher rates of unemployment than the 30- and 40-years-olds. If we add the further consideration of skin colour, we find that amongst ethnic minorities as a whole the percentage out of work is double that of white workers. A combination of the factors means staggering rates of unemployment among the younger members of the ethnic minority groups, as Table 20.9 shows.

The gap between the 'haves' and the 'have-nots' is multi-dimensional, and the bases of distinction between the two do not always neatly coincide. But the depressing fact is that by nearly every definition it is a gap which has widened, is widening and looks set to widen still further. This would not long ago have been a matter for deep concern, and there would have been calls for positive measures to reverse the process of widening inequalities between citizens. Now it appears that many people in Britain are either indifferent to the situation or willing to tolerate it. Some accept it as economically inevitable; some even regard the suffering as self-inflicted by those who are its chief victims.

In the 1960s and 1970s we had begun to question the desirability of using economic growth as an index of economic progress, and to ask about the *nature* as well as the mere quantity of work, about the *quality* of life in Britain and about the socially useful allocation of the globe's limited resources. Such questions have slipped down the agenda for serious discussion, or disappeared from it altogether. It is not clear that they have yet been replaced by equally serious and informed discussion of our present pressing problems.

LLLLLLLLLLLLLLLLL

Index

Note: t following a page number indicates a relevant table

FOR THE BEST IN PAPERBACKS, LOOK FOR THE

In every corner of the world, on every subject under the sun, Penguin represents quality and variety – the very best in publishing today.

For complete information about books available from Penguin – including Pelicans, Puffins, Peregrines and Penguin Classics – and how to order them, write to us at the appropriate address below. Please note that for copyright reasons the selection of books varies from country to country.

In the United Kingdom: For a complete list of books available from Penguin in the U.K., please write to *Dept E.P., Penguin Books Ltd, Harmondsworth, Middlesex, UB7 0DA*

In the United States: For a complete list of books available from Penguin in the U.S., please write to *Dept BA, Penguin, 299 Murray Hill Parkway, East Rutherford, New Jersey 07073*

In Canada: For a complete list of books available from Penguin in Canada, please write to *Penguin Books Canada Ltd, 2801 John Street, Markham, Ontario L3R 1B4*

In Australia: For a complete list of books available from Penguin in Australia, please write to the *Marketing Department, Penguin Books Australia Ltd, P.O. Box 257, Ringwood, Victoria 3134*

In New Zealand: For a complete list of books available from Penguin in New Zealand, please write to the *Marketing Department, Penguin Books (NZ) Ltd, Private Bag, Takapuna, Auckland 9*

In India: For a complete list of books available from Penguin, please write to *Penguin Overseas Ltd, 706 Eros Apartments, 56 Nehru Place, New Delhi, 110019*

In Holland: For a complete list of books available from Penguin in Holland, please write to *Penguin Books Nederland B.V., Postbus 195, NL–1380 AD Weesp, Netherlands*

In Germany: For a complete list of books available from Penguin, please write to *Penguin Books Ltd, Friedrichstrasse 10 – 12, D–6000 Frankfurt Main 1, Federal Republic of Germany*

In Spain: For a complete list of books available from Penguin in Spain, please write to *Longman Penguin España, Calle San Nicolas 15, E–28013 Madrid, Spain*

Lateral Thinking for Management   Edward de Bono

Creativity and lateral thinking can work together for managers in developing new products or ideas; Edward de Bono shows how.

Understanding Organizations   Charles B. Handy

Of practical as well as theoretical interest, this book shows how general concepts can help solve specific organizational problems.

The Art of Japanese Management   Richard Tanner Pascale and Anthony G. Athos   With an Introduction by Sir Peter Parker

Japanese industrial success owes much to Japanese management techniques, which we in the West neglect at our peril. The lessons are set out in this important book.

My Years with General Motors   Alfred P. Sloan   With an Introduction by John Egan

A business classic by the man who took General Motors to the top – and kept them there for decades.

Introducing Management   Ken Elliott and Peter Lawrence (eds.)

An important and comprehensive collection of texts on modern management which draw some provocative conclusions.

English Culture and the Decline of the Industrial Spirit   Martin J. Wiener

A major analysis of why the 'world's first industrial nation has never been comfortable with industrialism'. 'Very persuasive' – Anthony Sampson in the *Observer*

Dinosaur and Co   Tom Lloyd

A lively and optimistic survey of a new breed of businessmen who are breaking away from huge companies to form dynamic enterprises in microelectronics, biotechnology and other developing areas.

The Money Machine: How the City Works   Philip Coggan

How are the big deals made? Which are the institutions that *really* matter? What causes the pound to rise or interest rates to fall? This book provides clear and concise answers to these and many other money-related questions.

Parkinson's Law   C. Northcote Parkinson

'Work expands so as to fill the time available for its completion': that law underlies this 'extraordinarily funny and witty book' (Stephen Potter in the *Sunday Times*) which also makes some painfully serious points for those in business or the Civil Service.

Debt and Danger   Harold Lever and Christopher Huhne

The international debt crisis was brought about by Western bankers in search of quick profit and is now one of our most pressing problems. This book looks at the background and shows what we must do to avoid disaster.

Lloyd's Bank Tax Guide 1987/8

Cut through the complexities! Work the system in *your* favour! Don't pay a penny more than you have to! Written for anyone who has to deal with personal tax, this up-to-date and concise new handbook includes all the important changes in this year's budget.

The Spirit of Enterprise   George Gilder

A lucidly written and excitingly argued defence of capitalism and the role of the entrepreneur within it.

A CHOICE OF PENGUINS AND PELICANS

The Second World War (6 volumes)   Winston S. Churchill

The definitive history of the cataclysm which swept the world for the second time in thirty years.

1917: The Russian Revolutions and the Origins of Present-Day Communism
Leonard Schapiro

A superb narrative history of one of the greatest episodes in modern history by one of our greatest historians.

Imperial Spain 1496–1716   J. H. Elliot

A brilliant modern study of the sudden rise of a barren and isolated country to be the greatest power on earth, and of its equally sudden decline. 'Outstandingly good' – *Daily Telegraph*

Joan of Arc: The Image of Female Heroism   Marina Warner

'A profound book, about human history in general and the place of women in it' – Christopher Hill

Man and the Natural World: Changing Attitudes in England 1500–1800
Keith Thomas

'A delight to read and a pleasure to own' – Auberon Waugh in the *Sunday Telegraph*

The Making of the English Working Class   E. P. Thompson

Probably the most imaginative – and the most famous – post-war work of English social history.

FOR THE BEST IN PAPERBACKS, LOOK FOR THE

A CHOICE OF PENGUINS AND PELICANS

The French Revolution   Christopher Hibbert

'One of the best accounts of the Revolution that I know . . . Mr Hibbert is outstanding' – J. H. Plumb in the *Sunday Telegraph*

The Germans   Gordon A. Craig

An intimate study of a complex and fascinating nation by 'one of the ablest and most distinguished American historians of modern Germany' – Hugh Trevor-Roper

Ireland: A Positive Proposal   Kevin Boyle and Tom Hadden

A timely and realistic book on Northern Ireland which explains the historical context – and offers a practical and coherent set of proposals which could actually work.

A History of Venice   John Julius Norwich

'Lord Norwich has loved and understood Venice as well as any other Englishman has ever done' – Peter Levi in the *Sunday Times*

Montaillou: Cathars and Catholics in a French Village 1294–1324
Emmanuel Le Roy Ladurie

'A classic adventure in eavesdropping across time' – Michael Ratcliffe in *The Times*

Star Wars   E. P. Thompson and others

Is Star Wars a serious defence strategy or just a science fiction fantasy? This major book sets out all the arguments and makes an unanswerable case *against* Star Wars.

FOR THE BEST IN PAPERBACKS, LOOK FOR THE

A CHOICE OF PENGUINS AND PELICANS

The Apartheid Handbook   Roger Omond

This book provides the essential hard information about how apartheid actually works from day to day and fills in the details behind the headlines.

The World Turned Upside Down   Christopher Hill

This classic study of radical ideas during the English Revolution 'will stand as a notable monument to . . . one of the finest historians of the present age' – *The Times Literary Supplement*

Islam in the World   Malise Ruthven

'His exposition of "the Qurenic world view" is the most convincing, and the most appealing, that I have read' – Edward Mortimer in *The Times*

The Knight, the Lady and the Priest   Georges Duby

'A very fine book' (Philippe Aries) that traces back to its medieval origin one of our most important institutions, marriage.

A Social History of England   New Edition   Asa Briggs

'A treasure house of scholarly knowledge . . . beautifully written and full of the author's love of his country, its people and its landscape' – John Keegan in the *Sunday Times*, Books of the Year

The Second World War   A J P Taylor

A brilliant and detailed illustrated history, enlivened by all Professor Taylor's customary iconoclasm and wit.

FOR THE BEST IN PAPERBACKS, LOOK FOR THE 🐧

A CHOICE OF PENGUINS AND PELICANS

Metamagical Themas   Douglas R. Hofstadter

A new mind-bending bestseller by the author of *Gödel, Escher, Bach*.

The Body   Anthony Smith

A completely updated edition of the well-known book by the author of *The Mind*. The clear and comprehensive text deals with everything from sex to the skeleton, sleep to the senses.

Why Big Fierce Animals are Rare   Paul Colinvaux

'A vivid picture of how the natural world works' – *Nature*

How to Lie with Statistics   Darrell Huff

A classic introduction to the ways statistics can be used to prove *anything*, the book is both informative and 'wildly funny' – *Evening News*

The Penguin Dictionary of Computers   Anthony Chandor and others

An invaluable glossary of over 300 words, from 'aberration' to 'zoom' by way of 'crippled lead-frog tests' and 'output bus drivers'.

The Cosmic Code   Heinz R. Pagels

Tracing the historical development of quantum physics, the author describes the baffling and seemingly lawless world of leptons, hadrons, gluons and quarks and provides a lucid and exciting guide for the layman to the world of infinitesimal particles.

FOR THE BEST IN PAPERBACKS, LOOK FOR THE

A CHOICE OF PENGUINS AND PELICANS

Asimov's New Guide to Science Isaac Asimov

A fully updated edition of a classic work – far and away the best one-volume survey of all the physical and biological sciences.

Relativity for the Layman James A. Coleman

Of this book Albert Einstein said: 'Gives a really clear idea of the problem, especially the development of our knowledge concerning the propagation of light and the difficulties which arose from the apparently inevitable introduction of the ether.

The Double Helix James D. Watson

Watson's vivid and outspoken account of how he and Crick discovered the structure of DNA (and won themselves a Nobel Prize) – one of the greatest scientific achievements of the century.

Ever Since Darwin Stephen Jay Gould

'Stephen Gould's writing is elegant, erudite, witty, coherent and forceful' – Richard Dawkins, *Nature*

Mathematical Magic Show Martin Gardner

A further mind-bending collection of puzzles, games and diversions by the undisputed master of recreational mathematics.

Silent Spring Rachel Carson

The brilliant book which provided the impetus for the ecological movement – and has retained its supreme power to this day.

FOR THE BEST IN PAPERBACKS, LOOK FOR THE

A CHOICE OF PENGUINS AND PELICANS

Setting Genes to Work   Stephanie Yanchinski

Combining informativeness and accuracy with readability, Stephanie Yanchinski explores the hopes, fears and, more importantly, the realities of biotechnology – the science of using micro-organisms to manufacture chemicals, drugs, fuel and food.

Brighter than a Thousand Suns   Robert Jungk

'By far the most interesting historical work on the atomic bomb I know of' – C. P. Snow

Turing's Man   J. David Bolter

We live today in a computer age, which has meant some startling changes in the ways we understand freedom, creativity and language. This major book looks at the implications.

Einstein's Universe   Nigel Calder

'A valuable contribution to the de-mystification of relativity' – *Nature*

The Creative Computer   Donald R. Michie and Rory Johnston

Computers *can* create the new knowledge we need to solve some of our most pressing human problems; this path-breaking book shows how.

Only One Earth   Barbara Ward and Rene Dubos

An extraordinary document which explains with eloquence and passion how we should go about 'the care and maintenance of a small planet'.

FOR THE BEST IN PAPERBACKS, LOOK FOR THE 🐧

PENGUIN BUSINESS

Great management classics of the world (with brand new Introductions by leading contemporary figures); widely studied business textbooks; and exciting new business titles covering all the major areas of interest for today's businessman and businesswoman.

Parkinson's Law or **The Pursuit of Progress**   C. Northcote Parkinson

My Years with General Motors   Alfred P. Sloan Jr

Self-Help   Samuel Smiles

The Spirit of Enterprise   George Gilder

Dinosaur & Co: Studies in Corporate Evolution   Tom Lloyd

Understanding Organizations   Charles B. Handy

The Art of Japanese Management   Richard Tanner Pascale & Anthony G. Athos

Modern Management Methods   Ernest Dale & L. C. Michelon

Lateral Thinking for Management   Edward de Bono

The Winning Streak Workout Book   Walter Goldsmith & David Clutterbuck

The Social Psychology of Industry   J. A. C. Brown

Offensive Marketing   J. H. Davidson

The Anatomy of Decisions   Peter G. Moore & H. Thomas

The Human Side of Enterprise   Douglas McGregor

Corporate Recovery   Stuart Slatter